ENDORSEMENTS

"Get ready to explode whatever's in your way; the result being a richer, happier and more fulfilling life! The good news is that you really can blow up those walls that seem to be holding you back. The better news is that - in this book - you have an amazing teacher who will take you by the hand and help you to do it, step-by-step. There's a reason she's called 'Dixie Dynamite.' You're about to find out exactly why that is."

BOB BURG
Coauthor of *The Go-Giver* and
Author of *Endless Referrals*

"If you've ever found yourself wondering why you haven't achieved your dreams, told yourself 'I can't' or believed anyone else who may have said, "But not you," then you fully understand how limiting barriers can be. Here's your answer: Dixie 'Dynamite' Gillaspie has spent years providing people – myself included – the blasting caps needed to blast through their brick walls. In *Just Blow It Up* Dixie shares her insights, musings and proven process of identifying – then blasting through your walls. What once seemed unattainable, if not impossible, suddenly will come to life. Trust me – this works!"

Bill Ellis
Branding for Results

"If you have any fear, any doubt, or any thing standing between you and your greatness - this is the book for you! Dixie really does blow it up."

RANDY GAGE
Author of New York Times #1 Best Seller,
Risky Is the New Safe

"Dixie Gillaspie has a true gift for helping others to blast through challenges which stand in their way and create clear, workable plans to achieve in the areas that are important to them. I have known Dixie for years, and have witnessed her do this countless times through the work she does with her clients. In the pages of this book Dixie delivers her time tested techniques and strategies for all you need to achieve BIG in your life. This will be a welcome addition to your personal success library. Apply all that is found within the pages of this book, and you will have all you need to live an unlimited life."

JOSH HINDS
Entrepreneur, speaker, and
Author of *It's Your Life, LIVE BIG*

"Who knew tearing something down could be so elegant - *Just Blow It Up* is a blast!"

JOHN JANTSCH
Author of *Duct Tape Marketing*
and *The Commitment Engine*

"Dixie's book will help you blast through Kingdom Come to Kingdom DONE!"

TRACEY C. JONES
President of Tremendous Life Books
Author of: *True Blue Leadership*
and *Saucy Aussie Living*

"When it comes to inspiring people to make the changes they need to make in their life… Dixie Gillaspie is one in a million! Her stop-at-nothing commitment to help you blast through the things that are holding you back will be evident on every page of this book. But… be careful. By grabbing a copy of this book you are almost literally holding a stick of dynamite! Also know… *Just Blow It Up* could be the catalyst you need to make your big goals a reality!"

MITCH MATTHEWS
BIG Dream Gathering co-founder and
Author of *IGNITE - A little book to spark your big dreams*

"Willy Wonka, Robin Hood, Evel Knievel, David Lee Roth, The Punisher, Mother Theresa… and Dixie Gillaspie. Each for their own reason, are all hero's, no, SUPER hero's to me. Why is Dixie on that list? Because Dixie teaches you how to change the mind of fate itself. To understand that the barrier you're facing is actually the result of an opportunity presenting itself. I have met few who can do this. Inspiration wears off. Aspiration can change your DNA and stays with you your entire life. *Just Blow It Up! Firepower for Living an Unlimited Life* will leave you aspiring to be Dixie's brand of super hero!"

FRANK MCKINNEY
5x bestselling author,
including *The Tap* (www.The-Tap.com)

"*Just Blow It Up!* is a heartwarming and useful guide to living life above your expectations. Dixie communicates clearly and powerfully the wisdom we all need to succeed."

MARK SANBORN
Best-selling author of *The Fred Factor* and
You Don't Need a Title to be a Leader

"This book is a box of elegant super-power tools, delivered with the unique wit, wisdom, hard-hitting truth and deep compassion that is Dixie Gillaspie. Read it, work the exercises, and be amazed at your new world view--that expansive vista that's been waiting for you beyond all of your old psychological walls."

KIMBERLY V. SCHNEIDER, M.ED., J.D., LPC
Author of *Everything You Need Is Right Here:*
Five Steps to Manifesting Magic and Miracles

"Nothing says more about any sort of motivational or self-help book than the life of the person who wrote it. Five years ago I spent an hour parked on the side of the road getting to know Dixie Dynamite on a cell phone conversation. I have since watched her build her business, write the book she told me she would write, and inspire many people – including me – with her infectious commitment to blowing up walls with the word 'can't' written on them. Use Dixie's 'blasting caps' to just blow up the walls that stand between you and the achievement of your dreams."

JOE TYE
Author of *Never Fear, Never Quit*
and *All Hands on Deck*

JUST BLOW IT UP

JUST BLOW IT UP

FIREPOWER FOR LIVING
AN UNLIMITED LIFE

DIXIE GILLASPIE

Sound Wisdom
P.O. Box 310
Shippensburg, PA 17257-0310

For more information on foreign distribution, call 717-530-2122.
Reach us on the Internet: www.soundwisdom.com.

ISBN 13 TP: 978-1-937879-18-1
ISBN 13 Ebook: 978-1-937879-19-8

For Worldwide Distribution, Printed in the U.S.A.

1 2 3 4 5 6 7 8 / 16 15 14 13 12

"*It is when our true desires meet solid barriers that we are given the opportunity to be transformed into heroes.*"

CONTENTS

SECTION THREE
Four Walls Do Not a Prison Make

SECTION FOUR
The Dynamite Toolbox

FOREWORD
By Scott Ginsberg

Dreaming isn't dead.

Not if you have Dixie in your life.

The word *can't* doesn't exist in a conversation with her. She believes in everybody. And her unconditional positive regard is what feeds the heart and soul of all who encounter her. And the cool part is, if you're not blessed enough to have her in your life physically, this book is the next best thing.

Just Blow It Up isn't a book, it's a petition. It's a friend who believes in you more than you believe in yourself. It's a permission slip for lending an ear to yourself, calling bullshit on yourself, giving permission to yourself, doing work for yourself and trusting completely in yourself.

And with each page, with each of her ridiculously probing questions, which, by the way, are known to ruin your entire week, Dixie's words will applaud your risk, elevate your hope, disrupt your inertia, pours gasoline on your fire and help you fall in love with yourself.

Because she's the kind of person who adamantly refuses to let people stay where they are.

We all need to blow up our lives eventually.

Dixie is here to hold your hand when the world goes boom.

HELLO, my name is Scott, LLC - Writing, Speaking, Strategic Planning, Author of *Winking in the Dark*.

INTRODUCTION

"I just need someone to teach me how I can ..."

Sometimes the voice is frustrated, sometimes defensive, and sometimes, simply matter-of-fact.

Every time I've heard that sentence, the accent has been on "how."

What would happen if we change the emphasis? If, instead of focusing on *how*, we shift the focus to *I*?

Never mind how other people have done it.

Never mind if no one has ever done it before.

How can *I*?

How can *you*?

How can we do what we really want to do?

That is the foundation on which this work is built.

It's built on the understanding that nothing we want is out of reach, but just wanting isn't enough. There is a process we can follow that reveals our barriers, and provides the firepower to "just blow them up."

The stories I share here, and the lessons I have learned from them, have directed *my* path and informed *my* personal truth.

I hope you will discover your *own* path, and your *own* truth, using these examples as a description of how it *can* be done— not a prescription for how it *must* be done.

SECTION ONE

FABRICATING BRICKS—
BUILDING WALLS

—CHAPTER 1—

BABY DYNAMITE

*"Nothing is impossible;
some things just take longer."*

From the time I was able to understand language, my least favorite word was "can't."

I heard it a lot.

"Dixie, you can't do *that*, you're a girl."

"Dixie, you can't do *that*, you're too soft-hearted."

"Dixie, you can't do *that*, you aren't even good at math."

My usual comeback was, "I can too; just watch me!"

In spite of being a girl, I learned to change the oil and set the points on my Datsun B110. (Who even remembers the Datsuns? Or a time when cars had points?)

Soft-hearted I might be, but I learned to skin a rabbit. (I cried the whole time, and they do *not* taste like chicken.)

Although math was not my favorite class, when I was a sophomore in high school I let my teacher talk me into signing up to compete in a math theory contest. (I crammed for a week, placed fourth, then found out that the competition was supposed to be for juniors and seniors only.)

I still don't like cars, and what is under the hood of mine is mostly a mystery. I adore rabbits—with their skins on. I don't remember a thing about math theory, except that it was binary and fascinating, and I *was too* good at math, so there!

So why did I take on those challenges if I didn't care about cars, did care about rabbits, and didn't have any use for math theory?

Because hearing "Dixie, you can't do *that*" made my world shrink. Barriers cropped up where there had been limitless possibilities. I hadn't even decided what I wanted to do, and people were already saying that, for me, some things were impossible!

I've come to think of those "can'ts" as bricks, and the barriers as brick walls. Every time we accept that there is something we can't do, we add another brick to the wall. We limit our possibilities.

We limit our life.

We all knew this instinctively when we were kids. We challenged our limits every day.

Most of us started with the full support and encouragement of everyone around us. The first time we pulled ourselves up onto our tiny feet, legs trembling, mouth set in determination, there was a round of delighted applause.

No matter how many times we had to perform that feat, I doubt anyone said, "You can't *walk*—why, you can't even stand up!"

After a few ups and downs, we took our first step. More applause! And when we fell once again, no one said, "But you can't expect to learn to *run*—why, you can't even stay on your feet for more than a minute!

2

For most of us, our first attempts at the impossible were met with cries of, "Come on, you can do it! Just get up and try again!"

Because for adults, standing, walking, even running don't seem impossible. But for a baby trying to become a toddler, all those things *are* impossible. For now.

> *"Anything is impossible,*
> *until we do it once."*

So we proved that running wasn't impossible at all. And we started looking for new challenges. Then came that first time someone said, "No! You can't do *that*!"

Maybe it was the voice of experience: "You can't put your hand on that hot burner!" (Which is true, unless you're willing to have your skin singed.)

Maybe it was the voice of social norms: "You can't take off your clothes and run shrieking through the store." (Well, you can, but the adult in charge will likely be mortified.)

Maybe it was the voice of practicality: "You can't go to Disneyland by yourself; you're only six years old!" (Which isn't to say that a trip to Disneyland is out of the question— but the park does have rules about unattended minors, and is willing to enforce them.)

Whatever the source of that voice, as soon as we're told we *can't* do something, we have a choice. We can choose another destination, along a path that doesn't have a wall of bricks blocking our progress, or we can find a way over, under, around, or through the barrier.

Of course, as kids, we tried many methods. There was the pout and the full-on temper tantrum. There was the well-thought-out argument and the emotional appeal.

And there was the method I chose: full-on assault, until I

proved that I *could too*!

CHAPTER 2

NAVY BLUE SUITS DON'T SUIT ME

"Progress might be uncomfortable, but if it is painful you're likely progressing in the wrong direction."

I once had a successful career as a medical business analyst and management consultant. Many people would have told you I had great things ahead of me. At least that's what they told me.

My articles were being featured in national industry publications. I was lecturing. I was carrying a heavy client load, and training other analysts in the field.

I was miserable.

People handed me plenty of bricks during those years. I was too young, too feminine. I didn't have initials after my name. I was too bubbly, too intense. I didn't own a navy blue suit.

To comments like, "You can't even be 30 yet; what can you know?" I responded, "I've packed a lot into 29 years, but if I can't teach you anything new you can always fire me"—said with a smile and a wink that proved I was just bubbly enough to get away with sass.

The lack of initials I countered with a litany of what I'd learned through experience. I joked that most people pay to get their education; I got paid for getting mine!

I joked about the intensity too, reminding clients that they should be thankful I was only on-site two days a month, because no one could be expected to take any more of me than that.

When one manager coined the phrase "Dixie Daze" for the sense of overwhelm I left in my wake, I turned it into a compliment, taking pride in how much value I could pack into our time together. As for the navy blue suit—I bought one. And then another.

Every brick wall, I destroyed.

At last my path was clear: I could claim a place in my industry that few women had. Certainly few women my age, without a medical degree of any kind, had achieved what I had achieved.

I was still miserable.

You see, I'd blown up one brick wall after another, not because I wanted what was on the other side, but because someone had put them in my path and I didn't like the looks of them.

That turned out to be a less than effective use of energy.

Having burnt myself out destroying every brick wall just because it was there, I stopped blasting through any of them. I let them build up in front of me and all around me. I didn't connect with what I really wanted; I just went after what other people told me I should want.

I was doing something I had learned to be really good at doing, but I wasn't achieving my highest purpose. I wasn't feeding my passion. And my presence, the way I "showed up" in my business and in my life, reflected that.

I couldn't deliver what I promised my clients, because I promised them my best, and the platform I had built for my work didn't support me in delivering my best.

I couldn't be authentic in my relationships outside my business either—because I wasn't being authentic in my relationship with myself.

And there was one other problem—navy blue doesn't do a thing for my complexion.

—CHAPTER 3—

FROM DUD
TO DYNAMITE

*"Any success that does not allow you to be fully
yourself is not sustainable."*

It took a funeral to make me realize that my inner light was nearly burnt out, that being walled in behind the "can'ts" and "shoulds" was putting out my fire as surely as oxygen starvation snuffs a candle.

I sat there listening to eulogies for someone who had passed away at 52, only 10 years older than I was at the time, and I thought, "If that were me in that coffin, what would people say about me, about my life, about the impact I've made on the world?"

And I didn't have an answer.

It wasn't my funeral, of course, but reflecting on a life ended unexpectedly and prematurely made me realize that there was something dying inside of me, and I wanted to bring it back to life.

One of the songs played at this funeral was by the Flaming Lips. You might think the Lips an odd choice for a funeral (if you've heard of them at all), but Steve's children chose it because they and their father were big fans of the band, and the lyrics were a perfect testament to his life.

What is the light
That you have?
Shining all around you
Is it chemically derived?

'Cause if it's natural
Something glowing from inside
Shining all around you
Its potential has arrived.

~ "What Is the Light?" by THE FLAMING LIPS (1999)

Steve certainly had that "something glowing from inside" kind of light, and I remembered a time when I had had it too.

But that day, tears streaming, I asked myself, "What is my light?"

And realized the more pertinent question was, "*Where* is my light?" Because I was certainly not connected to it anymore. I wanted to get back to feeling connected to that fire. I wanted it to blaze as brightly as it had when I was the "Little Stick of Dynamite" who could do anything.

That wake-up call began a four-year journey of connecting to my passion and purpose, and rediscovering how I could tap into that fire. A journey of remembering how to let that light shine in my presence, how to create a business platform *and* a life in which I could fulfill my promise, both to myself and to others.

—CHAPTER 4—

REDISCOVERING THE DREAM

"In order to have true joy in your work, the
outcomes that light your fire must match the
outcomes you are paid to achieve."

I once dreamed of pursuing a career as a therapist. My well-intentioned mother said, "Oh Dixie, you can't do *that*! You'd take every client home with you! You'd never be able to handle the emotional stress."

What I heard was, "The greater your success in that field, the greater your personal pain."

But I wasn't thinking about that old dream as I sat, numbly listening to the question, "What is the light?"

I was thinking about the dream I'd been pursuing. And it was dawning on me that it wasn't *my* dream. It was someone else's dream for me.

I knew I had to change something.

I began by exploring ways to finish the statement, "What I *really* want to do is …"

11

The internal work I did to understand my passion and purpose is another story, but at the end of those four years I was able to say what I really wanted to do.

"What I really want to do is ... coach people who are ready to blast through their brick walls and tap into the power of their passion and purpose."

Of course, as soon as we discover the path we know we want to travel, our chosen path to success, the next thing we see is a brick wall. Right in front of our nose.

Immediately my mind became a battlefield of "can'ts." Whoever said to choose your battles wisely should have also reminded us that many of our battles are fought in our own minds.

"Dixie, you can't do *that*; you don't have a degree in psychology. You're a business consultant."

"Dixie, you can't do *that*; you'd have to deal with life issues! You aren't a life coach."

"Dixie, you can't do *that*; it took you years to figure it out for yourself."

Every time I said "what I really want to do is ... ," I followed it with "but I can't because ... ."

And finally, I said to myself, "I can too! Watch me!"

So now I coach. I do take every client home with me, and I handle it just fine. In fact, my deep personal connection to my clients gives me great joy.

Like most entrepreneurs, at first I struggled with doubts about my qualifications and my ability to reach enough people to create a profitable business. I even questioned whether my personality was suited to what I really wanted to do. I couldn't decide whether I was not calming enough, or not drill sergeant enough! I have found a higher calling than my original dream of becoming a therapist, but it took blasting through many brick walls for me to believe that I *can too* use my talents, create success for myself and my clients, and allow that deep personal connection without burning out or breaking down.

I'm still encountering and blowing up brick walls today. I expect I always will be, so long as I continue to grow and reach for something new.

Each time I share the story of that journey, I am reminded that I'm not the only person who has woken up and realized that the inner light has nearly been extinguished. I'm not the only person who has looked for a path, and seen mostly brick walls.

Perhaps you are reading this because you are also on that journey. Because you feel a flicker where you once felt a flame. Because you wake up thinking about what you should do and what you can't do, instead of what you *get* to do.

Perhaps you need to reconnect to your passion and purpose, but there are a few brick walls that have to come down in order to clear the way.

Perhaps you've even said, "I have a dream, and *now* is my time to make it come true!"

If that's what you're saying to yourself right now, if you're ready to blow up those brick walls, I want to share that firepower with you.

—CHAPTER 5—

THE ENTREPRENEURIAL MINDSET

"You are never given a wish without also being given the power to make it true. You may have to work for it, however."
~ RICHARD BACH

"Entrepreneur" is perhaps the most often defined and redefined, and still the most misunderstood, word in common business usage today.

Every consultant, expert, and guru seems to have a separate set of requirements you must meet before you can call yourself an entrepreneur. The literal translation of entrepreneur, from the French, is "one who undertakes." To say "I am an entrepreneur" is to say "I have chosen an undertaking."

"Your mission, should you choose to accept it."
~ MISSION IMPOSSIBLE

Your purpose, should you choose to undertake it. It is, indeed, your choice. To undertake, or to abdicate your power and live a limited life.

For many of us, entrepreneurship isn't about owning a business. It's about owning our outcomes, taking control of our own success, and making choices about how we work, how we live, and how we make an impact on the world.

Our *lives* are our undertaking; our businesses and careers are simply vehicles by which we achieve our purpose.

People with an entrepreneurial mindset aren't just big dreamers, they are big doers. To be fulfilled, it isn't enough to have ideas and dreams: we have to move forward boldly and with conviction. To many of our friends, family members, and colleagues, we always seem to be chasing the impossible dream, but without the great musical score.

Our well-meaning advisers often support the dream but not the doing. "What a beautiful dream—wonderful idea— sweet thought," they say, when we share our passion. But then they add, "Don't expect too much—maybe you'd better take it slow—I don't see how you can make money at that."

It isn't really surprising that I find so many entrepreneurs who are discouraged or even despairing, trying to hold onto dreams and ideas while seeing brick walls at every turn.

Even less surprising is the number of people I encounter who have the entrepreneurial mindset and spirit, but find brick walls in front of them every time they even consider taking the leap into an entrepreneurial life.

Of course, we don't have to be dancing on the cliff's edge of starting our own business to have people trying to save us from a fall. Brick walls get thrown up to "protect" us from training for marathons, moving to a different city, trying out for the community theatre, marrying someone older or younger, richer or poorer, than ourselves.

As soon as we share a dream, we take the risk that someone will label it "impossible."

Sometimes *we* label it "impossible" before we even share it, and it gets laid away in our emotional hope chest where we peek at it from time to time through the lens of what-might-have-been.

But what if Richard Bach is right?

What if we never needed to lay our dreams aside? What if we have the power to spin our wish, the one we've been given the power to make true, all the way from "what I really want to do is …" to "I can too. Just watch me!"

I believe he is right. We *do* have the power. But first, we must be willing to do the work.

CHAPTER 6

ARE YOU DEFENDING YOUR IMPOSSIBLE INSTEAD OF YOUR DREAM?

"What I really want to do is ..."

Everyone I know has made this statement at least once.

When my early clients said to me, "I know what I *want* to do, but I feel like I'm banging my head against a brick wall," and then went on to insist that their brick walls were insurmountable, I knew I had to figure out how to help these people attack their walls, without making them feel attacked by me. I noticed that most people seem conditioned to be defensive about their walls, to justify over and over their belief that they cannot do what they say they want to do.

They guard their "I can't because ..." statements as fiercely as any warrior ever defended the walls of a citadel. Which puzzled me, since I assume that people work with me because they *want* to discover how they "can too!"

Gradually I began to read between the lines of our conversations, hearing what they expected me to say that I wasn't saying.

"Can't is just another word for won't."

"If you can dream it, you can do it."

"Do what you love; the money will follow."

"If you want it badly enough you'll find a way; if you don't you'll find an excuse."

"Just do it!"

And the worst of all: "If you can't, you can't. No use crying about it!"

We don't like to say "I can't" because we usually get a lot of platitudes in reply, even put-downs.

What we need isn't rah-rah encouragement, or criticism. It isn't tough love, or even comfort. We need tools; we need ammunition; we need a plan of attack!

I wanted all of us (my clients *and* myself) to stop fighting to defend our walls, and start fighting to attain our dreams.

SECTION TWO

ANATOMY OF THE WALL— BRICKS, MORTAR, AND BELIEF

—CHAPTER 7—

ANOTHER BRICK
IN THE WALL

*"Shoulds and can'ts block your energy and destroy
your ability to see possibilities and opportunities."*

Admit it: All you Pink Floyd fans were just waiting for
me to use that quotation, weren't you? I'm a Pink Floyd fan
too, and I didn't want to let you down.

Besides, it's so apt!

Other people hand us bricks with the best of intentions.

In fact, the very people who are most firmly on our side
in every other way are often the most instrumental in helping
us build brick walls.

Sometimes they're speaking out of their own fear. Like
parents, afraid to let their child climb the jungle gym for
the first time, because they're sure their darling will suffer a
scraped knee or a broken skull.

These people have seen us fall before, maybe more than
once. They know our weaknesses, and they may really believe
the dream is impossible, for us. So they tell us we should do
something other than what our passion is driving us to do,
because they truly believe we are making a poor choice.

They think that because they know us well, and love us dearly, they also know what is best for us. They tell us we *can't* because they don't want to see us try—and fail.

Of course, the people closest to us are also the people who will be most impacted if we decide to "go for it." These are the people who will be most affected, emotionally if not materially, if we fail. Their lives will also be the most changed if we succeed.

Maybe they would be excited and impressed if someone else undertook something similar, but they hand *us* one brick after another to keep us from making the attempt.

And those are just the bricks offered by our nearest and dearest! We haven't even discussed the insecure haters, the envious detractors, the bitter naysayers.

Most of us meekly take those bricks of "can't" and "should," and mortar them into place.

We set aside our passion, we abandon the purpose we've been called to fulfill, and we follow the path of least resistance. Our passion dies, our light dims, and our dreams get filed away as fantasies.

Some brick walls are built over years and years, others in a single instant. Some are built from the external reinforcement of limited belief systems, others in response to the fear of failure, or of success.

Some have their origin in experiences we don't even remember, others in incidents so prominent in our personal stories that it has become difficult to see around them.

Often, brick walls are constructed of little things. Small disappointments and embarrassments, doubts expressed by a parent, a partner, a boss. Too much time spent in activities that do not feed our passion, producing outcomes that do not realize our purpose.

And then the time comes when we say, "I want *that*, and I can't have it because there is this barrier between it and me."

> *"Can't isn't actually a word.*
> *It is a contraction for cannot."*

And that is exactly our choice: We *can*, or we can *not*.

Other people will always have bricks to hand us, but we don't have to accept them.

Because, if we choose "can not," we have already accepted a limited life.

CHAPTER 8

SHOW ME WHAT YOU'RE MADE OF

"The easiest thing for anyone to do, is to think
themselves out of doing anything."

So what are bricks made of?

I knew that to create the firepower and plan of attack to blow up brick walls, I needed to understand their construction. I started making a note every time I heard "I can't."

I filled most of a notebook.

"I'm too old," "I'm too young," "I'm too shy," "I'm too scared," "I'm not qualified," "I'm over-qualified," "I don't have the money," "I don't have the time," "I'm not pretty enough," "I'm not tall enough."

The list went on for several pages. I think the only thing I didn't hear was "I'm not blonde enough," and I'll bet someone has said it—just not to me!

Then there was the "I can't just" list.

"I can't just quit my job—open a business—go back to school—move to Europe—join a band—become a consultant."

That one took up a few pages too.

Then there was the "if I do that" list.

"If I do that, my spouse will kill me—my boss will fire me—I'll lose my house—I'll lose face—I'll lose friends—I'll lose sleep."

And finally, the "if only I could" list.

"If only I could speak like Martin Luther King Jr.—write like Hemmingway—be creative like Steve Jobs."

I could practically hear the bricklayer's trowel scraping over the mortar as each brick was securely cemented into place.

I could *certainly* feel the energy ebbing away as these people told me all the reasons they were walling themselves off from what they really wanted to do.

With each "I can't because" statement, they reduced their expectations.

"When dreams and expectations are too far apart, the dreams are doomed to remain only fantasies."

—CHAPTER 9—

DO YOU HAVE A DREAM?

"Do not let your fears define your dreams, but rather let your dreams overcome your fears."

Martin Luther King Jr. said, "I have a dream."

I had the fortune, one of the times I delivered a keynote on how to blow up brick walls, to have a local radio announcer deliver that famous speech right before I took the stage.

His delivery was spot-on. I had to wipe tears from my eyes in order not to trip on the step up to the podium.

So I went with the flow, and asked the audience, "How many of you have a dream?"

Hands shot into the air. They were fired up and teary-eyed, just like me.

So I told them a story, of a little towheaded girl, all of three years old, back in 1966. She and her mother and father were about to take a trip, to Decatur, Alabama.

Now this little girl was well-loved, and she had several baby dolls. But her father only allowed her to take one baby doll on each road trip, so the dolls had to take turns. And this time it was Lily's turn.

29

Lily was the cutest little black baby doll you've ever seen.

And her daddy said, "Dixie, you *can't* take Lily on this trip! I am *not* taking you and a little black baby doll to Alabama!"

I was only three. I don't remember what I said (or how much of an explosion ensued), but I do remember the sense of horrible injustice. It was Lily's turn! It wasn't fair to leave her behind and take another baby doll!

He was only being prudent. Although it saddens me still, I understand that now.

"But here's the beautiful thing," I told my audience: "If I had a towheaded child today, and we were going to Alabama, I wouldn't have to tell her, 'You can't take that doll to Alabama!'"

"I have a dream ..."

I'll bet you do too.

Maybe you're starting to feel as if your dream is a long ways off.

Do you think Martin Luther King Jr. didn't stand there, with all that passion, all that eloquence, all that desperation, feeling that *his* dream was a long ways off?

But he didn't stop pursuing it.

And, though his dream has not reached the fullness of its potential, today we are living in a world that is much more like his dream than it was when he first shared that dream with us.

CHAPTER 10

"I WANT" COMES BEFORE "HOW CAN I"

*"There is a reason dreams are conceived while
sleeping—that is the only time the rational mind
cannot sneak in and abort them before they hatch."*

The rational mind gets in the way, doesn't it? When we're asleep and in the dream state, anything seems possible.

Kind of like being three years old. And not understanding that a prudent father can't go to Alabama in 1966 with a towheaded child, and a black baby doll named Lily.

When we're sleeping, anything can happen. Then we wake up. And the rational mind says, "What are you thinking? You can't do *that!*"

So what can we do to get the rational mind to go back to sleep—at least long enough for us to figure out what we really want to do? Then it can wake up and help us figure out *how*.

I did a single Blast Thru Coaching session with a woman I have never met, who transitioned away from a career in marketing to create her own business dedicated to helping girls and women embrace their feminine power through Facilitated Equine Experiential Learning.

With the passion evident in her voice, she said that what she really wanted to do was to take her work on a tour of other countries. When I asked how she filled in the blank after "but I can't because … ," she paused. Her voice cracked as she repeated to me what "everyone" said about her dream:

It wasn't what she should be focusing on. It wouldn't be profitable. And so on.

We stayed connected through Facebook, and I've read posts about her travels. In fact, the last post was from Italy, where she was working with women and horses via a translator! (I assume the translator was for the women—horses speak the same language in any country.)

The last time we talked, she told me that once she rejected all the shoulds, and made up her mind that she was going to pursue her dream, the pieces fell into place.

Remember that keynote when I asked the audience how many of them had a dream? And nearly all of them raised their hands? They not only *raised* their hands, they reached those hands high! They waved them at me! They knew they had dreams!

Later that same morning, I asked the audience to complete the statement "what I really want to do is …" on their worksheets.

And I asked them to share.

You would have thought I'd invited them to take my place on stage!

They were confident they had a dream, but when I asked them to write it down, they weren't so ready to commit.

*"What are dreams if not a blueprint
of what is possible?"*

A dream is like a house plan. You can't live in it, but you can use it to imagine what it would be like to live in it. You can look at it and say, "I love the windows, but the bedroom needs to be bigger."

This is your time to choose the dream you want, the one you're willing to put the energy into pursuing, the one that most lights your fire.

Until you've said "I want it!" there is no point in asking, "How can I make it happen?"

If you don't have anything to put in the "what I really want to do is ..." blank, you probably don't have much energy to do *anything*.

And, if what you put in that blank doesn't light you up, it doesn't matter how hard, or how easy, it will be. You won't put the energy into making it happen.

But what if you have been awake so long you've forgotten your dream? What if you don't know how to fill in that first blank, "What I really want to do is ..."

If you're like most of us, you're having trouble filling in that first blank because your mind is already filling in the second one. You're awake; your rational mind thinks it's in charge. It can come up with "but I can't because ..." responses faster than you can take a deep breath.

Here's a clue: In the years I've been coaching, almost every client replies to "what I really want to do is ..." with "I want to help ... ."

Does that resonate with you? Do you want to help people? animals? the planet?

33

Can you be more specific? What do the people you want to help have in common? What animals do you want to help in particular? What geographic area is closest to your heart?

What do you want to help them do—change something? create something? save something? How will they change because of your help? How will the world change? How will *you* change?

If you list every endeavor you've ever been part of, every accomplishment you've contributed to achieving, can you highlight the ones that really make your heart sing?

What themes do you see? Are they all connected to similar outcomes? Did they all require similar talents?

I've discovered that most of the outcomes that made *my* inner fire leap up were connected to people being able to do something they hadn't been able to do before. Usually something they didn't even believe they *could* do before we worked together.

When I do this exercise, I don't confine myself to listing career outcomes.

I have one life, and I'm pretty much living it all the time, so I don't differentiate between "life" and "business." My core purpose is my life purpose, and my business is just one segment of my life.

So I list interventions with friends and conversations with strangers. I note volunteer projects and random events. If it makes me feel good to remember it, it goes on the list.

What does your list look like?

Here's another clue: All the clients I've worked with wanted to do something they were good at, something that came naturally, and something that made an impact.

In fact, I've had several people tell me they pursued a career path simply because people told them they'd be wonderful at it.

They were filling in "what I really want to do is ..." with "something I'll be wonderful at doing."

But who *doesn't* want to do something he or she is wonderful at doing? You certainly shouldn't give up your dream in favor of someone else's dream for you. But knowing what other people think you're good at is an excellent place to begin your search for what you really want to do.

If you're struggling with "what I really want to do is ... ," ask "what makes people pay attention when I do it?"

What do you do, say, write, build, share, or contribute that causes others to say, "*Wow!* That's good! Can you do that again?"

Because whenever other people say that, you know you're making an impact. And that's what we get compensated for in life, isn't it? That's what fulfills us. Making an impact.

Let's try that again.

Tell your rational mind to go back to sleep. And complete this statement:

What I really want to do is

_____!

If you're still drawing a blank, then maybe you should write, "What I really want to do is figure out what I really want to do!"

> *"The good thing about not being sure of anything
> is that everything becomes possible."*

As children, we were programmed to learn through exploration. We learned to walk by exploring, we learned to climb by exploring, and we learned to fall by exploring too! So if you've been trying to figure out what you want to do by studying books and asking other people, maybe you need to look within, and let yourself explore something new!

Once you've completed that statement, go ahead and wake up. I know, I hate to do it to you.

Now complete *this* statement:

But I can't because

_____.

Write down everything you can think of. Not because I want you to build a lot of brick walls, but because they're already there and you can't blow them up until you can see them!

> *"Until you recognize it for what it is, you won't be able to change it into what it can be!"*

So if you believe anything is a reason that you can't do what you really want to do, or that you haven't done it yet, write it down. We'll blow up that list later!

CHAPTER 11

IS IT BIGGER
THAN A BREADBOX?

*"Our dreams are like puppies' paws—they start out
big so that they will support us as we grow."*

Does anyone know the dimensions of the "standard"
breadbox?

Neither do I. And there is no definitive set of dimensions
for a *big* dream either.

Brick walls don't just crop up in the path of big dreams.
They show up to test us when all we want to do is get the
garden weeded, or write a single blog post.

For the sake of teaching you how to blow up *big* brick
walls, I'll be talking about big dreams, major projects, life
aspirations, and the like. But remember that anything that
applies to a big wall applies to a little speed bump too.

CHAPTER 12

THE DYNAMITE DIALOGS PROJECT

*"Wholeheartedly pursue only that which you can
pursue wholeheartedly."*

In late 2010, I presented my dear friends and fellow mastermind members with a challenge.

"What I really want to do is start sharing my process for blasting through brick walls with *lots* of people. More people than I can reach through coaching."

Their response was unanimous: "Write a book."

I didn't give them reasons why I couldn't write a book. I gave them reasons why I didn't want to.

Books take time, lots of time. And once they're printed, they're printed. No edits allowed once they're sitting on that shelf.

Plus, I wanted to spend my time teaching. And learning. I just didn't feel that I could put my heart into writing a book.

Because of the intensity of my coaching style, I accept only a small number of private clients. So I didn't feel I had reached far enough, or deep enough, with enough people, to warrant writing a book. I knew that if I could reach more people, I'd learn far more about my process through being part of their experience than I could ever teach by writing a book..

I had already thought of creating an audio learning program as a way of reaching more people. I told them my idea.

The group was enthusiastic. Cheers all around.

Then I threw up a brick wall.

"But I don't like to just talk into a microphone. I get tired of the sound of my own voice, and I'd still have to write the content first. I'd rather have a conversation and just let it be organic. How do I do that?"

Every one of them offered to interview me. (I should call my mastermind group a booster club—they never let me down!)

Still, my gut said this wasn't quite the answer I was looking for.

Half joking, I said, "I'd rather interview you! You're as good at blasting through brick walls as I am."

Then I realized I wasn't joking at all. I've surrounded myself with a number of "Blast Thru Artists": people who have triumphed over their "can'ts" and achieved success doing what they really want to do. I *could* interview them!

The group was less enthusiastic. They brought me back to my original statement: If what I wanted to do was to share the process and methods I had developed, interviewing other people wouldn't achieve that purpose.

Then I saw the fallacy, what my friends (and Blast Thru Artists extraordinaire) John David Mann and Bob Burg would call "the unnecessary use of the word or."

The audios didn't need to be interviews *or* just me talking! They could be dialogs! Two people sitting down to discuss their ideas, stories, and observations about how we build walls—and blow them up.

And that's what we did. Me and 13 of my friends, heroes, and mentors. Blast Thru Artists all!

We called them the Dynamite Dialogs, and the energy we produced during those conversations would have kept a small country's lights on for a solid month!

(In fact, during a conversation with my long-time virtual mentor and now dear friend Richard Bach, we actually had a major tornado here in my home city of St. Louis. But we're not taking responsibility for that one!)

So I got exactly what I wanted: a forum to share what I'd learned, and to learn from others. And did I ever learn a lot! How could I not, with the caliber of people I had to talk to? I'll be sharing some of those stories, insights, and aha moments with you here.

My dream of reaching more people was realized, and this helped me arrive at a point where I could pursue writing this book with a whole heart. You're holding the next phase of that dream in your hands.

All because I said, "What I really want to do is ..."

And filled in the blank.

CHAPTER 13

THE NIKE MYTH

"I've never seen beating yourself up to be an effective form of exercise."

"Just do it!"

While the marketing geniuses who coined that phrase for Nike didn't create the problem, they've certainly helped their client far more than my clients!

My clients aren't slackers, looking for an excuse to sit on the couch all day. They're highly motivated, passionate, committed individuals. I'll bet you are too.

Here's something else I'll bet:

If "just do it" were enough, you'd have "just done it" by now.

I won that bet, didn't I?

So getting up in the morning and telling yourself to "just do it" probably isn't going to work.

Usually, when we figure out what we really want to do, there are things we need to learn, things we need to practice, even things we need to become, before we're ready to "just do it."

Remember that event when I asked, "Do you have a dream?" Hands went up. But when I asked the audience to write down what they really wanted to do, they weren't so sure.

I wasn't surprised. Want to know why?

Because having a dream is easier than doing the work.

Not because people aren't willing to work for their dreams, but because they don't know where to begin. The path between present-now and future-perfect is often hidden, and the part of it we can see is dotted with brick walls.

Giving a resounding YES to the question, "Do you have a dream?" That's easy.

Knowing how to fill in the blank that follows "what I really want to do is ..." means committing to action, and that gives us pause.

"The bigger the want, the higher the wall."

In my Dynamite Dialog with friend and mastermind partner Tom Ruwitch, coauthor of *Generation BIG*, he shares some stories about the bold, innovative, and generous (BIG) people featured in his book. These people certainly had dreams—dreams they were passionate about—but to actualize those dreams they had to *do* something.

As Tom says in that conversation, *"Passion* is a dime a dozen. Anyone can say they're passionate about helping someone or something."

"But the difference between that person and the BIG person is that the BIG person is going to do something about it. The BIG person is going to commit, not to be the person who says 'I want to,' but to be the person who *does* it.

"Are you passionate and interested? or passionate and taking action?"

But if you listen to that Dialog, you'll notice that Tom never says "just do it!"

CHAPTER 14

COMMITTED ACTION REQUIRES COMMITTED ENERGY

"What others call a miracle, is really just the power of the mind, and determined, directed action, coming together."

There are four prerequisites to "just doing" anything: Energy, belief, vision, and a plan.
In that order.
You thought the plan would come first, perhaps?

"Passion not expended in purposeful *action is just a lot of hot air."*

But it isn't about *just* taking action; you can take a lot of action and not actualize your dream. A plan is as essential to success as a map is to arriving at your desired destination.

But what good is a plan without the energy to implement it? Or without the belief that there is a plan that will work?

Or without a vision of where you want to go and what you want to accomplish?

Tom says it beautifully during our Dialog: "You have to keep coming back to the core vision, to that thing that really fires you up."

Energy comes from the connection to your vision.

I call it your "pilot light." Not only because it is that consistent source of a spark, but also because it "pilots" you in the right direction. If it flickers, you know you need to correct your course; you've waivered from your core vision.

During my Dialog with Tom, we talk about the challenge of coauthoring a book with two other people. Certainly, he agrees, the project has gone through several mutations, and the follow-up plan is still subject to change.

But he and his writing partners have one vital thing in common with the people they write about: they're uncompromising about their purpose, and flexible about the way it comes about.

"We've never wavered from our core vision [for] *Generation BIG*. But we *have* been willing to recognize that the path to get to that place, to get to that community of people who are working together to achieve their BIG vision, that path may not be anything like what we envisioned when we first started. The journey there is ever-changing."

> *"When the winds of change blow, some build walls, others build windmills."*
> ~ CHINESE PROVERB

Some of the stories featured in *Generation BIG* involve huge undertakings: bringing affordable transportation into third-world villages, putting computers suited for a rough-and-tumble environment into the hands of kids in developing nations, even selling shoes to fund heart surgeries for the thousands of children affected by Saddam Hussein's poison gas attacks on the Kurds.

Some of the stories are of dreams that started small, such as triumph in a personal struggle with depression or giving a coat to one needy child, and then mushroomed into multicity initiatives.

Tom and I agree that the stories all affirm that the desire must come before the plan.

Because nothing ever goes as planned.

Each one of the BIG people featured in the book, and every person I've ever talked to who has realized a dream, has a similar story.

They've moved from plan A to plan B to plan C. But they've stayed true to their vision, and they've found the energy to keep going on.

Will Austin, whose story is featured in the book, shared this insight about the "journey," the energy required to stay on course, and the rewards of the trip: "This journey is like an old, battered African road. It is exciting. There are beautiful views, great people, on the way. But there are also bumps. There are obstacles, there are washed-out roads. Sometimes you have to go back and retrace your steps, and go down to the next river crossing.

"It's a journey full of surprises. Some of those are really good. And some of those are really tough. But in the end, I'm always encouraging people to go for it."

When you connect to the purpose behind the dream, you tap into that fire, that energy. You build a windmill, to capture the power of the winds of change, instead of building walls.

CHAPTER 15

IMPOSSIBLE ISN'T IMPRACTICAL

*"If you aren't having impractical ideas, and
dreaming impossible dreams, then you aren't
reaching far enough, high enough, or deep enough!"*

In my Dynamite Dialog with Mitch Matthews, founder of the Big Dream Gathering and author of *IGNITE - A little book to spark your big dreams*, Mitch starts by putting a stake in the ground.

"There's a place and time for thinking bigger, but we need to start by dreaming bigger! People's ability to dream has taken a hit over the last few years: they're having a difficult time dreaming at all.

"But the core of the best products, [globe]-changing technologies, best comebacks, best moves by a company or a country: Those all started when one person, or a group of people, had a dream. And took action on it!"

Thinking, according to Mitch, kicks in later. If you start thinking too early, it shuts down the dream.

I tell him I call it "drowning in 'how.'"

If you start thinking about *how* before you've got the energy and belief, it's like quenching a candle before it becomes a bonfire.

Once that flame really catches, it will take more than a little "critical thinking" to drown it out.

Speaking of "critical thinking," Mitch and I decided there are two distinct types. One is a necessary part of dream actualization: analysis and planning.

The other is the thought trap we fall into when we listen to the "inner critic."

They sound a lot alike.

They say things like, "How are you going to make that happen?"

Or, "How do you plan to make a living doing that?"

But while the analytical mind asks those questions expecting that you'll have a logical, positive response, the inner critic expects you to respond with, "You're right, I probably can't make it happen, let alone make a living doing it."

Did I just hear you suggest that the inner critic might be speaking with the voice of experience? Maybe. But whose voice? Whose experience?

The voice of experience is always a voice from the past (unless you're remembering experiences from the future, which is a tad unusual).

So maybe, you say, it's the voice of social norms. Or the voice of practicality.

It might very well be either of those. Like the parents who would melt with embarrassment if their child shed her clothes and ran naked through a public place, your little voice might dread the frowns of others. (Although you know the child would be having a blast—no blushing or apologies from the little one.)

Or like the parent explaining that Disneyland is dead set against allowing minors to come play with Mickey and Minnie with no adult responsible for their behavior, your little voice may be concerned about the rules you'll have to break or circumvent in order to pursue your dream.

Wait, whose voice is that again? Do you care so much about the frowns of others that you'll abandon your dream? Picture that child streaking through the grocery store. Now picture the onlookers. Don't at least half of them have amused, indulgent, even envious smiles on their faces?

And about those rules. Whose rules? Most rules have exceptions. Are you willing to be the exception to the rule?

Often that little voice isn't on air "live," but is instead a rerun of "Might Have Been True Then." Isn't that show a bit outdated?

Whether you're hearing a recording of something first spoken by a parent, a peer, a teacher, a boss, a random stranger on television, or a previous version of yourself, that's not your voice today.

What does your little voice tell you? Today?

—CHAPTER 16—

DREAM BIG— THINK SMALL

"Sometimes it isn't about dreaming bigger, it's about dreaming truer. Bigger shows you possible futures. But truer reveals foundations on which we can build bigger dreams."

I know Mitch is right: a lot of people *are* finding it difficult to dream these days. But I still have many people tell me they have no problem dreaming big. What they need help with, they say, is implementation.

We don't implement dreams, we implement plans. We actualize our dreams by implementing plans.

Even when we're ready to create a plan, what often stops us in our tracks is the daunting prospect of determining what action to plan to take! Especially when that "little voice" whispers something like, "This is way too complicated—just call the whole thing off."

It's easy to listen to that little voice if you're thinking you have to have a fail-proof plan for that big dream.

The bad news is that there is no such thing as a fail-proof plan. The good news is that there is no such thing as a dead end without a detour.

Remember my Dialog with Tom, when we said plans always change? Remember what we do? We retrace our steps and go to the next river crossing. We check the map and find another path. Or we carve a path where there was no path before. If we find a river in our way, we build a bridge.

Plans change, but if we have that energy, belief, and vision, *we* keep moving.

So how do we begin, to begin?

As Mitch says, there is a time and place for thinking big. But, in my experience, the planning phase is the time and place for thinking small.

Small stages of the journey, small steps along the path, small tasks that can be checked off every day. If every step of your plan is still daunting, you're not thinking small enough.

—CHAPTER 17—

WHAT CAN YOU
SAY YES TO TODAY?

*"Take the first step in faith. You don't have to see
the whole staircase; just take the first step."*
~ MARTIN LUTHER KING JR.

The purpose of goals is to create motion. To move us from current reality to future possibility. You won't meet your goals if they require leaps that would span the Grand Canyon.

Which means goals need to be in step-sized increments.

In the Dynamite Dialog I shared with author, speaker, and speaking coach Ava Diamond, she tells the story of how she completed a 60-mile walk in only three days.

I suppose if you're a runner, or extremely athletic, that may not sound like much. But to most of us, it would rank somewhere between daunting and impossible.

When Ava signed up for the Avon walk, even *she* wondered how she would make it happen. She says bluntly, "You've seen me: I am several pounds overweight, and I was even more out of shape then."

Her "little voice" offered second thoughts. But Ava had learned long ago that thinking "what is the worst that can happen?" got her nowhere she wanted to go, while asking "what's the best that can happen, and what next step takes me in that direction?" propelled her toward success.

So she decided the best that could happen was that she would complete that walk. On time.

And the next step toward that goal was to create a plan. A list of little steps that she could take each day.

"Every time we climb a hill, we learn a little bit about climbing a mountain."

So she logged onto the Avon website and created her custom fitness plan. And that's all she did the first day.

The next day she bought new walking shoes. And that's all she did the second day.

The third day she walked around the block. And that's all she did the third day. It left her tired and breathless, but she wasn't about to give up. Because giving up wasn't the next step that would take her closer to the best thing that could happen.

"I still remember the day I walked a mile. I was like, I walked a mile! I walked a mile!" Ava has a musical speaking voice under any circumstances; now it rises with remembered joy as she sing-songs the words.

Before long she was hiking trails in Colorado, her native state. And when the time came to walk those 60 miles she did it. In under three days!

The weather didn't give the ladies doing the benefit walk any breaks—it was unseasonably hot for a Colorado summer and women were "dropping like flies." The ambulances were kept on stand by, and vans cruised the race route to rescue any participants who didn't feel up to finishing.

But Ava kept her eyes off the vans and focused on the next road mark. She kept moving, until the finish line was on her horizon. And she crossed that line, tired, but celebrating.

Remembered triumph resounds in her voice: "And it was AWESOME!"

> *"Nothing breeds big success like little successes."*
> ~ AVA DIAMOND,
> from The Dynamite Dialogs Project

Everyone knows you run a race one step at a time, but Ava knew you also have to prepare for the race one step at a time.

"I could have stayed powerless," she tells me. Instead she decided, "I have no idea how I'm going to make it happen. But what can I do today?"

> *"Horizons are only the limit of our vision, not the limit of our journey. If you've been looking at the same horizon for too long, it's because you aren't moving."*

"It's like driving down the highway after dark," Ava says, sharing her analogy for "thinking small" while creating a plan made up of step-sized goals.

She paints a picture of a night trip. Headlights cut into the blackness ahead, illuminating only a small section of the road at a time. But, because the car is moving, each section the light reaches is just a little closer to your destination, and you keep moving into the stretch of road you can see. Until there it is, in the light of your headlamps: the place you want to be!

Yes, a plan is vital, and so is action. But if your dream comes from your heart, you don't need to see the entire road to start your journey.

—CHAPTER 18—

WHAT CAN YOU
SAY YES TO EVERYDAY?

*"Balance is not a state of being, but a
moving art of becoming."*

Have you ever watched professionals walk a tightrope? How often do they stop moving?

Not often, because balancing on that rope at a standstill is much more difficult than putting one foot in front of the other. And if they do stop, you'll notice that they are never really motionless; they're constantly making little adjustments in order to remain balanced. Being rigid would only result in a fall.

Balancing all the aspects of our lives is like that. Momentum creates balance; balance allows momentum. Trying to hold on to the status quo creates tension; tension leads to a fall.

You've heard people talk about "work-life balance," right?

It's a myth. This *is* your life. Every single second of it. Seeing your work as something separate isn't balance; it's compartmentalization. And I've never heard anyone say, "What I really want to do is create a compartmentalized life."

During our Dialog, Mitch shares the story of one of his clients who found the prospect of balancing his current job (plus friends, family, and sleep requirements) with his future goals a bit overwhelming.

Kevin felt confident that he had a book in him—a great book! But he didn't feel confident that he had time to write it.

Mitch asked him how much time he could set aside every day to work toward his big dream. He couldn't honestly promise more than 30 minutes a day.

But when Mitch suggested that he start a blog and write one post every day, he agreed.

Writing came easily for Kevin, and he blogged consistently. His writing attracted a following, and the visitors and comments accumulated.

Eventually, Kevin wove his posts and the comments into a book. And the day that Mitch and I recorded our Dialog, Mitch's client was scheduled to appear on Dr. Phil!

It started with a commitment to write for 30 minutes, every day, and share the result with the world.

Mitch showed Kevin how he could create balance through forward momentum, not by taking one giant leap, but by a high-wire act—performed by making little adjustments and always moving forward.

So if you're wondering how you'll ever be able to balance what you really want to do with what you have to do right now, remember: It isn't necessary to take big steps to get to the other end of the rope, it's only necessary to *keep taking steps*.

—CHAPTER 19—

WHAT'S YOUR STATUS TODAY?

"If your day holds too few possibilities, just know that it is a limitation of your imagination, not a limitation of the day."

Perhaps you've heard of the phenomenon they call "social media?" It's hard to live in this decade without being at least aware of it, if not actively involved in it.

In my Dialog with the late Trey Pennington, a consummate storyteller recognized throughout the world as a master at teaching companies how to communicate through social media, he shares an observation about what most people post as their status.

"The significant opportunities available today are not so much about emerging technologies and techniques, but about purposefully, aggressively challenging and testing our assumptions about the way things are, the way things should be, and the way things can be!"

"And yet," he adds, "I see people post about the way things are. And the way things should be. But very few people post about the way things can be. And that's just sad."

How right. It is just sad. And completely unnecessary.

But sometimes even the exploration of what can be may mean blowing up a wall or two.

A client's wife once told me she had never had a dream for her life or her work. Her husband was an experimenter by nature; he had started so many businesses they nearly lost track before he found the one activity and business model that allowed him to live his purpose.

She had supported him in his search, and had financially supported them until that business began to be profitable.

Having been the breadwinner for so long, she was used to answering the "will it make money?" question before she even asked the "is it something I want to do?" question.

She had many brick walls to demolish before she could even give herself permission to embark on a journey to discover her own passion and purpose, let alone pursue her dream.

It is a natural human trait to dream of things we'd like to accomplish, achieve, and experience. It isn't practical to stop dreaming and exploring. Shutting down the creative dream state is demoralizing. Not allowing ourselves to even dream of doing something unless we can guarantee its success is a sure way to snuff out a light.

As a child, I was often criticized for having my head in the clouds. I didn't understand why growing up meant I had to be practical all the time. Now I'm grown up, and I understand that allowing myself "cloud time" is the most practical thing I can do.

Because that's where the opportunities are. By "purposefully, aggressively challenging and testing assumptions about the way things are, the way things should be, and the way things can be," I'm testing what I really want, and challenging the illusion of "impossible." If, from the outside looking in, that looks like my head is in the clouds, then I say, "Come on up, the air is fine!"

—CHAPTER 20—

HERE BE DRAGONS— BUT ONLY IF YOU BELIEVE IN DRAGONS

"We cannot see what we do not believe is possible."

Even if your pilot light is strong and your inner fire is burning bright, you'll be expending that energy on a treadmill unless you believe your dream is possible.

What if, one day, you saw a dragon flying overhead? Wings spread wide, scales glinting in the sunshine, and flames erupting from its maw—a real, live dragon. Would you say, "That is a dragon?"

I doubt it.

Your mind would struggle to make sense of the "nonsense" being fed to it by your eyes. Because your brain "knows" that dragons only exist in fairy tales and J. R. R. Tolkien stories. If we don't believe it's possible, we won't recognize it when it is right before our eyes.

Not believing in the "impossible" is a common barrier to living our dreams. Instead, we buy into things like "I'm not smart enough" or "I'm not creative" or "I'm too old," and add "so it is impossible for me."

What if it were possible? What if your age didn't matter and your creative abilities were validated?

This is called suspending disbelief—we do it when we read books or see movies. For instance, we don't really believe that dragons fly our friendly skies, but we are willing to believe in dragons in order to get "into" the story.

If *it were* possible, what else would be possible?

This is your story. If it has dragons in it, then believe in dragons.

What else do you need to see in order to create your happy ending? What belief is keeping you from seeing what is right before your eyes? What possibilities might exist that you can't see because you don't believe they are possible for *you*?

If you say, "The opportunity exists for me to use my skills, experience, and abilities to the greater good of mankind and make a good living while doing it," and listen closely for the "but I can't because …" that follows, you'll start to understand why you have never seen opportunities to realize that dream—your belief system is telling you that you are seeing geese, when in fact you're looking at a dragon.

You can prove yourself right, easily: just keep ignoring all those opportunities.

Or you can believe that dragons do exist in your world. As each "but I can't because …" comes to the surface, keep asking, "But what would I do if I *were* smart enough, or young enough, or rich enough, or creative enough?"

Knowing how you would behave or what action you would take, and then proceeding as if it were true, will open vistas to possibilities you would have never glimpsed before.

If you believe "but I can't because ..." then it becomes true.

But if you believe in dragons ... then "here be dragons."

—CHAPTER 21—

HOW MANY BABY ELEPHANTS CAN DANCE ON THE TIP OF A PEN?

*"Internal connections are the real game-changers—
everything else is either subsequential or superficial."*

You've never trained a baby elephant, have you? Neither have I. But I've been told that when trainers start working with a baby elephant, they chain it to a stake driven deep into the ground. The baby elephant, being a lot like Baby Dynamite, says "I can too! Watch me!" and tries with everything it's got to escape.

But it isn't strong enough to pull free of the stake. This goes on until the elephant "learns" that if there is a chain around its ankle, it is not free.

As an adult, the elephant has the strength to pull that stake out of the ground easily. But it believes it can't, so it chooses "cannot" and doesn't even try.

This is a story about belief.

About young elephants who didn't know they weren't free to dance.

And it's a story about vision. About having a vision and holding it steady until you can reach out and touch it.

And it's a story about passion, the energy you need to dance your way into that vision.

> *"The passion is the fuel that gets you there; the vision is simply the map."*
> ~ JOHN DAVID MANN,
> from The Dynamite Dialogs Project

No one would guess that John David Mann was a high school dropout.

He's been a musician, performing as a concert cellist while still in his teens, and continuing to perform for over a decade in orchestral and operatic productions, chamber ensembles, and solo recitals.

He's been a teacher at music schools and nationally recognized colleges.

He's been (and still is) a successful entrepreneur.

But John is best known as a writer. He's authored, coauthored, and ghostwritten more than 20 books, many of them best sellers.

I met John through my work developing the coaching program based on his books, written with Bob Burg: *The Go-Giver*, *Go-Givers Sell More*, and *It's Not about You*.

So there were any number of topics that John and I could have chatted about. But when I had the opportunity to record one of our conversations for The Dynamite Dialogs Project, I begged him to tell the story of dropping out of school.

At 16, he tells me, he and a group of his friends were kind of disaffected, bored with classes, and wished they had a more interesting education. So one fall they thought, "Hey, what if we started our own school?"

And that sounded great. So they did that.

They met on weekends and holidays and talked about what their school might look like. John even dropped out of school his junior year in order to focus all his energy on the project.

After a year's worth of effort, they opened a high school in central New Jersey. That high school went on to send its graduates to places like Harvard and Yale, and other major universities all over the country!

"How on earth do a bunch of high school kids start their own school?" I ask. He responds, "What can I say? It never occurred to us that we couldn't."

These kids believed in dragons all right!

They did have the blessing of a handful of parents who supported them. John's own mother always told him he could do anything he put his mind to; thankfully he had the good sense to believe her.

The youngsters hired a grown-up as a director. But they did the interviewing and hiring themselves, meeting with a series of adults until they selected a candidate to run their school.

John continued his active role, showing up every morning to work with the new director while his peers were in class. He remembers their first task together: fundraising. "Every morning, I'd get there around nine or ten, and Julian would be sitting at the typewriter with a paper bag full of letters he'd already written, addressed, and stamped."

I guess aloud: They must have sent letters to everyone whose address they could get their hands on, not just to people they thought might financially support their endeavor. John confirms my theory. They sent letters - to everyone

73

and anyone, with no emotional attachment to any *one* of the recipients making a contribution, only the expectation that enough of them would.

"We had a picture of what we wanted," he says. "And we filled in the pieces as we went. We knew we'd need adult support, and we assumed it would be there when we needed it."

The support was there, from their parents, the director, and the financial backers. After spending a year as a "high school dropout," John graduated from the school he had helped to found, and the rest, as we like to say, is history.

According to John, it came down to two basic elements: forming the picture in his mind, and acting as though it were true.

It isn't enough to have a vision, John reminds me. Anyone can have a vision. You have to hold that vision, day after day, hold it as real and true, until you step into it.

He used the same technique to master the cello. Long before he had the mechanical skills to perform difficult pieces, he'd lie awake and play them through in his mind, practicing in his head, creating the picture. Then, he says, he just played into the picture.

"It takes almost a fanatic level of devotion, energy, focus, persistence, patience, activity, and endurance, in the pursuit of that picture.

"But passion says 'it can't be true that I can't,' and if you listen to that, you stick with it."

While John had the kind of parents who believed he could do anything, and perhaps we didn't all grow up with that kind of programming, we do all have the option to choose to create the clear picture, and fill in the pieces as we go. We have the option to believe that support will be there when we need it.

We have the option to believe in dragons. We have the option to believe we "can too" dance!

If passion is the fuel, and the vision is only the map, then perhaps we could say that belief is the bridge that allows us to walk from "what I really want to do is ..." over to "I can too! Just watch me!"

CHAPTER 22

DO YOU HEAR WHAT I HEAR?

"What you say to yourself is the most important conversation you'll ever have. No one else's opinion will ever trump your own belief."

Martina Navratilova is a powerful personality, and a force to be reckoned with, on the courts and off. Her name is legendary in the world of tennis, known even to most people who don't follow the game. But she almost quit before anyone knew who she was.

It seems that, early in her career, Martina had a coach who tried to motivate her by saying things like, "If you play like that, you'll never be a professional champion," while telling anyone who asked that the only female player she was coaching who stood a chance was Martina.

Apparently this coach had been coached in what they call "reverse psychology" (which usually just puts people in reverse).

Martina, despairing of ever being good enough to please her coach, nearly left the game.

She didn't quit—in fact, she was the number one player for seven years and still plays on the World Team Tennis circuit as a guest celebrity. Her career wins include 18 singles and 41 doubles Grand Slam titles, including a record nine Wimbledons, and a total of 167 singles titles and 178 doubles titles.

Of course, her coach was only coaching Martina the way she herself had been coached, but it almost backfired. If it had, the world would have been deprived of some great tennis.

But many would say that great tennis is the least of Martina's impact. She has campaigned for equality in women's tennis, is an active supporter of animal rights programs, volunteers and contributes generously to organizations that advocate for underprivileged children, and serves as the health and fitness ambassador for AARP.

This impact would likely have been lost had Martina turned her back on a career in tennis.

> *"Words that are UP-lifting always inspire greater long-term success than those that are DOWN-putting."*

Martina listened to her own little voice. And that voice said, "You have what it takes to be a champion!"

I'm not a huge sports fan, but I have closely observed the traits of winning coaches. It's tempting to think that the boot camp approach of say, Bobby Knight, works well with some players, while others respond better to a quieter style, like Roy Williams's. But I have to wonder how much better people would respond if the "boot camp" were a little less brutal, and a little more uplifting.

I've had people in my life—maybe you have too—who seemed to think they could spur me to perform better by telling me all the ways I needed to improve, the things I was failing to do, and the shortcomings they could see so clearly. Others acknowledged my achievements and successes, even while pushing me to greater heights.

Those who offered negative prodding galvanized me to immediate action, but they didn't help me make a long-term transformation.

I didn't learn as much of what they had to share, because I was under tension to perform, and tension shuts down the learning centers.

More than that, they created recordings, other little voices, that pulled me down long after I stopped listening to their input.

As well-meaning as it may be, I've come to recognize this as a form of abuse. Boot camp, the original military training method, was designed to prepare soldiers to endure and overcome under extreme conditions. It is a taste of abuse to increase their chances of surviving greater abuse.

It is practical in that application, but to approach training for life and business the same way suggests that you expect your life to be a battle. Do you really need to be abused to be inspired to take action?

"You cannot achieve long-lasting positive results
using negative reinforcement."

"But it works!" you say. And you're right. It can be highly effective.

I've also seen many well-behaved children who didn't act out because they were afraid of the consequences. Consequences of choices like taking initiative, making mistakes, and going out on a limb. That fear may serve a purpose now, but it's creating a cacophony of little voices that won't serve them well in the long run.

One of my favorite "raves" on my testimonials page is a single sentence from Ana Gabriel Mann, an internationally recognized compensation consultant.

She writes, "Dixie has the amazing ability to hold her clients' toes to the fire and create realistic expectations and boundaries, while also being an authentic, respectful and loving presence."

I happened to read that quote from Ana just after I read the story about Martina. And my little voice said, "Maybe I need to be as good to myself as I am to others."

How about you? Might your little voice say the same?

I often beat myself up—how about you? I often set unrealistic expectations and boundaries for myself—how about you? I don't always respect and love myself—how about you? I've even been known to lie to myself—how about you? One of the greatest mistakes we can make is to look outside for what we need to discover inside. Tough love is one of those things.

The "tough" might get results, but alone it is a negative motivation at best, and often acts as a deterrent. The "love" part alone is comforting, but doesn't necessarily build us up.

Only when tough and love are fully interwoven do we create the confidence, validation, and impetus to reach continually higher than we ever thought possible.

So how do I love myself "tough?"

Through positive internal reinforcement.

Even if we have others in our life who offer uplifting words, if our internal dialog is down-putting, if we are abusing ourselves, the positive messages they gift to us will evaporate like soap bubbles on a windy day.

We all need coaches, they offer a perspective on our "game" that we can't get by looking inside.

We all need cheerleaders, they remind us of our power when we're feeling helpless and small.

But we must take responsibility for the conversations we have in the silence of our thoughts. Because it is these conversations that determine our winning record, no matter what game we play.

CHAPTER 23

BOUNDARIES, BARRIERS, AND BARRICADES

"Knowing the difference makes all the difference.
The basis of all intelligence is the
ability to differentiate."

If it looks like a brick wall and feels like a brick wall, it must be a brick wall. Right?

Maybe.

Let's say you've been offered a dream opportunity in San Francisco. The salary and benefit package is amazing and the job description is an exact fit, from the size of team you'd be heading up and the market segment you'd be serving right down to details like the color scheme in the corner office. But it requires that you be physically on-site at least 50 hours each week.

So you say, "What I really want to do is take that job, but I can't because I refuse to be away from my kids or move them to San Francisco."

That "can't" looks like a brick wall, doesn't it?

In reality, it's a self-imposed boundary.

That doesn't invalidate your reasoning. Nor does it mean you're using your kids as an excuse. We all have things we can't do, because we believe doing them would require doing something else we won't do.

We all live by a personal code. For most of us, it says we won't commit murder or theft, betray a friendship, or compromise the welfare of our loved ones. Of course, your personal code is likely far more extensive, but those examples head up most lists.

Do you know what boundaries you've established? What things are nonnegotiable —you simply will not do *anything* that requires that you violate this code?

Boundaries are vital to maintaining your integrity, and no boundaries are illegitimate. If moving beyond a certain point would compromise your ethics, erode your worth as a person, hobble your productivity, or in any way prevent you from being or becoming your highest self, then that boundary isn't a brick wall of "can't," but a fortress of "won't" that needs to be defended.

> *"There is a difference between establishing boundaries and accepting limitations."*

A boundary, then, is a wall you've built instead of drawing the proverbial line in the sand. Much as a barrier does, it prevents your progress down a certain path, but it's there because you want to honor your personal code more than you want what is on the other side of that wall.

Barriers are walls of a different composition. They're made up of beliefs that say you can't have what is on the other side, even though you want it more than anything that stands in the way.

Most of this book deals with what I've learned about blowing up barriers. But let's also take a look at another kind of wall that deserves a dose of dynamite. I call it a barricade.

"What impossible dream story are you telling yourself to avoid going after what you really want?"

A barricade, as you probably know, is something we erect to keep ourselves safe from someone, or something, that we perceive as a threat.

Seems counterintuitive, doesn't it? To think we would put up a brick wall to protect ourselves from what we say we really want?

Maybe you never have. But most of us have had at least one dream that is so big, a dream that would change our lives so much, that we tell ourselves we can't because, frankly, we're not only afraid to try—we're afraid to succeed.

So how do you determine whether your wall is a boundary, a barrier, or a barricade?

"Fear is a really big deterrent to desire."

I find that fear is also a great barometer.

I look to the source of my fear to help determine whether, and how, I need to blow up that wall.

If I'm afraid that moving forward means becoming someone I don't want to be, I know this is a *boundary*.

85

Nonnegotiable, non-assailable, non-budgable. Unless and until I change who I want to be, or change my belief about the outcome of pursing that path, that wall stands.

If I'm afraid of what the wall itself represents, the risks, possible consequences, personal growth, abandonment of comfort zones, or difficult conversations that will be required to bring it down, this is a *barrier*.

A *barricade* I recognize by the fear I feel when I imagine success. When I close my eyes and picture life after doing what I really want to do.

Will I still have control over my life? Or will my success mean being busier than I want to be? More in the limelight than I want to be? Less carefree than I want to be?

Will people still see me as I am? Or will they see only my success? Will they resent me? envy me? idolize me? patronize me?

And what if, after I'm living my dream, I can't keep it up? What if I fall from the pedestal, fall from favor, fall on my face?

It's easier, with those fears nibbling at my imagination, to rationalize why I "can't" and stay safely on this side of my barricade.

A barrier is something we'll fire at without reservation. Because we know we want what is on the other side.

A barricade, we build because we have mixed feelings about what is on the other side. So we duck behind that wall, peering out at what we say we really want, and telling ourselves (and anyone who will listen) that we *can't* because (insert reason here).

"Well, look," we say. "Can't you see this wall? I can't possibly get through that!"

"You'll never give 100 percent effort to achieving anything you aren't 100 percent certain that you want to do."

When you say, "I have mixed feelings, but I'll give it 100 percent for a month or two and see what happens," just know you will *never* give it 100 percent.

Giving it 100 percent isn't just about effort; it's about energy and belief. It's about being open to possibilities, being creative about alternate routes, being determined about forward momentum.

You can't have a mind that's open, creative, or determined when it's torn between two belief systems.

You may be pounding your fists on that wall, even pounding your head against it, but you won't put your full creative, problem-solving energy into finding a way over, around, under, or through it when you have mixed feelings about getting to the other side.

To blow up a barricade you must be mentally and emotionally clear and connected to your desired destination. You must be ready to embrace your success.

And to be ready to embrace your success, you may have to embrace your fear.

—CHAPTER 24—

TRUTH
OR FEAR

*"We aren't really afraid of the questions. It's the
answers that frighten us. But our answers are true
whether or not we have the courage to ask
the questions. Are you acting out of your
fears instead of your truth?"*

Few of us remember the first time we were afraid—of the
monster under the bed, the climb to the top of the slippery
slide, finding ourselves in the middle of a grocery aisle with
only strangers in sight.

But most of us remember being teased for our fears.
Feeling the blush of shame when we realized the monster
was only a bad dream, the ladder to the top of the slide was
easily worth braving for the thrill of the ride to the bottom,
the grocery store was a perfectly safe place, with Mommy or
Daddy only a shout away.

We've all heard the acronym "False Evidence Appearing
Real," and

Roosevelt's famous line, "The only thing we have to fear
is fear itself."

So we learn to hide our fears, even from ourselves, masking the fear that seems unreasonable with a brick wall that appears more real.

> *"Reality is merely an illusion,*
> *albeit a persistent one."*
> ~ ALBERT EINSTEIN

One of the most fantastic surprises I had during The Dynamite Dialogs Project was the opportunity to record a conversation with Richard Bach.

Richard is the best-selling author of more than 20 titles, including two iconic books that have touched the lives of millions: *Jonathan Livingston Seagull*, and *Illusions: The Adventures of a Reluctant Messiah*.

He is also known as a recluse, seldom appearing to sign books, speak, or do live interviews.

For several years, as part of a frequently requested keynote, I shared the story of how Richard's presence, in the form of the story he tells in *Illusions*, changed my life. How it, in fact, changed my perspective of my reality to the degree that I chose not to end my life.

And, since I knew his preference for staying out of the public eye, each time I told that story from the platform I said, "Richard Bach, a man I will never meet, shared his presence so authentically, so powerfully, that the course of my life was forever altered."

How Richard and I did meet is another story, but we both agree that we were brought together, in part, because of our fascination with barriers, our shared analogies of conceptual barriers as solid, physical walls, and our mutual understanding of those barriers as illusions that can be blown up or walked through with the power of desire, belief, and focused, purposeful action.

During our Dialog, Richard recaps a scene from one of his more recent books, *Hypnotizing Maria.*

The main character has an encounter with a performing hypnotist. Certain that he cannot be hypnotized, he agrees to be a subject in one of the master's demonstrations. So certain is he of his ability to resist suggestion, that, when he is led across the stage and perceives that he has descended into a room with walls of stone, he's still waiting for the "trick" to commence.

Then the hypnotist leaves the room, vanishing from view, and invites him to leave the room as well. But the door has disappeared, and all he can see are four solid walls of stone. He panics.

Of course, the audience sees him standing onstage with the hypnotist, no stone walls in sight!

Our fear is like that. The power of someone else's suggestion walling us in.

But, Richard also points out, as human beings, we've agreed to play by certain rules. It's like a game of chess, he explains, in which we say the knight can only move here, and here, and here.

In fact, the knight can be moved to the bureau, with no harm to the knight. Of course, once on the bureau, the knight is no longer in the game. If our objective is to win at chess, moving the knight to the bureau may seem an unacceptable risk, worthy of fear.

In just such a manner, we know that loss of face will not really harm us, but if we choose to accept it as important to winning the game, then losing face may be a price too high to pay.

The loss of home or health or physical life may be only an illusion to our spirit, but it's an unacceptable loss so long as we desire to continue our human existence and enjoy the advantages of a high-functioning physical body and our current lifestyle.

So, while our walls and fears may be illusions, for the sake of staying in the game, we allow ourselves to perceive them as real.

> *"Be transparent with your fear, and what*
> *you fear becomes transparent."*

I have observed that we create our thickest walls by trying to deny our fears. The memory of being shamed for showing fear, the expectation that we will be able to reason ourselves into not feeling fear, the dread of having our fears revealed as illusions, all create incentives to hide our fears behind blame.

When we're hiding from our fear, we look for other things to blame for our lack of momentum. We point to brick after brick, saying, "I can't because ... ." But we don't move those bricks, because we don't want to face the real fear that lies behind them.

When we're hiding our fear behind false bravado, we tend to blame ourselves. We lash ourselves into action with platitudes and competitiveness, saying, "Go for it; just do it; push through it; if so-and-so can do it so can you; just get over it."

Any time I find myself relying on blame, whether inward-focused or outward-focused, I ask myself, "So how's that workin' for ya?"

I've never been able to say it was working very well.

Perhaps, rather than saying "that brick wall isn't real—that brick wall isn't real—that brick wall isn't real"—while banging our heads against the wall in question—we would be better served by examining the wall and believing beyond doubt that we will discover a door, a window, a chink in the mortar, which will serve as a way over, under, around, or through it.

Fear has its function: It keeps us from jumping out of airplanes without a parachute, and suggests that nibbling on unidentified berries or fungi may not be the better part of wisdom.

It is part of our instinctive makeup to experience fear, and when we deny that instinct we create confusion. But when we acknowledge our fear, we can use that instinct to inform our truth. Only then can we differentiate the need for rational pre-cautions from the paralysis of conditioned panic.

Once we stop blaming outside elements for keeping us from our desires, once we stop blaming ourselves for not pur-suing our desires, then we can ask the right questions, and answer them truthfully. Then we can make choices based on our own truth, rather than our fear.

Facing fear doesn't mean rushing willy-nilly, head-down, battering-ram-style into the wall. Facing fear means looking it calmly in the eye, nodding with respect, and saying, "Yes, I see you, and I respect you, but you are between me and what I really want, so you're going to have to move."

CHAPTER 25

LEAVE THE CRATE TO THE CRABS

*"Keep away from people who try to belittle your
ambitions. Small people always do that.
But the really great make you feel that
you, too, can become great."*
~ MARK TWAIN

I've heard that there is no need to put a lid on a crate of live crabs. While I've not seen this phenomenon for myself, I'm told that if one crab tries to climb out of the crate, the others reach up and pull it back in.

Now I don't know whether their motivation is purely protective: "There's safety in numbers; it's a big scary world out there; if we all stick together we'll make it home in time for dinner." Or whether, being too lazy or too frightened to make a break for it themselves, they don't want to be shamed by one brave soul who's willing to risk it: "Oh no you don't! If *we* have to be part of someone else's dinner, you're going to be on that table too!" But I do know that whether we're escaping from a crate or blowing up brick walls, some "crabs" won't come with us. And some will actively try to hold us back.

To succeed, or even to fail, you'll have to choose to leave the crate to the crabs, and make a run for it!

Dafna Michaelson-Jenet knows all about escaping the crate and making a run for it. In 2008, she was working for a major hospital, and watching the decline of the economy. Tempted as she was to join in the conversations about how "our government needs to do something about ... ," she remembered a vow she had made to herself at 16, to never complain about a problem she wasn't working to solve.

Looking around, she saw not only a lot of people complaining about the problem and demanding that someone else do something about it, but also a lot of people who were working to solve problems in their own communities.

Then came the fateful moment when her fiancé (now husband) Michael Jenet said, "What would you do if we won the lottery?"

"I'd travel the country," Dafna declared, "and interview all those community problem-solvers, and share their stories with the rest of the world."

As she fleshed out her fantasy, she began to see the impact such an undertaking could have. Not only would the stories be inspiring to others, she'd also be proving that it *is* possible to solve our own problems without waiting for government intervention, and the examples she shared would offer blueprints for others who dreamed about solving problems in their own communities.

And she would be doing something to be a part of the solution!

Michael was caught up in the possibilities as well. Their conversation quickly turned from fantasy and dream into vision and desire. This was something they really wanted to do!

Of course, there were brick walls—towering fortress walls!

Their first concern was for Dafna's two children, whose custody she shared with her ex-husband. Traveling to do interviews, which they decided would be collected on video, would have to take place only on days when the children were with their father.

Then, because they did *not* win the lottery, there was the challenge of funding the undertaking. Dafna offered up her 401(k) as seed money, feeling confident that, with her background in fundraising, she could find the rest of the money she needed.

And of course, there were the "crabs." Her friends thought she was delightfully crazy. Her family just thought she was crazy.

As a perfect illustration of those who "support the dream, but not the doing," her ex-husband, with whom she has maintained a loving friendship, said, "I love the *idea*; I hate that Dafna is doing it. It's too hard on her; there's too much risk."

In spite of attempts to dissuade her, the plans developed. Dafna would travel to each of the 50 states over the course of a year, and capture video interviews of community problem-solvers.

She called her undertaking the 50 in 52 Journey. With Michael's help, she built a website. She formed a 501(c)(3) and recruited a board of directors. Of course, she knew she'd have to quit her job.

About that job ... "Timing," Dafna says to me in our Dialog, "sucked! In fact, it could not have been worse."

The day she left her job was the day the banks started to collapse. Friends, family, even members of her board advised her to drop her plans and go back to work. They said, "Crawl on your hands and knees if you have to, but *get your job back!*"

It might have been sound advice, but all Dafna could say was, "If you thought things were already bad, they're worse now. People need inspiration and hope even more than they did before."

But people also needed their security more than they did before. Contributions dried up. Brick walls loomed. Fear became a nagging companion.

Then came the morning Dafna woke up smiling. Well, she didn't wake up smiling; she just forced herself to smile as soon as she woke up. Because she woke up scared! And she'd read that body chemicals respond to facial expression. So she smiled as big and wide as she could, and headed for the sink to brush her teeth.

When she spit out the toothpaste, the sink filled with blood. She was spitting blood, then vomiting blood, and she could hear her kids up and about, so she tried to clean up the blood while pushing the bathroom door shut with her foot so the kids wouldn't know she was dying.

Because she was pretty sure that was what was happening. She wouldn't have to embark on the 50 in 52 Journey after all!

She called a friend who was a doctor, and, while he was reassuring about the blood, his diagnosis also evaporated that brick wall. She'd had a nosebleed, he told her. In her sleep. Probably due to stress. And the blood had pooled in her throat, and drained into her stomach. So it was just lying there, waiting for a chance to get out of her system, and out of her system it came. She wasn't dying. She wasn't even sick. Just stressed. Extremely stressed.

The first state she intended to visit on the Journey was Delaware. She had no interviews scheduled; she hadn't even booked her ticket. But, since she wasn't dying, she knew she had to go.

Dafna faced a lot of brick walls before she embarked on the Journey, and a lot more during the first six months. But she circumvented or blasted through them all!

"We are never given more than we can handle.
Just sometimes, more than we can handle alone."

Then came the day she knew she had to quit. She was out of resources, and out of energy. She had slept on the couches of strangers, and on the backseats of rental cars. She had spent every moment she was at home giving all she had to her children, and every moment she was away giving all she had to her mission. She had spent every dime of contributions and every penny of her retirement money. There was nothing left.

Tears flowing freely, she sat on a swing in the playground across from Michael's home, and pecked out a letter to her board of directors while her kids played on the jungle gym.

She wrote that it had been an amazing experience, and that she knew what she had accomplished so far would have tremendous impact. She told them too, that it didn't make sense to go on. It was time to throw in the towel. It was time to quit.

She asked Michael to preview her resignation letter before she sent it. He read it, then took her firmly by the shoulders and said, "*We* don't quit."

Three words. And in those three words, the opportunity to blow up a brick wall, and laugh in the face of one the greatest fears we ever face: the fear of being in it alone.

Because, alone, she had no responsible choice but to quit. Together, energies and resources combined, they celebrated a successful finish on New Year's Eve, 2009—50 states, in 52 weeks, and a collection of more than 500 interviews with incredible spirits that she, and the world, might never have met any other way.

CHAPTER 26

WHAT FACE DOES YOUR FEAR WEAR?

*"Two of the hardest things we will ever have
to deal with: Failure, and success."*

It seems to be widely accepted that the fear that most often keeps people from pursuing what they most want is the fear of failure.

And yet we're all familiar with failure, aren't we? It isn't pleasant, but it's survivable. And we already know what it takes to survive it.

But success? That's uncharted territory.

Fear of failure is easier to admit, and easier to express. We have words for it, and people can relate.

But if we are transparent with our fear, the brick wall often looks like this: "I'm afraid of doing what I really want to do, because if I succeed, I don't know whether I can handle the changes to my life, and to myself."

*"It is possible to survive failure completely
unchanged. But success transforms us forever."*

"All fear," Richard Bach taught me, "is a fear of loss."

Change, even positive, desired change, implies a loss. We give up the safety of the crate, and the company of the other crabs. We give up our usual routine, and our old worldview. Success can rock our foundations of truth, and push our known boundaries of *self* beyond recognition.

There are several techniques I use to lift myself, and my clients, over this barrier. They are all methods of applying what Richard taught in *Illusions*, and John David Mann demonstrated when he mastered the cello: First, you see yourself as already there—you accept that "it" is true—then you step into that truth.

And, taking that step, you have no fear of loss, because you've already fled the crate, released the routine, shed the boundaries, and embraced your future.

CHAPTER 27

CALLING ALL SAINTS

"It is in our truest dreams we find
reflected our highest self."

I'm no saint. I don't hang out with saints. I wouldn't even know how to have a dialog with a saint.

But I do have a community of friends I call my "angels."

They're the people who quietly take others under their wings, or who loudly and insistently campaign for their vision of a better earth and a brighter tomorrow.

They're the spirits who have touched me with their power, their grace, their clarity, their perseverance, their dedication to proving that one person, one voice, can change the now in which we live and the future that we face. And among them, they have touched the lives of millions more.

Dafna is one of those angels.

But when she told me about Michael's decision to fully partner with her in seeing the 50 in 52 Journey through, then added, "Can you imagine anyone more selfless?" I had to protest.

For all the good my "angels" do in this world, I don't consider them selfless. I honor their choices and contributions, but I know their choices serve them, and their contributions come back to them tenfold.

I realized this was yet another fear we face when we accept an undertaking. Sacrifices.

Our own, yes.

But often, the even greater fear is that we might require sacrifices of others.

"The pursuit of that which is most important is never a sacrifice."

I shared my realization, and Dafna quickly agreed. Michael chose to support the Journey because their shared vision was important to him. It was not only *her* true dream, he had made it his true dream as well. For both of them, seeing it through was a path to becoming their highest selves.

Which, by my definition, made Michael an angel. But it didn't make him selfless.

If we let go of the layers of meaning added to the word "sacrifice" over centuries of use, and refer instead to its Latin origin, we find it comes from *sacrificium*, which breaks down as *sacer*—meaning "sacred"—and *facere*—meaning "to make."

"To make sacred."

That is what Michael did; he made the achievement of their dream, the arrival at their destination, a sacred thing, worthy of his wholehearted pursuit. Dafna had already made that same choice.

Any path we pursue comes at a price. I don't think of it as a sacrifice, but as an opportunity cost. If we travel down one path, we give up the opportunity to travel down another.

During our Dialog, Dafna and I talk about the "sacrifices" she and Michael made to budget for the Journey.

Had they chosen to budget differently, they would have paid the opportunity cost of not being able to complete the Journey. Had they made other choices, Dafna's paying projects—consulting, teaching curriculums, speaking engagements that have taken her all over the United States, Ireland, and the United Kingdom, and an upcoming book—would likely not have materialized.

> *"Any time we choose to pursue that path of our highest right, there are things, and people, that fall out of our lives. Things that shift and change,*
> *and with that comes doubt and fear. You have to release yourself from that."*
> ~ DAFNA MICHAELSON-JENET,
> from The Dynamite Dialogs Project

I would suggest that neither Dafna nor Michael were self-less, but that they were highly self-aware. They knew what was most important. And they pursued it, not without fear, but responsibly and relentlessly, in spite of all their fears.

And yet, we are often afraid of accepting the help that is offered. Especially if we perceive that it will come at a cost.

> *"The most selfish decision you can make is any decision that holds you back from becoming your highest self. The second most selfish decision you can make is any decision that holds someone else back from becoming their highest self!"*

Have you ever considered that, when we refuse help freely offered, we might be throwing up a brick wall in the path of people who are only trying to live out their truest dream, to evolve into their highest self?

If your purpose statement begins, as so many do, with "I want to help ... ," How are you going to do all that helping if you don't first help yourself?

When I say "help yourself," I hear two interpretations. You need to *help* yourself, *and* you need to reach into the cookie jar and *help yourself*!

You're going to have to take some things from life in order to have more to give back.

If you want to help people, you can begin by modeling for them the strength and commitment of serving your purpose and realizing your dream. No matter how many brick walls get in the way.

Then you can allow them to be part of your journey, because being part of your journey might well carry them leaps and bounds ahead, on a journey all their own.

CHAPTER 28

AMANDA HAS SOMETHING TO SAY— AND IT IS NOT "I CAN'T"

"Everyone shares three universal needs:
to be heard, to be understood, and
to know that their life counts."
~ TREY PENNINGTON,
from The Dynamite Dialogs Project

Trey was known for applying those three tenets to create communication and social media strategies for companies all over the world, opening channels for customers to "be heard, be understood, and to know they counted."

But it wasn't a company that drove that lesson home for Trey. It was a little girl, a student at a school for special-needs children where Trey often volunteered. Her name was Amanda.

In our Dialog he says,

"My experience with Amanda was definitely transformative for me and the way I see the world.

"I was in the school one day, and walking down the hall, and Amanda came out of the speech therapy room and started walking down the hall with the speech pathologist.

"Amanda was 11 years old at the time, and doctors had diagnosed and characterized her as nonverbal, noncommunicative. Meaning that she could feel and think and hope and hurt, just like the rest of us. But her body simply would not cooperate with her for her to get her message out.

"So the speech pathologist had been showing her how to use an adaptive communication device, which was a computer that had pictures on it that Amanda could push, and the computer would talk for her.

"And so I was walking down the hall toward her, and she was coming to me, and she raised both hands and waved them wildly, so that I knew that this noncommunicative girl wanted me to stop and pay attention to her.

"So I did. And I said, 'Hello, Amanda. What is it?'

"And she looked at me. And then she looked down at the computer. She pushed a button. And the computer said, 'I have something to tell you.'

"And I said, 'OK Amanda, what do you have to tell me?'

"She looked up at me, and just really connected with my eyes. Then she looked down at the computer and looked up again to make sure she had my full attention. Then *very* slowly and deliberately, she selected a button. And the computer said, 'I love you.'

"I said, 'I love you too, Amanda.'

"Of course, I was touched by her expression of affection and affirmation. It was very valuable for me. But the most significant treasure, as it were, in that moment, was the look in her eyes as, for the first time in her life, she knew that somebody else knew what she was feeling."

Our Dialog has several seconds of silence after that story. In a sense, I realized, we are all nonverbal, noncommunicative; and we all need help being understood.

> *"The truth is, we don't do anything by ourselves.*
> *Even the things we do in solitude have their root*
> *in a shared experience."*

Amanda's story not only teaches the power of meeting those universal needs to be heard, be understood, and know our life counts. It also speaks to me of her desire to include others, her willingness to accept help, and her determination to follow her dream of being heard, being understood, and making her life count, down any path that presented itself.

Amanda could have "remained powerless," as Ava put it. No one would have been surprised, or thought less of her for it. She could have said to herself, "I can't express myself by speaking, so I can't express myself at all."

Instead, she accepted an unusual alternative to speech as a way to say, "I can too; just watch me!" And she accepted the help to learn to put it to use.

And when she was finally able to say "I love you," she was heard, she was understood, and she could see from Trey's face that her life, and her three little words, counted.

CHAPTER 29

WOULD YOU BELIEVE... TALKING MICE?

"All our dreams can come true, if we have the courage to pursue them."
~ WALT DISNEY

Ah, the things we fantasized about as children! Before anyone told us we were just being silly, when we still believed in talking mice and hobbits, and thought being a nurse or a firefighter would be exciting, but wouldn't really be work.

It was a time when we believed that the only reason we couldn't do anything was because a grown-up said no. And that when we were the grown-ups we would be able to do anything we wanted.

Then we grew up.

"I think one of the best guides to telling you who you are, and I think children use it all the time for this purpose, is fantasy."
~ PETER SHAFFER

Every time I speak about the importance of unedited fantasizing, at least one person says, "But some fantasies are just impossible."

And when they say that, a lot of other people nod sagely.

So I guess someone forgot to tell Walt Disney that talking mice weren't possible? Because millions of kids show up to talk to Mickey and Minnie every year.

And Peter Jackson created a world where hobbits come to life. Along with dwarves, elves, and orcs.

To some people, being a nurse or a firefighter might be so exciting and enjoyable that the effort doesn't feel like work.

"Indulging in a rich, unedited fantasy life is as essential to the creative wellspring as food is to physical function."

When we say "that's impossible" or "I can't," what we usually mean is "it can't happen exactly like that." That may well be true. I have yet to meet anyone who has gone on a romp through Wonderland with the precocious Alice, or sat down to a dinner of roasted dragon with King Arthur and his knights.

However, just because some flights of fancy have to stay in the realm of fantasy does not mean that we should edit them, or that we cannot choose the dreams worthy of pursuit based on the life we live in our fantasies.

The important thing is to learn what elements of a fantasy are really worth committing to.

For instance, a fantasy about owning a private island may be about the beach, but it may also be about a luxurious lifestyle, about status, about ownership, about seclusion. Or it may be about none of those things and about something entirely different. Knowing what about that fantasy keeps drawing you back allows you to create a reality that includes those elements.

There are all kinds of reasons we let what could be true dreams languish in dreamland. Commitments require courage; fear gets in the way.

We have "crabs" in our lives (often even in our heads), saying we'd better get back in the crate. We have naysayers who tell us that our dream is impossible, or that we don't deserve it. We may even have partners in our lives or businesses who do not share our vision. Sometimes, there *are* practical reasons for letting fantasies keep their "entertainment only" status.

However, when you make a commitment to turn your fantasies into dreams, narrow your focus to turn dreams into visions, and create a plan to turn visions into realities, you will find that your life undergoes a dramatic change. The energy gathers, you begin to allow yourself to believe, you begin to plan, and you begin to take action.

And things begin to happen that you thought only happened in fairy tales.

—CHAPTER 30—

MAGIC IS MADE UP OF LITTLE THINGS

"Success is not an attribute, but an
accumulation of achievements."

It's a common question, often asked by coaches as part of a client discovery session: "If you could wave a magic wand and change just one thing about your life, what would it be?"

Oh, don't we wish we had that magic wand, or magic pill, or magic spell! Then the only problem we would have would be choosing that one thing we most want to change. Right?

I've never made a magic wand, formulated a magic pill, or worked a magic spell. But I've read my share of fantasy and fairy tales. And, as I understand it, magic is a tricky thing at best.

You have to use exactly the right ingredients, say exactly the right words, at exactly the right phase of the moon. Magic, to people in the know, is a combination of little things.

In fact, it takes a lot of work to get it right! But, apparently, it makes everything else a lot easier once that work is done.

Like the work we've been doing here so far. Lots of little things. Work done now, to make life easier later.

If I were to write a spell for brewing a batch of firepower that will blow up brick walls, it would go something like this:

Select elements from the example(s) of others, but when formulating your method, ask, "How can *I?*" rather than, "*How* can I?" Methods that have worked for others may not work for you, and the method that will work for you may not work for anyone else.

Check the power connections before you accept an undertaking. Are you plugged in and fully charged with desire and energy? Can you commit to this purpose, mission, dream, or even project, with all your heart?

Listen for your little voice. It may be only a whisper under the cacophony of platitudes. It may be nearly drowned out by the shouts of crabs. It may be coming to you through layers of bricks. It may be muffled by status updates about the way things are, and the way things should be. But that little voice will tell you about the way things *can* be. If you are willing to make them so.

Focus your mind's eye on the desired result, never on the barriers, or the contingency plan. Tightrope walkers look ahead, not at the safety net. Magic-workers see what they really want to do as already done, not as blocked by brick walls.

Surround yourself with good witches. Coaches, mentors, role-models, and cheerleaders all add power to your spell, so make sure their magic is positively "white!"

Create an incantation that is your personal truth. If your words are based on platitudes, clichés, fear, blame, or doubt, your spell will surely backfire!

Name your demons. If you believe the stories, the presence of magic always attracts evil demons. But, those stories tell us, if you can learn a demon's true name you have power over it! Fears are the demons most often summoned by this kind of magic. Name them, and they will become much more manageable.

Invoke the magic of motion. No spell is complete without movement, and your magical concoction will be inert until you take action. Once you have committed to a path, decide what you can do today—what you can do every day—that will create momentum, and activate your powerful potion!

Oh, one more tip for deciding what to put in your cauldron: It helps to know what kinds of bricks your wall is made of!

SECTION THREE

FOUR WALLS DO NOT A PRISON MAKE

CHAPTER 31

SORTING OUT
THE BRICKS

*"The first wall you will encounter is your own
conditioning. The next wall, and the next, and the
next, will be the conditioning of other people."*

As I recorded the different ways I heard people complete the "but I can't because ..." statement, I realized that nearly all their "can'ts" could be sorted into one of four categories: Circumstances, Style, Consequences, and Design.

These are the names of the bricks we mortar into place until they become solid walls. These are the conversations we have with ourselves, as we once again lay our dreams aside to molder as fantasies.

Sometimes, just naming your wall reveals it as illusion, no more than a suggestion planted in your mind. Conditioning, programming, false premises ... an insubstantial barrier, constructed of ideas and solid air.

So we'll start there. But don't get worried or frustrated if your brick wall still seems solid after it has the proper nametag firmly affixed; being on a first-name basis won't keep us from blowing it up.

—CHAPTER 32—

THE WALL OF CIRCUMSTANCES

"It is what it is. What it will be is up to you."

"I can't because I don't have a degree."

"I can't because I'm not old enough."

"I can't because I'm not blond enough."

All those circumstances can be changed. It might take years, or just an hour in a beauty salon. It might take a lot of work, or just waiting around. But you can get a degree or change your hair color, and you will someday be old enough.

"I can't because I'm a guy."

"I can't because I'm too old."

"I can't because I'm married."

Those circumstances aren't likely to change, so unless you change the criteria, there's a good chance you "can't" compete for Miss America! I know I wouldn't qualify.

I'm sure you've heard the "Serenity Prayer":

> *"God grant me the serenity*
> *to accept the things I cannot change;*

courage to change the things I can;
and wisdom to know the difference."
~ REINHOLD NIEBUHR

The author left his verse untitled. So why has it come to be known as the "Serenity Prayer"? Why not the "Courage Prayer" or the "Wisdom Prayer"?

Surely knowing the difference, and changing what you can, comes before accepting what you cannot change!

As Trey points out, most people focus on the way things are, and the way they believe things should be. But the opportunities lie in exploring the way things *can* be!

"Not accepting 'can't' begins with not buying into
the way things are or the way they should be, but
challenging the way things can be. If we are
willing to make them so."

Of course, you don't have to change everything at once!

—CHAPTER 33—

CHOOSING "CAN TOO" — JUST NOT RIGHT NOW

"A bridge is not a destination."

I remembered Lynne Wilhite as a redhead.

Later, I realized that my perception was partly due to an optical illusion, caused by the lighting in the office space where we first met. But I still think it was partly because she has all the sass and spark of a natural redhead!

In any case, Lynne's curls are naturally blond, but her fire-and-bubbles personality is bone-deep, along with the most "can do" attitude I've ever encountered.

Which was a good thing for both of us. Because she had to blow up some brick walls just to work with me.

Lynne and I met at a networking event. We quickly became no-longer-strangers during a brief conversation in a swirling tide of people. Some minutes or hours later, we realized we'd been ignoring the rest of the room completely, so engaged were we in our discussion. We decided we'd better circulate, but we knew it wouldn't be our last conversation.

What I didn't expect was that our next conversation would be her phone call to me with a single question: "What does it cost to work with you?"

You might think this would be a perfectly natural next step after meeting someone at a networking event. But, you see, Lynne was not my typical client. Not only was she not self-employed, she wasn't employed at all. Lynne had introduced herself to me as a "seasoned sales professional in search of a new opportunity."

So, after assuring Lynne that I would love very much to work with her, I added, "But I'm not a career coach."

She said she didn't care.

I told her that my strength as a coach was not in helping people decide what job they should pursue—I had absolutely no expertise in helping someone find a sales job, and she didn't have to hire me in order to tap into my network; I would be happy to make any introduction that would be beneficial to her.

She said that wasn't the point.

Every wall I threw up, Lynne answered with some variation of, "But I like you, and I trust you, and I want you to be my coach."

It finally got through to me that I was making a lot of assumptions. I was assuming that the coaching Lynne needed would center on finding employment opportunities. I was assuming that she wouldn't be able to pay my usual fee. I was assuming that she was mistaken in her desire to work with me. And I was making all these assumptions because of one circumstance—Lynne didn't have a job.

You've probably already noticed that Lynne didn't try to change the circumstances. She just redefined the criteria.

Once I stopped assuming, I posed the question I usually ask in the beginning (when I'm not busy throwing up the Wall of Circumstances). "Lynne," I asked, "What is it you'd like to accomplish by working with a coach?"

Lynne laid out two sets of circumstances. One she wanted to change immediately. The other she wasn't ready to change, but she wanted to prepare for the time when she would be.

She'd been in medical sales for about 20 years, she told me. And she knew she had developed some patterns and beliefs that were costing her dearly. She wanted to use her time between positions to create new patterns and retire old habits and belief systems.

"Isn't that what a coach does?" she challenged me. Feeling humbled, I agreed. Yes, that was an appropriate objective for us to partner on.

The other objective had to do with Lynne's true dream. She didn't intend to be an employee forever.

She and her husband had an agreement, she explained. He was self-employed, and they had two young children. She had committed to maintaining traditional employment for the stable income and medical benefits, until the children were older. Then it would be her turn to explore entrepreneurship.

She wanted to be strategic about the opportunities she pursued during those years, building the resources, skills, connections, and character traits that would best serve her when her circumstances at home changed.

Lynne and I had a wonderful coaching relationship for more than six months, and we have a rich friendship to this day!

"Dreams are like eggs; they'll hatch
only when the chick is ready."

Lynne says the greatest gift our time together offered was teaching her not to edit her dreams, even if she isn't pursuing them right now, because, by dreaming both true and big, she's been able to think small, making choices that will take her closer to where she really wants to go. That egg may still be in the incubator, but she's going to be ready for it when it hatches!

In fact, Lynne discovered that the purpose that really lights her fire isn't selling. "What I really love to do is help people do deals," she says during our Dialog.

And that is exactly what Lynne is doing now. She's still in traditional employment, but she is coaching and mentoring sales professionals, helping them write proposals and present to clients, and teaching the secrets she's mastered in over 20 years of never failing to meet her sales goals.

Our Dialog makes it plain that Lynne's secrets to "doing deals" aren't so different from my method of blasting through the Wall of Circumstances. We negotiate our dreams much the way we negotiate a purchase.

In any deal, Lynne explains, there are things that you can change and things you can't. The key is learning the client's priorities.

Usually, the first objection offered by clients isn't the real reason they aren't buying. They may not even know the real barrier. So Lynne teaches her protégés to play the "what if" game.

"What if we could add value here?"

"What if we could reduce the delivery time there?"

She calls it "leveling the playing field." I call it "exploring the way things *can* be!"

When was the last time you played the "what if" game with the circumstances of your life?

Lynne understands that constructing a complex proposal means distilling what the client really wants, and adjusting the offering to give the client as much value as possible.

Which is exactly what Lynne and I did together: distilling the essence of what she really wanted from both her long-term and short-term opportunities, and adjusting circumstances to align as closely as possible with her path from A to B.

We had a grand time, during our Dialog and other conversations, comparing the sales and buying process to the way we conquer our brick walls.

But it was *this* comment of Lynne's that really gave me chills:

"If you don't know what they want, and why they want it, then you get caught up in *how*; you're competing on price alone, and you're automatically stuck. The deal is as good as dead."

You can either change the circumstances or change the criteria. But if you don't know what you want, or why you want it, then your circumstances really don't matter. Not one bit!

CHAPTER 34

THE WALL
OF STYLE

*"Are you using 'I am what I am' as an excuse
for being less than you can be?"*

"I can't do it the way my idol does it."

"I can't do it the way the book says to do it."

Do you often think, "Wow! I wish I could do it like that!" And then finish that thought with, "But I can't, so I'd better not even try?" Why do we tend to put an equals sign between "I can't do it that way" and "I can't do it at all"?

Believing that there is only one way to do anything is what my friend and mentor Bob Burg calls a "false premise."

Bob is a speaker and author, and the perfect person to join me in a Dialog about the Wall of Style. Because "I can't do it the way Bob Burg does it" could so easily have become a brick wall for me.

I got to know Bob because of a powerful little parable he coauthored with John David Mann. *The Go-Giver* was such a perfect illustration of the mindset and values that I believed were the basis for success in life and business that I recommended it to a client.

The client responded with an impassioned request that I create six workshops, based on the Five Laws of Stratospheric Success from the book. Not willing to create such a body of work based on someone else's material without permission (that, by the way, is a boundary, not a barrier), I sent emails to Bob and John asking for permission, and advice.

A few emails later, we were working out the details of a dream relationship—I would not only create the workshops my client had requested, I would use those materials as the basis of a program to train coaches, consultants, and speakers how to share the Five Laws with others!

I would not only be coaching and teaching *my* clients, I would also be coaching and teaching the Certified Go-Giver Coaches! And I would be licensed to use all Bob's materials, including his previous best seller, *Endless Referrals*, and any later books. And that's where I run into the Wall of Style.

Because I've heard Bob present on his work more times than I can count. I'm always blown away by his stage presence, his polish, his *style*! And I *can't* do it the way Bob does it. Not even close.

Fortunately, I've studied the material until it's part of my natural language, and I've developed my own style of sharing it. That has been possible largely because of the support Bob has given me, and the insights he's shared.

During our Dialog, Bob and I talk about how our unique, authentic style is more valuable than our ability to imitate anyone else.

> *"Never let the generalities offered by others*
> *define your unique possibilities."*

"You have value," Bob asserts. "You may not know what it is, or how to market it, yet. But you are already enough! Of course, that doesn't mean you stop growing."

One thing that Bob feels has helped him grow into his distinctive style could easily have become a Wall of Circumstances for him. For much of his young life, Bob often felt like he was "going crazy." That was explained when he was diagnosed with obsessive-compulsive disorder.

That's not a personality style, he clarifies, but a chemical imbalance that was a "bear to deal with."

But it helped him develop empathy for the struggles of others, and a style of showing his concern for them, that is so much a part of what he is known (and loved) for today that no one would suspect it wasn't always part of his makeup.

But Bob *has* jokingly played with imitating someone else's style. For our Dialog recording, I asked him to tell how he "did Zig" better than Zig Ziglar himself.

During his years as a sales professional, Bob listened to his sales hero's training audios hundreds, maybe thousands, of times. As his own speaking career took off, he often quoted Zig, doing a dead-ringer imitation of Zig's distinctive style.

Then came the opportunity to be Zig's "opening act." Bob arrived in the city where they were to share the stage and, moving through the airport, he heard someone "doing Zig."

"The nerve!" he thought. "I'm the only one who does Zig, and I do a better job of Zig than that!"

So he retraced his steps, glanced into the pay phone cubicle where this "imitator" was, and realized the person "doing Zig" was Zig himself!

If Bob had said, "What I really want to do is become an iconic thought leader, author, and speaker," he could easily have finished the sentence, "but I can't because I can't do it like Zig Ziglar."

Fortunately, he didn't build that wall. He did it like Bob Burg. And the world is better for it!

"Model your mentors, but master doing
your own thing your own way!"

We'd all love to be able to measure up to our idols. Whether we want to sing, act, dance, write, play a sport, or just make a grand entrance, we have models in our mind of pure perfection.

Can you look at what those people are able to accomplish by being who they are, instead of the way they accomplish it? Perhaps begin by asking yourself what you admire most about their style.

Is it that they can make people laugh? or cry? Is it that they're cheered by thousands of fans? or booed? Is it that they've made discoveries? captivated an audience? Or maybe they're just sweet.

"A yellow rose bush will never put out red
blossoms. That doesn't make it any less a rose.
Or any less beautiful."

My only sister is 16 years older than I am, and I believed she was perfect in every way.

Of course, that might just have been my perception, since by the time she moved out of our house I was all of two years old, and I worshipped her. But it was also because she was one of those people who could make anyone comfortable. *Everyone* loved her.

In a word, Kathy was sweet.

And people, meeting me, would say, "Oh, you're Kathy's little sister! Kathy's so sweet; we love Kathy!"

Before long, somewhere in the conversation, they'd say, "You're not much like your sister, are you?"

Nope. Not much. There's a reason I got the nickname "Dynamite."

So I grew up thinking I wasn't a sweet person. It just wasn't me.

As I got older, people would say things like, "Thank you, that was so sweet of you." And I would think, "Nope, not me; I've scientifically proven I'm not sweet. You're thinking of my sister."

Of course, I have come to understand that I *am* sweet (most of the time), but I don't "do sweet" the way my sister does "sweet". I have my own style, my own brand, of sweetness.

> *"When you do what is natural and authentic*
> *you will find that you are able to do it more*
> *effectively, more efficiently, and more consistently,*
> *with less effort, and more joy!"*

Style isn't always about performance or personality. It's also about natural strengths.

A person whose strength is to be highly organized and systematic will never be the natural juggler who can be interrupted from 10 tasks at once and still complete them all with ease. If you're hardwired to learn kinesthetically, you'll never do your best work by studying a textbook.

If your wall is a Wall of Style, ask yourself, "*What* about the way he or she does that thing that I want to do makes me admire him or her so much?"

Is it a powerful presence? Maybe it is grace under pressure or a turn of phrase. Maybe the person can make people smile, cry, laugh, or dance. Whatever it is, you *can* find your own style of doing it.

Finding your own style, as Bob says at the beginning of our Dialog, may require that you do some growing. That you develop character traits and strengths by adopting what you learn from others into your own manifestation of self.

I call it "intentional becoming." We leverage what we are authentically, the strengths that come most naturally, what we've learned from the examples of others and from our own experiences, and we use all that to become the person we can be, to do what we want to do, and to go where we want to go.

CHAPTER 35

THE WALL OF CONSEQUENCES

*"Life gives us all kinds of messages that can be
used as inspiration or excuses. It's the
interpretation that matters."*

"I can't do that because my spouse would kill me."

"I can't do that without quitting my job."

"I can't do that without mortgaging my house."

We all face consequences when we pursue a dream.

"I can't make that choice without something else happening" is inevitably true.

Because we cannot make a change without consequences. Good or bad. Usually both.

Consequences are really just outcomes, and every choice—including refusing to choose—results in an outcome.

"Your life," Ava points out to me during our Dialog, "Is a result of all the choices you've made up until now."

And our choices are governed by what we believe will happen as a result of making each choice.

If we believe that asking for a raise will result in an increase in salary, no doubt we'll schedule that conversation as quickly as possible. But if we believe our request will result in a confrontation with management or human resources, we are likely to postpone that review.

So what do you believe will be the result of your choice? What if you believed in a more positive outcome?

Often our beliefs are informed, however subconsciously, by what I call "contingency thinking."

"What's the worst that can happen?" we ask, by way of reassuring ourselves. "And can I survive it?"

The theory is that we'll find courage in knowing that, if worse comes to worst, we'll be just fine. My observation is that we condition ourselves to expect the worst.

Ava says the same thing about her choice to sign up for the Avon walk. "I learned that asking myself, 'What's the worst that can happen?' didn't work for me. So I asked, 'What's the best that can happen? And what do I need to do *today* to move in that direction?'"

Ava could have focused on the possibilities of failure, and none of them would have meant the end of the world. But she chose instead to list the possible positive outcomes, and take action to bring them about.

Changing what she believed about the probable consequences of her choice, gave her the power to complete that walk in spite of her initial fears.

Of course, only you can decide whether the risk is worth the reward. While most people do not become homicidal over a decision made by their business or domestic partner, it has happened. While quitting your job may be something you want to do, this may not be the right time to do it.

*"Are you trading your future success for
an illusion of present security?"*

No future success is guaranteed, neither the success of the path you are on nor that of the path you want to be on. But choosing "cannot" without exploring another avenue of reaching your desired destination does guarantee failure.

A word of caution: blasting away at a wall just to prove you "ain't skeered" of the consequences is not likely to yield a positive outcome either.

If your wall is a Wall of Consequences, how confident are you that the contingencies you're thinking of are surefire outcomes? How can you affect the probabilities? How can you alter what you believe is the most likely outcome of any particular choice?

—CHAPTER 36—

THE WALL
OF DESIGN

*"If you still believe you can't, you haven't
exhausted all the possibilities."*

"I can't play pro football, be an astronaut, dance at the
Metropolitan Opera as the prima ballerina in *Swan Lake*, or
become a Motown recording artist."

Really. I can't.

The life of your dreams, the way you have designed it in
your mind, may very well not be possible.

Few people, no matter how hard they train, practice,
or network, will have the opportunity to play as a pro in
any sport, travel to the moon or to the stars, dance in Swan
Lake or any other ballet, or become a Motown recording
artist—even if the label were to split from Universal and
begin signing artists again.But that doesn't mean you can't
design a career in pro sports, or even play at some level. Or
you might pursue a career with NASA, or with a company
that contributes to the space program, or become a science
teacher who inspires the next generation of astronauts.

You see where I'm going? Figure out what about that dream inspires you, and find another way to design that outcome. You can achieve your purpose once you discover it, but you may have to rethink your method.

Years ago, I worked with a client who had purchased a business from his father after working as an associate for several years.

He had dreams of creating a bigger business: He craved the public recognition, the respect of his father, and the financial independence that he believed would come with that success.

However, for his entire career, he has resisted expanding his business to the extent that it can support another service provider. He says he fears not being able to provide enough business for both of them—failure—less than he fears that the business would become so busy that he would no longer be able to make sure all the clients are cared for and standards for excellence are met—success. He's continually seeking new avenues to gain what he craves, but as long as he chooses "cannot" he just can't get there. I've watched him spend hundreds of thousands of dollars starting new businesses, getting additional degrees, learning new techniques, and hiring new marketing professionals.

He has designed his dream so specifically that it cannot happen.

So long as he clings to his fears, his business income is limited by what he is personally able to produce by providing services.

So long as he resists replicating what he does, he will hit the wall of his personal ability to provide services before he reaches the level of success he says he desires.

One of the best examples of redesigning or reframing is tackling the statement "I can't fly."

The implication is that you don't have wings and you can't move yourself from place to place by flying.

But, if your objective is to get from point A to point B as quickly as possible by moving though the air, you can purchase a ticket or charter a plane.

If your objective is to experience the sensation of your human body moving through the air, you can skydive, hang glide, or paraglide.

A simple redesign, and see! You *can too* fly!

CHAPTER 37

NEVER PUT OFF UNTIL TOMORROW WHAT YOU CAN ENJOY TODAY

"If your heart isn't 100 percent in it, it is 100 percent harder. No matter what it is.'

I was chatting with audience members after I'd given a talk on blasting through brick walls, and one of them said, "My brick wall is procrastination—what category does that belong in?"

Instant silence. All eyes turned to me. Clearly more than one person wanted an answer to that question.

Procrastination, I explained, is not a brick wall. It's a symptom of a brick wall. I mean, think about it—if you knew that moving forward would cause you to bang your head against a brick wall, you'd put it off as long as possible, wouldn't you?

I could write an entire book on procrastination, but I don't have time for that. (I'm going to procrastinate doing it—see how it works?)

So here are just a few of the problems that show up as procrastination. This will be enough to get you thinking about the walls that might be causing you to put off until tomorrow what you would have benefited from doing today.

Keep in mind, most of these conversations aren't conscious "notes to self." They are the subtext behind your choices to fill your time with something other than the thing you know you need to do to get where you want to be.

Let's start with the Wall of Circumstances—the "I can't do that right now" statements.

"If I wait, I might have more money—time—focus …"

"If I wait, I might be skinnier—smarter—more successful …"

"If I wait, I might be more confident—educated—credentialed …"

But *wait*—aren't those all descriptions of where you want to go? How are you going to go there without doing what you need to do?

What about the Wall of Style—the "I can't do it that way" statement?

Kathy Kolbe, the theorist and scientific mind behind the Kolbe Assessments and Kolbe Wisdom, says, "Procrastination is the mind's way of protecting itself from what it does not do naturally."

Anything you ask yourself to do that is unnatural, or too far outside your comfort zone, is likely to get put off for a lot of tomorrows.

The Wall of Consequences is a major culprit in causing procrastination. This is the "I can't do that because such-and-such will happen" statement.

Every choice you make comes with an opportunity cost. If you commit to one thing, you cross off other things as possibilities. If you went to the Cardinals' playoff game, you missed the concert. If you bought that new couch, you had to put off buying the new grill.

Every step taken in one direction is a step not taken in another direction.

But if you put off taking steps, where do you think you'll end up?

Which leaves the Wall of Design—the "I can't do it exactly the way I have it pictured so I can't do it at all" statement.

Oh, boy—perfectionism and procrastination go hand-in-hand. They're twin souls. Maybe Siamese twins. Separable only by a miracle. Right?

If it's got to be a certain way, and you're not convinced you are ready or able to make it that way, you'll not do it for as long as you can get away with it.

Now, can you slap a nametag on that wall? What is holding you back from pursuing your desired outcome?

To stop your procrastination, and get yourself moving, focus on the outcome of doing whatever it is you're not doing.

Remember it's not getting the lawn mowed—it's having a neatly mowed lawn. And it's not having the thank-you cards written—it's relationship development with everyone who will receive a card.Chances are, when you've clarified your true objective, and been honest with yourself about your barrier, you'll find a way to blow up that wall and stop putting off your reward!

SECTION FOUR

THE DYNAMITE TOOLBOX

CHAPTER 38

SMALL EXPLOSIONS— MAJOR BREAKTHROUGHS

"It isn't always about what it's about."

I have found that, like most of the issues that challenge us on a fundamental level, what we say about our brick walls isn't necessarily what we mean.

Often, there is the "but I can't because ..." that we tell the world, and there is also the "but I can't because ..." that we hide.

Even from ourselves.

For instance, a client who came to me for an initial Blast Thru Coaching session said, "What I really want to do is go on a tour of Italy, but I can't because I can't afford it."

We followed my usual line of questioning, and she confessed that she hadn't even checked the total cost of the tour she had selected. Once we unveiled all the illusions of brick walls, we were able to blast through the real one. Another client went through a litany of reasons he couldn't leave his job and start his own company. After my questioning process, he circled back and confessed that he felt as if he *should* want to be an entrepreneur, but really he likes having a company

151

structure around him. It gives him the freedom to focus on his own success, without feeling responsible for anyone else.

I'm not suggesting that any of these people weren't being honest with themselves. Those illusions of brick walls were valid considerations. They just weren't the heart of the matter, the solid barrier that needed to be destroyed.

> *"A* **blasting cap** *is a small sensitive primary explosive device generally used to detonate a larger, more powerful and less sensitive secondary explosive such as TNT, dynamite, or plastic explosive."*
> ~ WIKIPEDIA

To strip away the illusionary barriers, and to attack the real brick wall, I built an arsenal of four "blasting caps." Fired off in order, with the dynamite ignited at the end as the coup de grace, they truly do have explosive power.

They look a lot like questions. (That curvy little "?" mark at the end of each line is deceiving.) They're actually powerful devices designed to set off real TNT, and blow up the brick wall.

These charges can be used to challenge any "I can't" statement. Set them off in the order I've shared them here, and keep coming back to them again and again. You might be surprised to find that your responses change, and that each round of explosives weakens that wall just a little bit more, until you're blasting right through.

—CHAPTER 39—

BLASTING CAP #1— DO I REALLY WANT IT?

"Do you want what you want?
Or only what you want *to want?"*

That might read like a circular riddle with no answer.

But it is grounded in a common reality: We often pursue something because someone said we should want it, or because we believe it would be best for us to want it, or even because it would be easier to want it.

We *want* to want what is attainable.

We *want* to want what other people want us to have.

We *want* to want what will ruffle the least feathers.

Perhaps you want to be a good employee, because that is what you've been told you should want. Or maybe you want to be a business owner, because you come from a long line of entrepreneurs. You might want to be a doctor, because your parents were both medical professionals. Or you might want to volunteer for an organization because you really believe in its cause.

You might even say you want a certain level of success, when in fact you are afraid of the changes that success would bring into your life.

You might not want it enough, because you want something else more. Maybe you're really saying, "I can't because I'm not willing to put that kind of time and money into it." You're not willing to incur the opportunity cost.

During one workshop, I had a participant tell me she had always wanted to be a recording artist, but she couldn't, because her voice was never good enough.

We began to challenge it. We set the first blasting cap: Did she really, really want it? She was sure she did; she would always regret not going for it.

What did "be a recording artist" mean to her, and why did she want it? She could just imagine hearing her voice coming over the radio and everyone saying, "Is that you? Cool!"

"So," I asked, "what about the voice training, the studio time, the live performances, working with other musicians, promoting your work?" What about that appealed to her? Nothing.

It came out during our discussion that her mother used to praise her voice. She would tell her that she had such a sweet voice, someday that voice would be coming over the radio and everyone would be so proud.

Truly, she didn't want to be a recording artist; she wanted to make her mother proud. She wanted to be recognized for her talents. She wanted to perform at her highest level. But she did not want to be a singer.

We had a blast working through her talents and all the ways she could perform at her highest level and be recognized for her talents. All of them, she agreed, would make her mother proud.

It is OK to not want "it" enough to be willing to contribute resources to make it happen. But then you'll need to turn away from that path, and move on to something you want more.

Maybe you're even telling yourself you don't want something because getting it will be really hard. I find that often people choose to want one thing because they think it will be easier to attain than their true heart's desire.

> *"Hard is when you have to*
> *do it someone else's way."*

Things can be difficult in terms of effort, challenge, or energy, but they don't have to be hard on *you* in terms of suffering. You can choose how you expend your effort.

For instance, some people choose to stay fit by running long distances, while others prefer to lift weights or do yoga. There is always more than one way to achieve your goal. So if the way you are going about yours is tortuous, then change your approach—but don't change your goal.

Bill Ellis, the brain behind Branding for Results, left his position in marketing and brand integration with Anheuser-Busch when he was 50, after more than 20 years.

In our Dynamite Dialog, Bill—who has been a client, is now a mastermind partner, and will always be a dear friend and respected go-to expert—says that when he left, he had no clarity. He knew he didn't want to return to a corporate environment, but he didn't know what he did want to do.

"I was a little dazed. ... I was only focused on what I *should* do."

He selected a path traveled by many new entrepreneurs. "I decided to do what I had been." He found office space, had cards printed, and, anticipating bringing in additional consultants, became the Conrad Ellis Group.

But he found that being a brand manager and marketing consultant wasn't very satisfying.

"I was wanting to want to be a marketing strategist and brand manager, the way I had been at Anheuser-Busch for all those years. Because I knew it, and I knew I was good at it.

"But I had a lot of conflict."

In fact, I was only one of the people who called the symptoms of that conflict to Bill's attention. Many of his friends and colleagues noticed that when he introduced himself, in spite of his track record and tremendous credibility, he didn't sound convinced.

During one of our coaching sessions, I made a note and shared it with Bill.

"If there is no conviction in your message, there is either too much fear, or not enough love."

He agreed. In spite of all his success creating consistent brands, his own brand message was mushy.

It came down to this: he was doing what he was doing because it seemed like what he *should* be doing. And he knew that any time you're only doing something because it's what you think you should do, you should probably stop and explore your options!

During our Dialog, I ask Bill what gave him the courage to explore his options and embark on the path toward what he really wanted.

"It *is* a journey, but then I look at branding as a process too. I don't believe that a brand is something you create, then put on the shelf. It's part of my role for my clients, to examine, not only what the company is offering in products and services, but also what the market is looking for. You have to adapt; you have to be able to change."

As he would for any client, he first examined the name he'd chosen for his enterprise. "People have to understand what you do," he chuckles, "but because of my corporate background and mindset, I'd chosen this very corporate-sounding name. So I had to spend the first five minutes after meeting someone explaining what it was that I offered— the name did nothing for me at all."

At the same time, he began to clarify what he really wanted to do, his whole reason for being in business. "It became pretty obvious to me that what I wanted to have happen, was for people to take their brand and get results."

He realized that few businesses, and even fewer individuals, understood branding—what it could do for them, how it could hurt them. And even fewer knew how to manage their own brand.

He knew this was a problem he could solve—a problem he wanted to solve. By using the "do I really want it?" blasting cap, Bill created a new brand and a new approach. He now teaches "The Seven Cs of Branding," the first two of which are Clarity and Conviction.

In our Dialog, Bill says he believes that knowing what you want, Clarity, leads to the second C: Conviction. I agree, and add that there is another C to consider, and that is Courage.

Bill and I both work with many clients who have internal conviction: they know what they really want to do. But they are afraid to externalize it.

While Bill's lack of conviction about the Conrad Ellis Group was born of a lack of love for what he was doing, for many, the lack of conviction in their message—the way they communicate their value to the world—is fear.

> *"Your physical energy will follow your emotional energy like a raft over a waterfall. Where are your emotions taking you on your journey?"*

Whether you're trying to want something because you think you should, or you're trying not to want it because you're afraid that you can't, your emotional energy is taking you nowhere but down, and people can tell.

An outcome, goal, dream, or mission that you really, really want has the energy of desire behind it. Not just a that-would-be-nice kind of energy, but a that-is-what-I-really-want-to-have-in-my-life kind of energy.

So when you ask yourself, "Do I really want it," gauge the strength of your answer.

If "that would be nice" is a one and "that is what I really have to have in my life" is a ten, where is your level of desire?

Listen to your little voice, and allow it to tell you *your* truth. There's no shame in realizing that what you've been calling your big dream for years is no longer what you really want to do.

If you're not at an eight, nine, or ten, you're not going to put the energy into making it happen. It *might* still happen— but not because you gave it your all.

Maybe there are parts you want, and parts you don't want.

Maybe you aren't sure you're willing to do what will be necessary to get it.

Maybe you aren't even sure what will be necessary to get it.

The "I want it" factor may be a 10, but then the things you don't want pull it back. "I don't want to take the risk— take the time—take the test ..."

Make a list of the things that pull you back, things that you're afraid of, things that you think you'll have to do to get where you really want to be. If you've said, "What I really want to do is ... *but* ... ," write that "but" down.

You may discover that what you've been saying you really want to do isn't something you want to do at all. But you thought it was what you wanted to do because you believe it would lead to something you want to have, or something you want to accomplish. The Law of Consequences in reverse!

To name your brick wall, you may need to change how you fill in the blank after, "What I really want to do is ... ."

I had a dear friend and fellow coach say to me, "What I really want to do is write a book, but ..." and in fewer than five minutes of conversation it became clear that she didn't really want to write a book. There was no emotional energy around the writing.

It took 10 more minutes to discover that what she *really* wanted to do was to bring the gifts she had been given, from her experiences and the lessons she had learned, to as many people as possible. Knowing what she really wanted to accomplish allowed us to blow up the real brick wall, instead of throwing dynamite at an illusion.

Chances are, once you've written out the things you want, the things you don't want, and what you believe the outcome of moving forward will be, there will be circumstances you can change, a different style you can develop, consequences that would be "worst case" but aren't really probabilities, even a way to design around those things you don't want to do or don't want to have in your life.

CHAPTER 40

BLASTING CAP #2— DO I HAVE PERMISSION?

"Playing by your own rules isn't being irrational.
It's just refusing to knuckle to
someone else's rationale."

If you're able to give yourself at least an eight on the desire scale, but your wall is still looking pretty solid, the next blasting cap is a game of "Mother May I."

Once you're sure that you really do want what you want (and not just what you *want* to want), and you've named and addressed your fears, you should feel yourself gathering the energy to move forward.

If you find yourself stalling or moving forward just to encounter yet another wall, the problem may be that you don't believe you have permission even to go for it.

Who is playing Mother in this game?

As part of the Dynamite Dialogs Project, I had the pleasure of chatting with Kimberly Schneider. Known as "The Manifestation Maven," Kimberly has been studying consciousness and manifestation pretty much all her life. She is the author of *Everything You Need Is Right Here: Five Steps to Manifesting Magic and Miracles,* and has been my coach, mastermind partner, and mutual mentor for several years.

With her background in counseling and psychotherapy, as well as her past as a practicing attorney, Kimberly knows a little bit about the mental (and legal) issues we have with permission.

Kimberly and I start our Dialog with the story of how her husband, David, asked her permission to learn to fly.

Over lunch one day, David casually mentioned he'd always dreamed of getting his private pilot's license. Kimberly immediately replied, "Why haven't you ever done it?"

"You mean you wouldn't mind if I did?"

Kimberly explains, "It turned out he had a story in his head about how I would be scared of him flying. That I'd be afraid of losing him or whatever."

"So how did you feel when you found out you'd been built up in his mind as his brick wall?" I ask her, pretty much knowing the answer.

Kimberly agrees that it didn't feel so great, but she adds that she felt grateful he was brave enough to bring it up and ask the question.

It comes to us almost simultaneously: sometimes the first thing we need to give ourselves permission to do is to have the conversation!

"It's such a vulnerable thing to do, to open yourself and ask the question."

I agree with her: We're like children psyching ourselves up to ask, "Mommy, may I?" Because one "no" and our dreams are dashed! How many times have you watched a child craft an appeal, bursting to list all the reasons Mommy should say yes, only to deflate like a balloon when the yes comes so quickly the child never needs to present the case?

Be clear about the stories you're creating. What is your story? Is it based on your truth, or on your fear?

Who do you trust enough that you can be that vulnerable? Who can you sit down with over lunch and say, "I've always dreamed of flying," even when your story says that this person won't support you in pursuing that dream?

I know that often, regardless of our ability to be vulnerable and to trust, we walk away with a feeling that we didn't get permission. But was this person really in a position to give or withhold permission? If so, *who gave the person that power?*

Do you start your "Mother May I" conversations prepared for the worst? Remember that most people with whom you share your dreams, ideas, and aspirations are processing from a position of, "How does that affect me?" If they love and care for you it may even be, "How does that affect you, because anything that affects you, affects me!"

The fact that your choices will affect them does not mean you are dependent on them for permission to move forward.

Is it possible that what you are really seeking isn't permission at all, but confirmation, validation, and encouragement?

Kimberly suggests establishing a dreaming place that is separate from your problem-solving, planning, doing space. Keeping the activities in different spaces, she says, can help us stay clear in our heads about when it is appropriate to have conversations about permission.

The lightbulb that appeared over my head doesn't show up in the audio, but it was there!

*"You never need to ask permission to dream! So
the question is, 'Who do you need to
ask for permission to do?'"*

Kimberly and David finished that lunch discussing the logistics of how David could live out his dream. What lessons and classes would he need to take? Where were they available? What were the appropriate next steps?

With Kimberly's encouragement, David took his first lesson within two weeks, and today he has his private pilot's license.

The more flying David does, and the more Kimberly sees how much the realization of his dream feeds him, the more supportive she has become.

As we discuss the sequence of events in that story, I realize how often this is true. If we just get started, if we begin to manifest our dream, then people around us wake up and see our dream as real. They feel safer putting their energy behind it.

So perhaps you don't need permission or validation to pursue your dream; you just need permission or validation to take the first step! If your dream is to become a professional singer, it may be difficult for those who love you to support you, because they can see all the possibilities for you to be disappointed. But if you begin with singing lessons, that's easier for them to support.

Do I hear you saying, "Taking steps won't make any difference to them?" Is that your truth, or your fear? Are you telling yourself a story?

In *Everything You Need Is Right Here*, Kimberly writes about ways we project our power onto other people. Building up another person as our brick wall is a perfect example of projecting your power!

So let's say you've taken back your power, and you have that conversation, and you're told, in no uncertain terms, "No!"

> *"A relationship with anyone who says NO to your dream is a relationship at risk."*

Kimberly and I agree that your next step is to examine that relationship. Perhaps it's time to do what I call a "Permission Audit."

It's an easy exercise really, but it may reveal some unpleasant truths. Begin by making a list of everyone with whom you'd like to share your "what I really want to do is ..." statement. Your family, friends, colleagues, community—everyone.

Beside each entry on your list, write one of these words:

VETO
I have consciously and intentionally given this person or group the power to veto my choices.

LIMIT
I have consciously and intentionally given this person or group the right to limit when, where, how, or how often I take any particular action or pursue any particular dream.

SABOTAGE

I have consciously and intentionally given this person or group the right and ability to undermine my efforts to pursue my dream.

DISCOURAGE

I have consciously and intentionally given this person or group the ability to affect my energy and enthusiasm to the degree that I can be discouraged from pursing my dream.

INFLUENCE

I have consciously and intentionally given this person or group the power to influence whether, and how, I go about pursuing my dream.

RELEASE

I have consciously and intentionally released myself from allowing this person or group to have any impact on my choices regarding the pursuit of my dream.

"Can you give those who are not able to support you the permission to live their lives, even to exit your life, but not to limit your life?"

It's something Richard considers beyond price: the Power of Consent. Our Dialog closes with his story of how, in spite of "knowing" he would never be a pilot, he learned to fly.

He says flying was, for him, the ultimate freedom, proof of his Power of Consent. Once in the sky, at the controls of a plane, no one can tell you what you can or cannot do, where you can or cannot go. There may be consequences to your choices, but the freedom is yours to choose as you will.

As you go through the Permission Audit exercise, remember Richard's lesson: only you can give or withhold consent. Others can impose consequences, from voicing their concern or displeasure to leaving or even threatening your life. But no one can impose limitations against your will.

> *"Your free will is only as big as your consciousness.*
> *You cannot choose consciously to create the*
> *kind of life you desire if you're operating*
> *unconsciously out of a belief system that is*
> *not supporting those desires."*
> ~ KIMBERLY SCHNEIDER,
> from The Dynamite Dialogs Project

As you release your attachment to receiving permission, validation, or support from the people around you, you begin to be really clear about what you do need.

Kimberly frames it beautifully: "We put so much pressure on ourselves, thinking that what we need has to come from a particular source, situation, or person. But sometimes, when I'm clear about what I need, I've found that I got what I needed from a song on the radio, or the cashier in the checkout at the grocery store —somebody I have an encounter with who gives me a new piece of information or confirmation."

She continues, "Or sometimes a new relationship comes into my life. But again, it's about that responsibility for saying, '*This* is what I need in my life.'"

But it's so important to remember that you set yourself up for disappointment, even disaster, when instead of saying "*this* is what I need," you say "this is what I need from *you*!"

You may need validation, encouragement, support, and endorsement from someone, and when you release your need to receive it from any particular source you will likely find it's there for you from a source that was completely unexpected. But do you really need permission from anyone, except yourself?

Don't ask for anyone else's permission until you know that you have given yourself permission, and that you believe in yourself, in your worthiness. Why wouldn't you give yourself permission? There are two brick walls I often discover related to the Wall of Circumstances and Permission Audits.

"I can't because I'm not ready."

"I can't because I'm not worthy."

If you say "I'm not qualified—I'm not ready—I don't deserve it," what do people say?

"Of course you deserve it."

"You're wonderful; you're the best."

"Just go for it!"

Does that help? It's nice. But is it meaningful?

I'll bet you've heard all that before, and if it were going to work, it would have worked already.

Perhaps instead of trying to convince yourself of something you don't believe, you might challenge your belief system by asking some brutal questions.

"Am I willing to do the work?" If you're not, then you don't deserve it. See, that was easy.

What do I mean by "do the work?" It depends on what you are trying to achieve, but there is always an internal component and an external component, an insight component and an action component.

You'll have to develop your character and skills, and you'll have to take risks and perform tasks.

"Doing the work" means showing up fully in the moment, forming new connections inside and outside. It means going after opportunities that seem impossible, and being prepared to grab the brass ring when it comes in view.

"Doing the work" means challenging yourself every time you say, "But I can't because … ."

Are you willing?

"Am I saying I'm not worthy just to get people to reassure me?" If you are, then you need to conquer your need for reassurance. You're telling yourself a story of your own unworthiness every time you tell others that you don't deserve success. No amount of reassurance in the world will counteract the story you tell yourself.

What do I mean by "conquer your need for reassurance?" I'm not saying you shouldn't need other people; we all need our support structures and teams. We all need validation and reassurance from time to time. But no support structure can make up for what you aren't doing for yourself.

If you're demeaning and belittling yourself in order to get other people to offer their support, then you are manipulating others into giving you what you need to learn to give yourself.

> *"What is there about me that makes me worth*
> *less than all the other people who have*
> *achieved their dreams?"*

Write it down!

What do I mean by telling you to write down every reason you are worth less than other people? I mean exactly that. Put down every single thing you have ever told yourself about why you don't deserve what you want in life.

Because if you're having that argument with yourself, I want you to win it. And you can't even challenge it until you get it out where you can see it.

If you've said "because I'm not smart enough" or "because I'm not pretty enough," write it down.

If you've said "because I don't have enough initials after my name" or "because I haven't been doing this long enough," write it down.

Now, I want you to challenge EVERY SINGLE ITEM ON THAT LIST!

I want you to set aside your preconceived notions, and other people's cautions, and ask yourself why you ever bought into them. Odds are that when you're done, you will have three categories:

It's simply not true.

It simply doesn't matter.

It simply needs work.

You may find some things that will make your goal more difficult for you to achieve than it might be for someone with more money, more education, or blonder hair. But you aren't likely to find anything that makes you inherently less deserving.

I've worked with so many people who believe that they have already forfeited their chance to achieve their dreams because of choices they've made in their lives. It is never too late, until you believe it is.

Maybe you do believe that you deserve to pursue your dream and achieve success, but you still haven't given yourself permission to do it now.

If you have asked, "Do I have permission?" and the answer came back "NO," you have to decide whether you are going to allow circumstances, or other influences, to put your dream on hold.

Not that there aren't circumstances that make certain choices more responsible than others. But that doesn't mean you need to let the brick wall stop you in your tracks.

Just as Lynne Wilhite demonstrated, you can explore bridges that lead you toward your ultimate goal without compromising the commitments and relationships you are maintaining in the present.

When you ask yourself, "Do I have permission," think about what giving yourself permission will mean. Is it scary? Are you saying "cannot" to your dream so that you don't have to say yes to your fear?

Maybe it is time to say yes to your fear. "Yes, it is scary and a lot could go wrong, but a lot could go wrong if I do nothing."

Are you ready to give yourself permission?

—CHAPTER 41—

BLASTING CAP #3—
IS IT TRUE THAT I CAN'T?

*"We often discover our hidden power only when we
need it to recover from failure."*

We've all been baby elephants.

Believing that we "can't" is something we learned. What
have you learned? When did you learn it?

Was it under a *circumstance* that limited your strength?
Did you "learn" that you weren't strong enough, and have
you never tested your abilities since? How have your circumstances changed since then?

Were you using a different *style*? Maybe you modeled
your efforts on someone else's success, and that wasn't a model
that was natural to you. Have you considered other ways to
accomplish the same goals?

Were there *consequences* of your decision then that you
don't want to suffer now? Perhaps being mindful of that
experience will allow you to be better prepared, or to miti-
gate the side effects.

Did you discover that you don't always get exactly what
you thought you wanted, and the way you *design* your goals

doesn't always match your outcome? Can you accept that plans change? In fact, sometimes the house that we build is far better because of a "change order.

If you're saying "I can't" because you've tried it before and failed, does that really mean you can't? Or does that mean you haven't yet?

> *"Champions say 'I can' after every win.*
> *They also say 'I can' after every defeat."*

Top athletes win consistently because they evaluate consistently. They review what worked and what didn't work. Then they build on what worked, and modify what didn't.

Martina didn't become the champion she was by saying, "Well, I lost in the quarterfinals at the US Championships, so there's no need to compete at Wimbledon." Neither did she get there by believing her coach when she told her, "You'll never be a champion playing like that!"

Choosing "I can too" begins with changing what you believe to be true. But that isn't enough. In our Dialog, Richard and I discuss one of the themes from *Hypnotizing Maria*: "Attitude, Choice, and the Desire to make it true." Your attitude, and your choices, must support your desire. And your desire informs your attitude and your choices.

If you examine your attitude—your belief system, your thoughts—what do you need to change to support your desires? What you want to do; who you want to be?

What choices are you making? What actions are you taking? And how do they support your goals? What choices can you make that will change the answer to the question, "Is it true that I can't?"

Scott Ginsberg is the most challenging person I know.

Not only in the way he challenges me, but in the ways he finds to challenge himself.

Scott is a speaker and the author of more than a dozen books, including *The Power of Approachability* and *The Nametag Principle.*

Every time we meet, Scott explains his latest method for challenging himself.

So it wasn't a surprise when, during our Dynamite Dialog, he shared his latest challenge. It *was* a surprise to learn that the challenge had been a case of writer's block.

I've worked with a number of writers and other artists, and having the creative well go dry, or even sludgy, is their worst bad dream. Not for Scott.

He didn't enjoy it, but, like a champion athlete, he says, "I *can*; I just need to figure out what isn't working."

He adopted several subtle changes, such as mixing up his daily routine and changing the locations where he did his writing. He revisited his success techniques, including a customized guided meditation that had been recorded for him by his therapist.

"It wasn't working for me anymore." (You can almost hear the shrug.) "So I went back to him and said, 'Man, we need to redo this,' and he did and it was like BOOM!"

> *"Argue for your limitations, and sure*
> *enough, they're yours!"*
> ~ RICHARD BACH

What do Richard, John, Kimberly, Bob, and Scott have in common with Martina Navratilova?

They don't argue for their limitations. They embrace their potential, knowing it to be limitless.

Bob and I discuss potential in our Dialog as well. "Early in my career," he says, "I wouldn't have said this potential was in me." But each time he's been faced with the question, "Is it true that I can't?" he's chosen to challenge what can be, and push his understanding of his potential just a little bit, in order to say, "Of course I can!"

For myself, I have found that the more deeply I tap into my potential, the more potential I discover that I have.

Perhaps I can't do "it" today, but I can see the potential in me to do it in the future, if I take steps today to build my strength, increase my knowledge and ability, surround myself with the right people, and amass the right resources.

It's just a matter of supporting my desire with my attitude and my choices.

Limitless.

There is a piece of advice from my Dialog with Bob that I added to my journal, and revisit often.

> *"Become aware enough of your own value that*
> *you cannot be budged from it just because*
> *someone else can't see it."*
>
> ~ BOB BURG,
> from The Dynamite Dialogs Project

Right below it I've written an entry from my Dialog with Scott. It comes from our chat about being creative, overcoming writer's block, and nurturing your inner artist.

We created it together, as often happens with us, the way two pizza chefs might work together to stretch dough. One of us tosses it up; the other catches it and turns it into something different. Listening to the recording, I can clearly hear Scott say, "You have to believe that you have something worth expressing." But this is what I heard:

> *"To create art, you have to believe that you are*
> *something worth expressing."*
> ~ SCOTT GINSBERG WITH DIXIE GILLASPIE,
> The Dynamite Dialogs Project

Attitude.

I learned from Richard that, when flying, the direction the plane's nose is pointing (up, down, straight ahead) is referred to as attitude.

The direction the nose is pointed is the direction the plane will fly. Attitude determines altitude.

What is your attitude toward yourself? Is it an attitude of limitation?

If your attitude isn't supporting your desires, you can make the *choice* to change it. To change to a positive attitude in a small plane you pull back on the stick. The choices that will change your attitude may not be as obvious, but Bob and Scott both offer their wisdom concerning choices that affect attitude—and altitude! Bob refers to choice as the decision to "act as if." The more you behave in a way that is consistent with your desires, the more your mind accepts these data as your truth. For instance, try smiling for even one full minute without feeling your attitude shift slightly toward the sky!

Scott recommends choosing the people you associate with as one way to adjust your attitude (and your creativity).

"Surround yourself with people who are honest, but who totally support you! And, to keep a great perspective and an open mind, surround yourself with people who have a different life experience than your own."

These are two examples of choices you make every day—your facial expression and the company you keep—that can support your desires, or sabotage them.

Another method of increasing altitude by improving attitude is to take inventory of choices you've already made, lessons you've already learned, and changes you've already implemented that support your desire.

Perhaps you think you can't build a successful business because you tried and failed. Surely you learned something from that experience besides "I can't build a successful business."

Maybe you learned something about business models, or which time-management methods don't fit your style. That teaches you a lot about crafting a model or designing a work flow that does work. For you!

Maybe you learned something about what you need from partners, advisers, coaches, outsource service providers, and other support structures. Maybe you learned something about being more flexible, agile, willing to shift when a shift is required.

One of my first consulting clients was William Payne. He isn't a client any longer only because he sold his dental practice and retired.

Today, he and his wife, Teresa, and their three amazing offspring count among my dearest friends and my "family-of- choice." But when we started out, we had a lot of brick walls in our way.

Shortly before engaging me to work with his McPherson, Kansas, dental practice, Bill brought in an associate doctor.

In anticipation of the growth it would mean for his business, he built a new facility—with nine treatment rooms.

People said, "You can't do *that*—it's too big; it's too expensive; you'll never be able to pay for it."

Bill said, "I can too." And he did it.

It wasn't the first time Bill had heard, "You can't do *that*!" He'd heard it loud and clear when he elected to no longer place amalgam (metal) restorations, years before his industry embraced the composite and porcelain materials that replaced them.

His colleagues were horrified! How dare he force his patients to accept his new-fangled methods? Why, he'd lose patients! He'd go out of business!

He did lose some patients. And gained some. And he did not go out of business.

Then the associate's wife decided she wasn't cut out for small-town living. They moved to Wichita, and Bill was left with a beautiful new building, a staggering debt load, and no associate.

He contracted with an agency to find another associate, with the option of selling the practice if the doctor preferred ownership to employment.

People said, "You can't do *that*—it's almost impossible to get young doctors to come to a small town."

Bill knew that was true, but he wasn't going to give up. He did what he could to make the practice attractive and promote the opportunity he was offering. And he hired me.

It's probably a good thing that I was still new to consulting. If I'd had more experience, I might have been one of those people telling him, "You can't do *that*!"

Because producing enough to pay for that building with only one dentist and a part-time hygienist, in a small Kansas town where fees are low but overhead costs remain high—well, let's just say it was a little daunting.

Fast-forward to the day I received the celebratory call: "Today is my first day of official retirement! I wanted to share it with you!"

Together, Bill, Teresa, the staff, and I went through many adjustments to attitudes and choices. We made mistakes, we course-corrected often, and we apologized almost as frequently. But we held true to our desire.

And all those things people said he couldn't do? Done!

The debt was paid. By building the practice to an exceptional level of performance, excellence, and efficiency, we were able to maintain a gross income level of more than $1 million a year for several years running.

The practice was sold, at a fair and mutually favorable price, to a young dentist whose wife and kids love small-town living. And Bill had the opportunity to continue working as an associate, on his own terms, as he phased out of practicing dentistry.

The purchaser has already attracted a new associate to take Bill's place.

Oh, and he never did place another amalgam restoration!

Whatever you've achieved, learned, or changed, remember that it has caused you to grow. Just like the baby elephant, you've gotten bigger, stronger, and more able to pull that stake out of the ground and choose your own path.

Whatever growth your experiences have afforded you, now is the time to test yourself. Tug on the chain. Does it still hold you back, or are you more powerful than you once were? More ready to own that power and put it to work for you? More able to choose "can" instead of "cannot?"

After all, what's the best thing that can happen?

CHAPTER 42

BLASTING CAP #4— HOW CAN I REDESIGN IT?

"If your eyes are full of tears from the past, your future is likely to look blurry."

Have you ever set your sights on something you didn't get? I don't know anyone who can (honestly) say no. Of course, we're disappointed when that happens. Of course, we grieve. But if we hold on to that state of grieving, we miss the opportunities that the future holds.

When we give ourselves over to that disappointment, we also close our eyes to the successes that were part of the experience.

When we focus on the loss, we forgo celebrating a game well played. When we focus on the small audience, we forgo celebrating a song well sung. When we set our hearts on a method rather than an outcome, we forgo celebrating the achievement.

So how can you redesign your definition of success? How can you redesign the method by which you realize your dreams?

My dear friend, author, speaker, and massage therapist, Annette Karr, is doing exactly what she wants to do—but she's had a few brick walls to blow up.

First, she's itty bitty.

Second, she's over 60, and has just now written her first book, although it is something she's wanted to do for a very long time.

And third, she has epilepsy. So she's heard "you can't do that" a lot.

"You're little, you're nearly retirement-age, you have epilepsy, you'll never be able to … ."

To which Annette said, "I can too! Watch me!"

And she did. Her successful career as a massage therapist has spanned decades, and allowed her to be part of hospital teams and head up her own private massage practice.

Her first book, *Wink the One-Eyed Wonder*, written with the cooperation of Wink, her French poodle born with (you guessed it) only one eye, has taken her into schools and nursing homes and put her in front of town councils and state governors to share her message: "Think Wink. You ARE worth a million!"

Even in my earliest conversations with Annette, she expressed a desire to be a public speaker. She knew she wanted to share a message about the precious, unique beauty we all have, not *in spite* of our differences, but *because* of them.

But her massage practice kept her busy. She wasn't sure how to frame the story of living with epilepsy to make that message simple and powerful enough to reach the people she wanted to reach.

Then her long-time companion, Rosie, left her physical body. Soon after, Annette got a call from her vet asking whether she was ready for another dog.

"It's a poodle. A French poodle. He was born prematurely. One eye is missing. He needs a home."

Annette wasn't ready for another dog. And she didn't like poodles. But she went in to have a look at the poor little fellow.

And came home with Wink—a nearly infinitesimal ball of white curls, surrounding an uncontainable personality.

I'm sure there were people who said, "You can't raise a puppy, and a sickly one at that, while you're running your massage practice!" But Annette is no more minded to accept "can't" than is Dr. William Payne.

Even though Annette's big heart had plenty of room for one tiny puppy, she couldn't have guessed that he would provide the "voice" for her message, and the vehicle for the pursuit of her dream.

Wink's story—of being a reject, nearly put down because of his missing eye and dismal chances of survival, only to be welcomed by his "Momma" and given the opportunity to spread his special brand of love to all her friends, her massage clients, and the community—has provided the perfect parallels to Annette's own story. And the perfect platform for her to share her message.

Now, through the book and Annette's speaking engagements, Wink is able to share his story and his larger-than-life spirit with the world at large.

The dream was redesigned, but the purpose speaks loud and clear!

Annette also provided me with another story about redesigning dreams. She told me the story of a professional football player who had to have part of his leg amputated because of bone cancer.

What this man really wanted to do was play professional football. And he had permission—not only his own permission, but the permission of an entire league. And he knew he could. At least, until the surgery. Then he knew he couldn't.

The cancer robbed him of that option forever.

Annette tells how the man had sessions with a therapist at the cancer center where he was being treated. The therapist asked him to draw a picture representing how he saw himself.

He drew a crude vase. And then he drew jagged lines across the vase.

"What are those lines?" the therapist asked.

"Those are cracks. I was a perfect vessel; now I'm flawed."

As this man continued his treatment at the center, he began to redesign his dream. Perhaps he realized that the reasons he wanted to play football didn't have to do with the game. Perhaps they had to do with winning, with achieving. Perhaps they had to do with having an impact on people's lives.

I don't know what went through his mind, how he found purpose and fulfillment in what he was able to accomplish there at the center. But I do know, through Annette, that he began to work with other patients, helping them face the challenges of their own battles with disease.

Eventually he met, and married, a woman who was a patient at the treatment center. When the therapist asked him to repeat the exercise of drawing a picture to represent how he saw himself, he drew the same crude vase. With the same jagged lines.

But then he added little lines radiating out from the cracks. And when the therapist asked what those represented, he said, "That's the light that pours out of me now. No one could see it when I was perfect."

By redesigning the method through which he could achieve the outcomes central to his purpose, he ended up contributing far more, and living a more fulfilled life, than he might have as a professional athlete.

Not only were others able to see his light, but he became aware of it in a new way.

When you open yourself to asking, "How can I redesign it?" you are committing to seeing your future possibilities with a fully present energy that is free from past emotion.

Clinging to the exact model of your dream makes you like a child who has a tantrum because the circus has left town. The opportunity to see *that* circus in *that* place at *that* time no longer exists.

But there are other performances, other circuses, other opportunities. Maybe it isn't about the circus at all; maybe it's about the animals, or about the high-wire act, or just about the excitement of the crowd. Those desires can be met in other ways. The "success model" can be redesigned.

What outcomes are you committed to achieving? What is most important to you? Is it fame and fortune? Is it a sensation or experience? Is it an environment or people? Is it the impact it has on you or on others? What, specifically, makes pursuing your dream worthwhile?

How can you design a model that achieves those things?

> *"Uncovering buried treasure may require*
> *digging through a lot of dirt."*

This exercise may require digging deep, though layers of past experiences, celebrations, disappointments, dreams fulfilled and dreams cast aside. But it's essential to blowing up this brick wall!

Let the excavation begin!

What are you looking for?

Artifacts.

That's right. Artifacts of your life as you've lived it, of your life as you've dreamed it.

In the same way that archaeologists look for clues about past cultures—the way the people interpreted their world, the way they worked and played, the things they prized, the things they threw away—you're looking for clues about your own culture, your own choices.

What dreams have you brought to life? What about them thrills you still, and what would you not choose to do again? What dreams have you laid away? What about them calls you still, and what finds no answer in your heart?

In your answers to these questions you'll find themes: clues to what has the greatest meaning for you, and what offers the greatest satisfaction.

Now ask yourself which elements of your "what I really want to do is ..." statement are vital to creating the culture you want for your life. What would it do for you; what would it do for the world? What doors would it open? What about it really lights your fire?

From this, you'll create a list of nonnegotiables. These are the elements that must be present for you to be fulfilled, and boundaries that you will not violate in order to achieve your purpose.

This is the blueprint of what is possible, the heart of your dream. Working from it, how can you design a method, vehicle, and platform that will allow you to surround yourself with the physical, emotional, and spiritual elements you most prize, while fulfilling your core purpose?

—CHAPTER 43—

THE REAL DYNAMITE— WHAT AM I GOING TO DO ABOUT IT?

"Affirmations clear the road for action, but an open road left untraveled still takes you nowhere."

Each time you find yourself saying, "But I can't because ..." your first step is to identify the wall. Is it a Wall of Circumstances, of Style, of Consequences, or of Design? Keep challenging your answers until you have that lightening-strike moment and say, "Yes! That is the real barrier."

Make the four blasting caps a continual part of your plan of attack, too. Go through them in order, without moving to the next until you're sure you've done all the damage you can with the one you're on.

That will keep the way clear, but only action will take you down the path.

We've been using some controlled explosions to loosen the bricks, but those blasting caps won't move your wall or take you further down the path unless you ignite the real charge.

187

What are you going to do about it? Because that decision, that plan for taking action, is the real TNT!

Don't fall into the trap of "ready, fire, aim!" But don't let yourself get caught in the endless loop of getting ready to get ready either.

Taking action without a plan will certainly blow something up, but the brick wall may not be the thing that comes tumbling down. On the other hand, creating a plan, then failing to take action, is like stringing out your fuse with only a firecracker attached to the other end.

How do you know you're ready?

First, you must claim your power, give yourself permission, and escape from the crate, leaving the crabs and naysayers behind.

You'll have people predict that you "can't," and people who are afraid you'll fail. You'll encounter people who refuse to accept your definition of success, or who resent you for pursuing or attaining it. But only you have the power of consent, the power to determine your attitude, control your choices, and claim your heart's desire!

Second, you must do the work, challenging each brick wall as it goes up, and maintaining momentum despite the "change orders" that come along.

Being committed to your outcomes, and flexible about the method of achieving them, may be the most difficult requirement, but it is a requirement nonetheless.

Third, you must leave where you are, and know where you want to go.

As Stephanie Frank, serial entrepreneur and author of *The Accidental Millionaire*, reminds me during our Dynamite Dialog, there are really only two things you have to know.

You have to know the "what": your destination.

Then you have to figure out "how."

"People get it backwards!" Stephanie's frustration is clear. "Most people will not take a step in the direction of their dreams until they know how they're going to get there. But here's the problem: Until you know the 'what,' the destination, pretty much *any* how will get you somewhere. Just maybe not where you want to go."

If you know the "what," Stephanie asserts, the "hows" start showing up by elimination.

If you're trying to figure out transportation options, for instance, and you don't know where you're going, the possibilities are overwhelming. But if you want to go from Phoenix to Orlando, then you can cross off going by ship, and walking doesn't sound too appealing. Until you are prepared to leave where you are, and until you decide on your desired destination, the "how" is meaningless.

Once you've met those three requirements, you're ready to light the fuse for the dynamite—the plan!

Stephanie says she has found that the brick wall that stops the most entrepreneurs is the belief that the plan, and everything that follows the plan, must be complete and perfect before you say "go!"

Call it perfectionism, call it procrastination, call it fear of not being good enough, or just call it a barrier to "getting it done"; much of Stephanie's ability to build one multimillion-dollar enterprise after another is due to her refusal to fall into that trap.

Stephanie's story about how she began her speaking career is a perfect illustration. She'd no sooner decided that what she really wanted to do was to become a public speaker, when she came across a brochure for Skillpath Seminars, a company that paid speakers to deliver training.

"When I decided to become a professional speaker—and the *decision* is the key here—I had no idea how to do that. So I started looking for a sign, a signal. I started looking for the 'hows.' I made the decision, and the hows started showing up.

"Of course, here's the thing. As soon as you make a decision, and the hows start showing up—guess what? You're gonna get scared. It's a little freaky!"

As a believer in taking advantage of seeming accidents, and refusing to let herself get freaked out by how fast the hows showed up, Stephanie took that brochure as a sign and gave the company a call. "How do I become a speaker for Skillpath?"

Skillpath wanted a list of topics she was qualified to teach, and a video. "This is how stupid and green I was," she laughs: "I said, 'of what?'"

Of her teaching, they said. Something. Anything. She could be teaching someone how to tie shoes; they just wanted to see her in action.

Of course she didn't have a video of herself teaching. So she recorded one.

She tells me, amusement bubbling, that she recently came across a copy of that audition video. "I gotta tell ya, how

I became a speaker with *that* video—" she pauses in remembered amazement—"it's beyond me!"

Her background is in high-level technology, so she recorded a video of herself teaching a bunch of engineers. She was wearing a blue checkered suit, and her '80s appropriate, poodle-curly hair was sprayed within an inch of its weight tolerance.

"All three of those things are don'ts if you're a speaker, right? But the worst part of this video was, I would go and teach them a little bit, and then I'd walk out of the screen. So the majority of this video I wasn't even in the frame!"

But off it went, and soon Stephanie was being trained as a public speaker by a top-notch institution. Most of us would pay big bucks for that kind of training. Stephanie was receiving it as part of a paying gig!

Her speaking career has come a long way since then, and at each point she has asked the same questions: "What do I want? What do I need to do next?" Sound familiar?

Once you know those two things, you *are* ready for "just do it!" As Stephanie says, "Perfectionism is a form of fear. Get it 80 percent there, guys, 80 percent *if that*, and it's ready to go!"

Don't be concerned about having your plan fully fleshed out. Make a decision, and start watching for "hows." Find a place to begin, and get started. Like Martin Luther King Jr.'s staircase, or Ava's drive in the dark, keep your desired outcome clearly in your mind's eye, and the path will become clear as you move toward it.

And once you've made the decision to move toward it, hold nothing back!

*"Why cross your fingers when you can
spread your wings?"*

You laughed. But it isn't a joke.

So often, when we go into any situation, whether our dream is to land a contract, land a job, or land a date, we go in with fingers crossed instead of arms spread wide. Not only does that posture impede forward progress, it's also awfully hard to receive or hold onto anything with crossed fingers, isn't it?

Now, about that starting place, that action plan.

Since determining even your next step depends on what you really want to do, the type of walls you've built, and how you've responded to the blasting caps, I won't try to craft one for you here.

However, I know that powerful questions yield powerful answers, so I will offer some of the questions I would ask you if we *were* crafting your action plan together.

What resources do you think you lack? List the people you need to know, the skills you need to hire for or master, the financial stake that will be required.

Make a plan for getting connected, for mastering the skills or finding a service provider you can outsource them to, and for generating the financial stake, or phasing the launch to reduce the initial investment.

Where is the area of greatest resistance? First, what resistance are you meeting within yourself? Then, who else is likely to be frightened by your decision to pursue your dream? Who is likely to resent the time or financial investment? Begin to have those conversations. Honor and respect others' concerns, but be firm about your commitment.

Who is on your success team? Who will support you, advise you, challenge you, and celebrate with you? Connect with these people and ask them to help you stay on the path.

Do you need to create a bridge? If there are circumstances you cannot change right now, boundaries you will not cross, you may need to take temporary stabilization measures. How can you make sure that the bridge takes you closer to where you want to go, and that you don't get too comfortable and turn the bridge into a rut?

What is the one thing you could do next that would have the greatest impact? Is there one brick that's holding up the rest of the wall? One "I can't" that you can move to the "can too" column that would let everything else break free?

What is the one thing you could do right now? What can you do tomorrow or even next week? Is there a wall that can be demolished easily and quickly? Hit that one, hit it hard, and just keep going.

What part of the plan is the most challenging for you? Is there something you dread doing? Something you fear most? Can you outsource it? Can you ask someone to help you prepare for it? Can you find another approach to getting it done?

Finally, who will you need to become in order to do what you really want to do?

> *"Self-control, without self-awareness,*
> *results in misery."*

Kimberly included this powerful advice in our Dialog: "Ask yourself, 'Who do I want to be right now?' Then ask,

'What would that person do in this moment?' Because that person you want to be is already alive inside you, and they have answers to share with you if you'll only ask."

Discard the "I am what I am, and that's all that I am" belief. Because it's not about what you are. The power to blow up any brick wall lies in *who* you are, which includes your past, present, and future selves.

Limitless.

"In 1917, there was no Charles Lindbergh."

Richard's storytelling voice is instantly captivating. I know he's about to share a story that has informed his own attitudes and choices.

"No one [had] ever heard of Charles Lindbergh. He was an air service pilot flying Jennys, and later he was an airmail pilot flying Standards and VH Fours.

"*No one* had ever heard of Charles Lindberg. And no one had ever crossed the Atlantic. So as this man flew, he decided.

"I don't think he consciously said, 'I'm going to become Charles Lindbergh, an icon for the twentieth century.'

"He was saying, 'Now there's a challenge! Can a person fly across the Atlantic? Would they need a biplane or a monoplane? Would they need a multi-engine? Would they need a crew? Or would they do it alone?' And this was something to pass the time. While the fields of the Midwest rolled beneath him. While he carried the mail.

"The more he thought about it, the more he thought, 'That could be done!' And his own individual sense started manifesting.

"And if *I* were going to do it, I'd do it in a monoplane. And I wouldn't do it with a crew; I'd do it alone!" And as that thought continually escalated and cycled in his mind, it drew in other people.

"At first it drew in other people who thought he was crazy! 'You can't possibly do that! No, you'd need a big airplane with three engines on it. You'd need a crew! That's a long way to go! No, we won't even think of financing you, Slim Lindbergh."

"And then he went to St. Louis, and he met some people there who said, 'We *will* finance you! We think you can do it. Your desire, and your series of choices, and your skills that you've already expressed, have so impressed us, we're going to help you become the Charles Lindbergh that you want to be."

They had no clue that it was actually going to work, and that 'Charles Lindbergh' would become a name that everyone in the 20th century would know.

"Step by step by step!

"He went out to meet Claude Ryan in San Diego, began the sketches to design the Spirit of St. Louis. Talked with the Wright Engines Company about installing one of their new Whirlwind engines, and step by step by step …

"Flew it across the country! Sure enough! It was a flying fuel tank! And they figured out how much fuel it would need, and all the fuel had to be at the center of gravity of the airplane, so the pilot can't see a thing! You had got to look out the little side windows. So he got a periscope so [he] could see ahead.

"'A flying fuel tank! That's the way we do it!' While meanwhile, others were trying, and failing, and dying, in the Atlantic Ocean.

"Finally, all his planning, and all his skills, came together. And an icon [was] born in our culture. The idea of flight overcoming space, overcoming time, connecting cultures, connecting continents—all because of this mail pilot, for the fun of it, thinking, 'How would *I* do it?'

"That's true of every one of us. We don't know who we're going to be 10 years, 50 years from now. All we know is what our desires are.

"If we don't have desires, if we don't have passions, it probably won't be something that will touch a whole lot of other lives. But if we do have passions and desires, and if we do follow them, effort is required. Work is required. And sometimes danger is required, to be vaulted over.

"But sure enough, we can reach the end of a lifetime and look back across it, and say, 'Yeah! I did what I came here to do. And, as a kid, I didn't even know what that was! All I had was this yearning to …'

"You fill in the blank: 'to express my art,' 'to fly airplanes,' 'to somehow make a difference in the world around me.' And as we follow that which we most love, those desires require of us certain steps, certain actions.

"There's always action involved! And sure enough, we live through, we make our lifetimes come true, to become the person who, at the beginning of a lifetime, we wouldn't have believed we could possibly become."

As I listen to his story, I think back on what I learned from *Hypnotizing Maria*: We hypnotize ourselves into success or failure, sickness or health, wealth or poverty. All as a result of the suggestions we accept.

Charles Lindberg faced many suggestions. Some said "of course you can do this," others "you can't do this." He had to make a choice between the two, over and over, weeding some suggestions out and nurturing others in order to do what he did and become the person he became.

Who do you need to become to do what you really want to do?

When you make the attitude-choice-desire loop, consistently, over and over, with the same answer, you become the person of your desire.

You create the path through desire, and travel it through attitudes, through choices. Yes, that path will have the occasional outcroppings of brick wall. But you know how to just blow them up.

Proceed with confidence: You have the personal power, and the firepower, to make it happen!

> *"It is one of the most ironic truths about the human creature: he is unable to measure his own potential, therefore he believes it to be limited."*

You won't make that mistake.
Will you?

DEDICATION:

Dedicated to all those brave Blast Thru Artists who are blowing up brick walls every day, and dancing through the rubble into the life they deserve!

ACKNOWLEDGEMENTS

No one blasts through barriers without borrowing firepower from the arsenals of others.

If I listed all my sources of inspiration, motivation, education, and illumination it would double the size of this book. So I'll resign myself to acknowledging a few who have been a constant and consistent source of firepower for me.

My inner circle of friends and mentors – Bob Burg, John David Mann, Scott Ginsberg, Bill Ellis, Tom Ruwitch, Kimberly Schneider, Dafna Michaelson Jenet, Jeremy Nulik, Caren Libby, Barbara Abramson, Lynne Wilhite, James Stafford, Rachel Lapin, Philip Penrose, and Dr. William Payne and the entire Payne family who have adopted me as "family of choice."

Three gentleman without whom the "dynamite" may never have ignited or made it to the page:

Tom Gillaspie, who's known me the longest, put up with the most, raised an eyebrow when I said "I can't", and cheered every "I CAN TOO" explosion.

Richard Bach. The man whose book, Illusions – The Adventures of a Reluctant Messiah, shaped my life. The man who "by pure coincidence" downloaded the ebook that was the basis of this work, read it, and suggested I might have a gift.

Finally, Nathan Martin, whose quiet intensity and conviction led me to believe that Sound Wisdom was exactly the right publisher to help me bring the work of years of experience, exploration and explosions into book form.

So many people have touched my life, directly and indirectly - you may have even been one of them. And if you hadn't yet, you are now. By reading, thinking, sharing, responding, and by changing even one small bit of your world, you touch me. And I thank you.

ABOUT THE AUTHOR

Dixie Gillaspie has been called a muse, an alchemist, and a blast through artist, but most people who know her just call by her by her childhood nickname; "Dynamite." In *her* words, she has been a coach, business consultant and analyst, and a general trouble-shooter to entrepreneurs and business leaders for more years than she is willing to admit.

She is also the author of *Doses of Dynamite - Firepower for Capturing the Inspiration in Everyday Things* with photography by Caren Libby, and is a contributing author to *The Thought That Changed My Life Forever*, with Dr. Bernie Siegel and Dr. Joe Dispenza.

Check Out

http://dixiedynamitecoaching.com/mini-lessons/

For free mini-lessons from Dixie!

Two-Dollar Pistol

"Compelling . . . Be prepared for a fast ride."
—Historical Novel Society

"An entertaining Depression-era adventure with
echoes of *Bonnie and Clyde.* Good fun."
—*Booklist*

Panhandle

"There's an earthy realism and attention to detail
in this first novel that sets it apart . . . Cogburn has
a deft ear for planting emotion and honesty in his
rhythmic cowboy dialogue."
—*AudioFile* magazine

"You'll need a hanky for this one, but you'll be glad
you picked it up because it grabs your undivided
attention when you least expect it."
—"Best Westerns of 2013," Kmart book reviews

"This well-written novel offers up a cast of complex
characters . . . far removed from the simplistic
caricatures so common in traditional Westerns."
—*Roundup Magazine*

"A gritty read."
—*Oklahoma Gazette*

"Throughout the book, Cogburn treats familiar
subjects with freshness and originality, spinning
engaging tales true to the Western tradition but
told in his own distinctive voice."
—*Roundup Magazine*

PINNACLE WESTERNS BY BRETT COGBURN

Rooster

Panhandle

Destiny, Texas

Widowmaker Jones

Buzzard Bait

Look for more great titles from Brett Cogburn
coming soon!

BUZZARD BAIT

A WIDOWMAKER JONES WESTERN

BRETT COGBURN

PINNACLE BOOKS
Kensington Publishing Corp.
www.kensingtonbooks.com

PINNACLE BOOKS are published by

Kensington Publishing Corp.
119 West 40th Street
New York, NY 10018

All Kensington titles, imprints, and distributed lines are available at special quantity discounts for bulk purchases for sales promotions, premiums, fund-raising, educational, or institutional use. Special book excerpts or customized printings can also be created to fit specific needs. For details, write or phone the office of the Kensington sales manager: Kensington Publishing Corp., 119 West 40th Street, New York, NY 10018, attn: Sales Department; phone 1-800-221-2647.

PINNACLE BOOKS and the Pinnacle logo are Reg. U.S. Pat. & TM Off.

ISBN-13: 978-0-7860-4166-4
ISBN-10: 0-7860-4166-8

First printing: September 2017

10 9 8 7 6 5 4 3 2 1

Printed in the United States of America

First electronic edition: September 2017

ISBN-13: 978-0-7860-4177-1
ISBN-10: 0-7860-41776

*All sides involved in the Apache Wars
committed atrocities and made missteps.
You who judge, place blame where you will and call
your villains by name, but there are always good men
to be found within every such narrative,
even if they are sometimes shrouded by the fog
of history and buried by their own sins
or the sins of their fellow man. . . .
Those times were violent and bloody
and imperfectly heroic, and so is this story
of three men who lived them.*

Chapter One

It was well past sundown, and the big man had come a long way afoot over the desert when he finally saw the campfire burning in the bottom of a canyon below him. A single grunt that could have meant anything escaped his chest while he loosened his pistol in its holster and started down the ridge with the tattered soles of his boots grating on the gravel beneath them, one long, wrathful stride after another.

Their fire was a white man fire—the kind you build up big and sit way back from, and the kind any fool could see for miles. An Indian or a smarter set of bandits would have built it different—small fire, sit close, and live to build another fire another day. The men he hunted were either confident that they weren't being followed, or else they didn't give a damn. Either way, on top of not being cautious fire builders, they were all asleep or had stared into the fire so long that they were night blind. That was why they squinted and blinked at him as long as they did when they should have been getting up out of their bedrolls pulling their pistol poppers.

Thing was, by the time they got right with the fact that they had a visitor, the big man was already squatted down across the fire from them with the flickering flames dancing across the scarred face revealed beneath his hat brim.

"Where the hell did you come from?" The bandit to the right of the big man reared up his head from the folded saddle blanket that had been his pillow. The little tufts of hair on the sides of his bald head stuck out so that they added to his incredulous, confused look. It went without saying that he didn't like being surprised, and he liked it even less that both his arms were outside the blanket over his belly with no easy way to get to the pistol he probably had covered up under there.

The big man didn't answer him, instead turning his head slowly to look at the other bandit, a young, bony Mexican, maybe seventeen or eighteen years old. The big man's right hand moved to rest on top of his thigh, closer to the Smith & Wesson revolver both of the bandits could see holstered on that hip. "Kid, you keep digging around under your blankets like that, and you're going to make me nervous. Maybe you got fleas, or maybe there's a pistol under there you're itching to take a hold of."

The young Mexican quit squirming but remained propped up on one elbow and the other arm hidden under his blanket. He tried to play dumb, or maybe he didn't speak English. "*Que?*"

"You heard me," the big man said. He reached out with his left hand and took up the coffeepot from beside the fire, keeping careful watch on the Mexican. "I see you guessing whether you can get a pistol out before I can lay hand to my own shooter. Tricky business, that guessing, and a game I'm thinking you don't have the experience for."

"You ought not come sneaking up on a camp that way," the bald one threw in. He scooted himself to a sitting position. "Ain't no friendly way at all."

The big man turned up the coffeepot and took a gulp from it, grimacing at the heat of it. He took two more deep swallows while he stared at them over the tilted pot.

"You boys caused me a long walk. Time or two there I thought I might not catch up to you," he said after the third drink. "Two days, and nigh forty miles or better across that out yonder." He gestured with the coffeepot in the general direction of the rough country that lay behind him, as if that said it all. "And a dry trip it was without even so much as my canteen you took with my horse and saddle. Puts a heavy thirst on a man, a walk like that. Enough to make him plumb peeved if he were a man given to holding grudges."

"Mister, I don't know who you are. What we got here is some kind of misunderstanding." It was the bald one who spoke again—the older of the two acting as the spokesman, or maybe the Mexican kid didn't speak English.

"Where's your partner?"

"Ain't nobody but us."

The big man glanced at the empty bedroll beside them while he sat the coffeepot down. He then looked into the dark beyond them at the shadows of several horses tied to a picket line strung between two stunted, twisted juniper bushes. "What I know is that your man out there probably fell asleep when he was supposed to be taking his turn at guard. By now, I'd guess he's trying to Injun around until he can get a rifle gun on me. What *you* ought to know is that the second he lifts that rifle I'm going to put a bullet into you. Not the kid here, not that man out there. You."

The bald fellow had eased his blanket down to his knees and made like he was going to get to his feet. He paused at those words, and then longer, as if measuring whether the big man would let him up or not. When he finally stood, he made sure to do it slowly.

The kid followed suit but only got to his knees. He had taken his pistol off when he lay down for the night and couldn't keep his eyes off it lying there on the ground beside him, half exposed under the brim of a straw *sombrero*, one of those great big hats that the Mexicans favored.

"You better call your man in. I admit I came down here promising myself the awful things I was going to do to you for stealing my horse like you did, but sitting here with some hot coffee in my belly I've had time to think on it some." The big man's attention went back to the picket line. "You out there, it ain't like I don't see you standing there behind that rock. You put that rifle down and saddle my horse and bring him here."

"*Que?*" the Mexican asked the bald fellow. "*Está loco?*"

"Yeah, I think he's crazy," the bald fellow answered.

"Just trying to live and let live where I can," the big man said. "This Gypsy girl I met a while back stressed to me that I need to reform."

"A Gypsy girl?" The bald outlaw seemed to find that funny. "She read your fortune with them cards?"

"No, she wasn't that kind of a Gypsy."

"What'd she want you to reform from?"

"My wicked ways."

"How's that working out?"

The big man straightened the slump in his back, and the former weariness to his posture was gone. His right hand hung just below his Smith .44. "You might say it's been mixed results so far, but I haven't killed anybody lately."

The bald fellow's tongue flicked a rotted front tooth. It was a long few seconds before he took a deep breath and gave what sounded like a forced chuckle. "Mister, you got some moxy to you, I'll give you that. But no matter how salty you think you are, you ain't getting all three of us. You know that, and that's what worries me about you."

The bald-headed bandit wasn't the only one to be thinking that the big man might have some help out there in the dark. The Mexican made a study of the dark ridge rising up behind the big man, searching for who else might be lurking about.

"Who you got with you?" The bald outlaw ran his tongue over that blackened tooth again. "Ain't no man comes down here talking like you're talking without he's got some insurance."

"Just me. That's always been enough."

The Mexican kid put one leg under him and braced a hand against the ground like he was going to push himself up. The pistol under his hat wasn't six inches from that hand, and he glanced twice at it.

"Your man out there can't make up his mind. Liable to get us all killed fidgeting around like he is," the big man said.

"Don't you listen to him, Pete," the bald fellow said over his shoulder to the man hiding near the picket line. "You stay right there. He so much as bats an eyelash wrong and you plug him. I need time to think on this. He thinks he's got some kind of edge."

"I'm watching him, Seebo," the man out there in the dark called back to the bald fellow.

One side of the bald fellow's shirttail was untucked, and he made as if to tuck it back in. "I think maybe you got a man or two up there on that cliff."

The big man didn't answer.

The bald fellow went on, working it over out loud and shaking off his first thought. "No, what I think is you're the damnedest bluffer I ever did see. You want us to think you got some help, elsewise you wouldn't be sitting here talking, not if you had the numbers and the drop on us."

"I want my horse." The big man kept his voice matter-of-fact, like he had all along, but there was a hint of a harsh edge creeping into it.

"You come all that way after us just to get yourself killed over one damned horse?"

"He's the only one I've got."

The bald fellow chuckled again and kept working at the tail of his shirt like he was having trouble with it, needing an excuse to get closer to the holstered Colt he was carrying. "I ought to give you the son of a bitch. Tried to ride him and the bastard bucked me off. Nasty piece of horseflesh, that one. I don't cherish us bleeding each other over the likes of such an animal."

The big man almost looked sad. "That horse and me have come a far piece together, and so happens that you picked a bad time to steal him. See here, I've got to be in San Antonio two days from now to meet an old friend who's up against it in the worst way. She did me a good turn once when I was down and out, and I'm not the kind to go forgetting something like that."

The bald fellow's laugh was genuine that time, louder than it needed to be, and it echoed off the stone canyon walls. "You hear that, Pete? First that Gypsy girl, and now this woman in San Antonio."

"I heard him," the man near the picket line called back. "Regular ladies' man."

"What's your name, big man?" the bald fellow asked. "You're damned sure one of a kind."

The big man's mouth tightened and he shook his head ever so slowly. "Are you going to bring that horse here, or are you going to go ahead and pull that pistol?"

As quick as that, the bald fellow quit making like he was trying to tuck his shirt in and went for his Colt, and the kid reached for his shooter under that *sombrero.* Across the fire from them, the Smith pistol rasped against leather and appeared in the big man's fist without him even seeming to have drawn it—a blue-black oily thing, dark as sin in the orange glow of the fire.

The bald fellow's Colt stuck in his holster, and he was having such a hard time yanking at his belt to try to free it that the big man didn't bother to shoot him first. Instead, he shot the shadow of a man at the picket line. Did it kind of nonchalantly and shot him so quick that all that one managed to do in return was to let a round off into the ground at his feet, and then he tipped over face-first into the dirt at the edge of the firelight with an awful groan.

By that time, the bald fellow had grunted and jerked enough to get his Colt free, but he never got to use it. The big man clacked back the hammer on his Smith once more and put a bullet into the bald fellow's belly that knocked the air out of him in one drawn-out groan. That first bullet was probably enough to do him, but the second one took him for good measure right through that black tooth as he was falling.

By the time the Mexican kid got a good hold on

his own pistol and drug it out from under his hat, he found himself looking up into the bore of that Smith .44. The big man was aiming at a spot right between his eyes. An instant before things had been all gun roars and hellfire, and now there was nothing but dead quiet except for the sound of the Mexican's heavy breathing and the wounded man by the picket line still groaning and writhing in pain.

"You're a frog's hair away from bad things, boy. A frog hair," the big man said. "You let go of that gun, or I promise you it's going to hurt."

The Mexican kid let go of his pistol like it was red hot and crabbed backward, shaking his head. "*Por Dios, no me dispare! No me mate!*"

"I ain't going to kill you." The big man kept his aim for a long moment, then uncocked that Smith with another clack. "Might save somebody some trouble someday if I did, but I ain't going to."

He kicked the kid's pistol into the fire and then went over and toed the bald fellow's corpse over to make sure he was done for. Satisfied, he bent over and scooped up the man's Colt and pitched it in the fire with the other.

When he turned back to the kid he gestured once more to the picket line. "You go saddle my horse. *Ensille mi caballo. Pronto.*"

The Mexican did as he was told, stumbling twice because he didn't want to turn his back on the big man, and giving the wounded outlaw on the ground near the horses wide berth. Nervous or not, he had the horse saddled quickly and soon led it back to the fire while the big man snapped the Smith open and let his empty cartridges eject on the ground. He replaced his spent rounds with three from the loops on his cartridge belt. The Mexican stood holding the bridle reins of the horse.

It was a plain, brown gelding, with not a single white mark on him. The only distinguishing or unusual feature on the animal was the brand burned on his left hip revealed in the firelight—a circle the size of your palm with a dot in the center of it. The gelding cocked one ear and eyed the body of the bald fellow cautiously, but held its ground.

The big man holstered his pistol and walked to where he had shot the man at the picket line. The gut-shot outlaw quit moaning and took one bloody hand off his belly to reach for the big man's pants leg.

"Damn you, help me or finish me. I can't take this hurt," the outlaw said.

The big man brushed free of the wounded man's grasp without stopping. "You asked for it."

He picked up the big-bore '76 Winchester rifle laying on the ground where the gut-shot outlaw had dropped it, and then he examined it before coming back and shoving it in the rifle boot hanging from the saddle on the brown horse.

"Sorry man that will try and shoot you with your own rifle," the big man mumbled while he took the reins from the Mexican and put a boot in the stirrup and swung up astride the horse.

"*Cómo se llama, señor?*" the Mexican asked softly in Spanish, and then in halting and heavily accented English. "I would like to know your name."

The big man seemed to think that over before he answered. "Jones."

"Jones? *No mas?*"

The big man gave the brown gelding's belly a bump with his heels, and the horse left the firelight at a trot.

"You no tell me your real name," the Mexican repeated.

From the darkness and almost muffled by the sound of the horse's shod hooves on the rocky ground, the big man called back to him. "Some call me the Widowmaker, but I never set much store by that."

"Widowmaker Jones." The Mexican repeated it as if it explained much. And then he looked at the bodies of his friends and made the sign of the Cross before he saddled another horse and rode in the opposite direction that the big man had taken. He crossed himself three more times on his way out of the canyon.

Chapter Two

Two nights later, Newt Jones, the man some out West called the Widowmaker, slept in a rundown, abandoned adobe warehouse on the outskirts of San Antonio, Texas. It was raining and near to midnight when he rode into town, and he didn't have the price of a room in his pockets. So he led the Circle Dot horse under what remained of a section of roof that hadn't collapsed and then lay down in one corner and wrapped himself in some newspapers he found there.

It was a restless night, and he awoke early and rode out into a drizzly morning. He found the private train car not long after daylight—parked on a siding a hundred yards from the depot house—and he rode straight to it.

A man in a fancy Prince Albert coat and smoking a cigar stepped out on the platform at the end of the car. He propped one of his button boots on the ornate cast iron banister and puffed on a cigar while Newt dismounted and draped a bridle rein over the railing. He went to the foot of the stairs and looked up.

"I take it you're the one she's waiting for," the man with the fancy shoes said, then he inhaled deeply and let out another cloud of smoke. "You don't look like much."

Newt stared back at him through the rainwater running off the brim of his hat. "I don't feel like much. She in there?"

The fancy man took his boot down and stepped a little to the side so Newt could come up on the platform under its awning and out of the rain. "We've been waiting for you for three days."

Newt went up the stairs and stopped at the top of them. He took in the fancy man's oiled and combed hair, the silk ascot tie adorned with a diamond stick pin, and then took another glance at those patent leather button boots. "Well, you ain't waiting no more."

"I take it you had some trouble getting here."

"What? No trouble."

The fancy man ground his cigar against the handrail and pitched it to the ground, and then he opened the door and went into the Pullman. Newt followed him, stepping aside when barely through the door and putting his back to the wall. The interior of the private passenger car was as fancy as the man who led him inside, all ornate brass and exotic wood. Newt was suddenly conscious of the fact that his rundown boots were muddy and that he was dripping water on the oriental carpet.

A woman in a high-collared, plain black dress

came through the doorway of another room at the far end of the car. She was a comely woman. Although most of her blond hair had turned to gray, she was of a kind and beauty that made it hard to guess her age beyond that she was somewhere past her middle years. "Hello, Newt."

Despite what one would guess about a woman who could command such rich surroundings, there were pieces to her that didn't fit. Her skin had seen too much sun for a gentlewoman, and there was a country twang to her accent that no amount of money could refine.

She gave him a careful examination, and took a long while doing it. He knew what she saw: a big man, not a giant, but well past six feet tall; more big boned and raw frame than heavy, with a face as battered and worn as the raggedy clothing covering him. He didn't even have a coat or a rain slicker.

"You look almost as tired and down on your luck as the last time I saw you." She put some effort into the smile she gave him, a smile that was somewhere between weariness and genuine happiness to see him.

"I came as fast as I could. Your telegraph didn't find me until a week ago."

"I think we sent that telegraph across four states and three territories. I had no idea where you might be." She took a seat on a sofa under a crystal chandelier in the center of the room, at the same time gesturing at a table to his left. "You're probably hungry. Help yourself."

He went to that table and lifted a silver lid. The dish below it held the cold leftovers of their apparent breakfast. There were scrambled eggs and a few sausage patties. He took a piece of the sausage and worked at it while he turned back to her. The fancy man had closed the door, and he went and took a seat beside her on the sofa.

Another man came from the back of the coach, dressed as impeccably as the first, and the only difference between the two was that he was black and he had some kind of a white napkin or towel draped over one forearm. The black man gave a polite nod to the woman and the gentleman on the couch before he went to the table and poured a mug of coffee. He offered the coffee to Newt with an air of servitude, and Newt guessed him to be some sort of a butler. He'd heard of such, but he had never seen one.

"That will be all, Hiram," the fancy man on the couch said. "Leave us now."

Newt took the mug of coffee, and the butler disappeared into the back room where he had come from.

"We were about to give up on you," the fancy man said.

Newt finished the sausage and wiped the grease from his fingers on his leg, quickly aware and ashamed that he had done so. "Like I said, it took a while for me to get that telegraph. I was down to Laredo waiting on a boxing match they were trying to get up for me."

"The newspapers said you were on a weeklong

drunk and they had to cancel the match," the fancy man replied.

"I was under the weather for a spell, had the croup or something, you know. They should have waited until I was up on my feet again."

The woman gave both of them a glance, noting that they had taken an instant dislike to each other. "What do the papers know?" She focused her attention solely on Newt once again. "I see you're still wearing my Amos's hat."

He took off the black felt hat he wore and turned it by the brim in his hands, examining it and the hitched horsehair hatband around its crown. It was a fine hat, almost too fine for the rest of his rundown outfit. "It's been a good hat. I've tried to take care of it, but it's seen a bit of hard living since you gave it to me."

She nodded, and it was plain to him that she, like him, was thinking back to the day she'd given it to him a year before, standing over a freshly dug grave on a lonely stretch of the Pecos River. He'd been half starved that day, too, and with a bullet wound in his chest to make things worse.

Not that Matilda Redding didn't have troubles of her own at the time. He'd found her by herself and with a lawman husband recently murdered by the very same Mexican outlaws who had put the bullet in Newt's chest.

"I also see that you don't have his pistol anymore," she added.

"Oh, I've still got it." He gestured out the door

behind him with a nod of his head in that direction. "It's rolled up in a piece of oilcloth in my saddle-bags. Didn't want to get it wet."

"I halfway regret that I ever gave you that gun, and I don't know if I should be happy that you take care of it so or if I should be disappointed that you don't let the thing rust away. My Amos always stood on the side of law and order, but a pistol isn't anything but the Devil's right hand, no matter who's packing it. Carrying one is like carrying your sin in a holster, and a man that gets used to wearing one usually finds he has a hard time putting it aside."

"Matilda, you didn't send me that telegraph because I'm a gentle man. You don't need a gentle man for this thing."

She nodded in reluctant agreement. "Back when I was a girl, folks used to have a term for a man like you. They'd say you were a man with the bark on, and I need a man with the bark on in the worst kind of way."

"How long ago did the Apaches get your grandson?"

"Seven days ago."

"How did it happen and where?"

The fancy man leaned forward on the couch. "This is all a waste of time. I don't know what you think he can do—"

Newt interrupted him with an upraised palm. "I don't know who you are, fellow, but me and Ms. Matilda were having a conversation. I can't figure you and this fancy train car, or what business this is of yours. But you can have the good manners to stay quiet while I'm talking to the lady."

The fancy man stiffened, and when he spoke he was almost stammering. "What business is this of mine? The child you speak of is my son, and the woman you are speaking to is my mother."

Newt frowned.

"Newt, this is my son, William," the woman said. "And this train car is courtesy of the Southern Pacific. William owns considerable stock in the company."

Newt nodded to the fancy man and gave a grimace that was meant as an apology, and then his attention went back to Matilda. "Never would have guessed you for a rich woman back when I met you."

"Oh, I'm nothing but a farm girl at heart. Just a lawman's widow biding her years," she said. "It's William here that's rich."

"What about the boy? Your grandson?"

The fancy man looked to the woman and shrugged as if it didn't matter. "You tell it, Mother."

She nodded, then took a deep breath and gestured for Newt to take a chair across from them. When he did, she began, "Very well. Among William's other holdings is a mine near Tombstone, Arizona Territory. William Jr., Billy we call him, was to travel with his mother from Tombstone to meet his father at that mine. They went overland by buggy with three mine guards escorting them, but they never arrived. A search party found the burned ruins of their buggy and the bodies of the escort where the Apaches ambushed them."

"The boy's mother?" Newt immediately regretted asking that question, because the look on both of their faces confirmed the worst.

Matilda needed time to gather herself, so her son took over. "A posse sent out from Tombstone lost the trail of the renegades south of Skeleton Canyon. Currently, the army has patrols out all over the border from Arizona to Texas, and their leadership is trying to get permission to pursue the hostiles into Mexico."

Newt looked to Matilda. Once more, she took a deep breath before speaking. "And how many times has the army ever recovered a captive child? Oh, yes, they occasionally barter for one years later and make sure they get plenty of press for it, but I put no faith in them."

Newt could tell that this wasn't the first time they had argued over how to best handle their predicament, and he didn't envy them the decision making.

Matilda once more focused her intense blue eyes on Newt. "I've got no right to ask you this, but I will anyway. Get that boy."

"You have every right to ask," Newt answered.

"You owe me nothing."

"Have you a photograph of him?"

She nodded and looked to her son, who produced a cardboard-backed photograph from the inside pocket of his coat. Newt took it from him and studied it.

"That photograph was taken three months ago," William Sr. said.

"How old is he?" Newt asked.

"Ten."

"Is he a strong boy?"

William paused as if a little perplexed. "I'm not sure what you're asking."

"I'm asking if he's strong, 'cause he doesn't have a chance if he isn't."

"He's a good boy. Reminds me of my Amos sometimes," Matilda said.

Newt got up out of the chair, and William stood to face him.

"Miz Matilda says you're a railroad big shot," Newt said. "Can you get me and my horse on a boxcar going west?"

"I can."

"Well then, anything else is wasting time that we don't have." Newt made as if to go.

"Hold on," William said.

Newt stopped with one hand on the doorknob. "What is it?"

"There are ten men waiting at the Menger Hotel. They're well-armed, well-equipped, and ready to ride at a moment's notice."

"What men?"

"I hired them personally, and they've been waiting for your arrival. Anything you need in the way of equipment you may purchase here, and I will give you a letter of credit and some coin should you incur further expenses along the way."

Newt shook his head wryly. "You got any idea where I'll be going?"

"I assume you'll be going to Mexico."

"Do you think your letter of credit is going to get me anything down there? And it won't be money or equipment, or all the men in China, that will get your boy back. You can't buy what it will take. No sir, I'll need your credit about as much as I'd need a piece of paper to start a fire in hell."

"Lead the posse he's put together, Newt," Matilda said in a soft voice.

"No, I figure to take the train as far as I can and then go overland to one of the Apache reservations and hire a tracker."

"Alone?" William asked. "I've voiced my opposition to my mother's plan to hire you many times. As I understand it from my sources, you're little more than a barroom brawler, pistol-fighter, and small-time pugilist with no qualifications as a tracker other than a gory tale that claims you hunted down some Mexican bandit. That's enough to give me due pause as to your character, but now, sir, you give me fear that not only are you incapable of recovering my son, but that you could endanger any chance that we may have of regaining him."

"I'll get your boy back, or I'll see to it that those that did this pay for it."

William Sr. looked to his mother and held in whatever he had been about to say. Instead, he smoothed the passion in his voice. "Have your try then. My mother and I don't always agree, but she thinks very highly of you. Despite my objections, you misjudge me if you think I wish you anything but the best in this endeavor. I love my son very much."

He turned and walked to the far end of the salon before Newt had a chance to reply. Matilda came to the door and took his place.

"Take the men," she said. "Don't be stubborn."

"Good-bye, Matilda."

He stepped out the door and went down the steps. She followed him outside but stayed on the platform. She tried to cover her laughter with a polite hand on her mouth when she saw what he was looking at. The Circle Dot horse had lain down on its side, never mind that it was raining and that it was saddled.

Newt toed the gelding gently in the rump three times before it would get up. When it did, Newt's saddle was coated in mud.

"I see you're still riding that crazy Indian horse," she said. "And I see he's still vexing you."

"He suits me most of the time. The other times I try my best not to scold him, and he does the same for me." He swiped the worst of the mud from his saddle seat, tightened his cinch, and swung aboard.

"Take this." She held out a leather wallet to him. "William was going to give it to you, but he's upset and forgot."

"I'm not doing this for pay. That's not why I came."

"I know, but you might need money along the way. And knowing you, you don't have the price of a piece of rock candy in your pockets." Her smile and her sincerity stopped short the refusal he was about to give.

He nodded and took the wallet. "Got holes in my pockets. Every time I get hold of some money it falls right out."

"You were the only one I could think of to turn to," she said.

"Why me, when you've got all those men down at the hotel?"

"I don't know those men."

"You barely know me."

"I know enough."

"I'm no good man."

"You're more than you know."

"Miz Matilda, like I told your son in there, I'll bring that boy back or I'll die trying. That's all I can promise you."

"I know you mean that. That's what William doesn't understand, and that's why I'm pinning my hopes on you and not those men at the hotel or the army."

"I'd best be going."

"Don't misjudge William or take insult at anything he said to you. He's out of his element with this, but he is a good man and no coward."

"I wasn't judging him."

"He's going to take those men you refused

and go after Billy. You know that don't you? He thought you would lead them, and he was going to insist that he come along with you."

"That's part of the reason I refused. Best he takes those men and bungles around the border while I see if I can get the boy back. I've got enough troubles without toting along a fretting father, and a tenderfoot at that."

"My Amos could have done it, but William is cut from a different cloth. All the schooling we paid for back East was enough to give him a better life and make him a fortune, but you don't learn what it's going to take for this in a schoolhouse."

"No, ma'am, you don't."

"I'd go with you myself if my old bones could stand the saddle."

"I know you would, and I'd gladly take you along." Newt turned the horse and rode away. "So long."

His next stop was at a livery, and then he made call at the nearest mercantile. When he reappeared at the railroad depot he was leading a little red dun pack mule. According to William Redding's offer, he had outfitted himself for the journey and put his purchases on the Southern Pacific Railroad's tab. His clothes were the same except for a new pair of boots and an India rubber rain slicker, and the packsaddle's pannier contained a new cotton duck coat, two hundred rounds of .45-75 ammunition for his rifle, another fifty rounds of .44's for his pistol, a pound bag of salt, another pound of coffee, five pounds of flour, a dozen cans of tinned fruit and vegetables, a coffeepot, and a frying pan. Thusly equipped, he loaded his livestock on a boxcar and took the noon train headed west. Few people ever knew he was in San Antonio, and even fewer would miss him if he never came back.

Chapter Three

The train crew let him off in the middle of the night some twenty hours later at a water tank stop west of Willcox, Arizona Territory. The boxcar he rode in was not a normal livestock car, and the crew had no ramp to unload his horse and mule. He jumped them from the open door, and the last the train crew saw of him he was headed across the desert under the moonlight.

He rode into the San Carlos Agency three days later, both he and his saddle stock covered in road dust and gaunt from hard travel, having come over nine hundred miles, the last hundred of it overland.

The agency lay on a hardscrabble desert flat at the confluence of the Gila and San Carlos Rivers. He crossed that flat at a long trot, aiming for the cluster of stacked stone and adobe brick buildings. Apache women paused from their work in the middle of little irrigated fields of corn and shielded their eyes from the sun and watched him pass. The wind blew dust and bits of gravel in rolling waves across the flats and bent over the shin-high, sickly yellow stalks of corn.

A band of Apache was gathered in military-style ranks before the agency house, and an army officer and another white man were calling roll and checking number tags for attendance. Two other white men sat at a table under a brush arbor to one side of the agency house.

Newt reined up alongside that arbor and parked his horse in the edge of its shade. It was a hot day, and neither man at the table moved from their slumped, languid poses in their camp chairs. One was an older man in a sweat-stained flannel shirt. He had both boots propped up and crossed on a stool in front of him and was pretending interest in the large rowels of his Mexican spurs while he gave a study to Newt out of the corner of his eye. The other man, much the younger of the two, had his legs propped up in a similar manner. He had a little piece of rope that he had fashioned into a toy lariat, and he would swing his loop a few times and rope the toe of his boot. He did this three times before he stopped and finally tilted his head back far enough to reveal his face beneath his hat brim.

"Looks like we got company, Al," he said.

The older man spat a stream of tobacco juice into the dust, then squinted up into the sunlight at Newt. "It do, Tom."

Newt kept his attention on the Apaches lined up in front of the agency house. Of the sixty or seventy Indians gathered, about a third of them were adult men. They stared straight ahead from their ranks, their faces hard and still, and so stoic as to be made from stone itself.

"Don't look like much, do they?" the older man beside him said with a touch of an accent that sounded like it might be German. "But don't let their looks fool you. Those little brown men are the fighten'est sons a bitches this side of Hades."

"You seem to admire them," Newt said.

"I do," the older man retorted.

No two Apache men were dressed alike. Some wore white man clothing, some a mix-match of that and the traditional Apache wear of a headband to hold their long hair back, a belted cotton shirt, long cloth breechcloth, and high moccasins. Others wore little more than the moccasins and a headband, with only a cloth breechcloth in between. They ran mostly to the short side, and not a man among them would weigh much more than half of Newt—mustang lean, weathered little men, with bandy arms and legs like racehorses. Yet, like the man beside him had said, Newt knew without being told not to misjudge them.

While he watched, a potbellied, naked boy child ran through the ranks laughing and squealing. An Apache woman called for him to come back while she held up the brass nametag on the necklace she wore for the army officer to see.

"What are they doing?" Newt asked.

"Taking roll and giving out rations," the older man with the big spurs said.

"Is that army man there in charge?" Newt asked.

"That's Lieutenant Davis. That other fellow with him is the agent," the older man replied while he worked his chewing tobacco around in his cheek, as if contemplating spitting again.

"Who should I talk to about hiring an Apache scout?" Newt asked.

Both men looked up at him when he said that.

"What would you want a scout for?" the older man asked.

"Going hunting."

The older man took his feet down off the stool and stood. He nodded at Newt's rifle resting across his saddle swells. "What kind of hunting are you aiming to do? I got a feeling you ain't going after elk meat."

"I'm going to Mexico."

"Are you the one they sent the telegraph about?"

"What telegraph?"

"The lieutenant got a telegraph from some muckety-muck with the railroad. It said one of their hired men was coming here and requested we give him an Apache scout."

"Didn't know about that. Where's my scout?"

"You picked a bad time. You talk to the lieutenant if you want, but they won't give you a scout."

"Why not? I'll pay him fair wages."

The older man pointed at the lines of Indians, as if they said it all. "You got any idea what this place is? It's a bomb is what it is. Those are Chiricahuas. Know what they are? They're Apaches, and then they ain't. Meanest of them by far, and we've got them and all kinds of other bands to keep on this reservation and to make sure they act halfway civilized. Every time we turn our back or so much as take a sneeze, there's a dozen of them slipping away and going off raiding. The Apache don't like us, they don't like each other sometimes, and they least of all like starving on this patch of hell we've forced them to live on."

"I just want to hire a scout."

"And I said you won't get one. Talk to the lieutenant if it makes you happy, but you won't."

The younger man threw a loop on his boot again and chuckled. "Don't you read the papers?"

Newt looked to the older man. "I'm not much of a reader."

The older man frowned at the younger before he continued. "What he means is that Crook's army just spent two months chasing all over hell and half creation trying to get these savages back on the reservation. We got Chato's bunch and most of the miscreants, but it's a touchy thing right now keeping them here. And we've still got the problem of the ones down in Mexico that haven't turned themselves in yet like they promised."

"Your problems don't concern me. All I need is a tracker."

"Mister, don't you know who you're talking to?" The younger one threw in. "This is Al Sieber, Chief of Scouts, and the man who knows more about Apaches and hunting them than any white man west of anywhere and more than most Apaches to boot."

"I've got a hundred dollars, gold coin, to the Apache scout that will hire on with me," Newt said. "And you and Mr. Sieber here can sit and talk about Apaches all you want while I go to Mexico."

"General Crook knows about the Redding boy's capture." The older man ignored the rising temper in Newt's voice and continued as calm as he had been before. "There's already two companies of cavalry on the trail. Last we heard they were camped at San Bernardino Springs on the border, and have thirty White Mountain scouts out looking for the boy."

"The Reddings didn't send me out here to wait on the army," Newt replied. "I don't know much about Apaches, but I know enough that I need an Apache to catch one. And that's what I aim to do."

"Say you could hire one? Any Apache you get to go with you is liable to turn on you once you're on the trail. You thought about that?" the younger asked.

Newt stepped off his horse and brushed past them and headed toward the lieutenant calling roll.

"Stubborn, ain't he?" the younger man said when Newt was out of earshot.

"You better watch that talk, Horn. That ain't no pilgrim there," the older replied.

"He's going to get himself killed, pilgrim or not."

"Probably, but killing him will take some doing, if I don't miss my mark." The older turned to the younger with a twinkle in his eyes. "You don't have a clue who that is, do you?"

"Big ugly cuss with a face that looks like a bear worked it over."

"How many big ugly fellows packing a Smith pistol with blue crosses in the handles have you heard of?"

The younger man took a second look at Newt, as if reappraising him. "Is he the one that tamed the mob in Shakespeare?"

"That's him. Made him a name for that, and prizefighting in the mining camps. Bareknuckle or with gloves, they say he don't care."

"Then he's the same that got Cortina?"

"That's him."

The younger grunted as if slightly impressed. "Well, fist-fighting or locking horns with Cortina is child's play compared to hunting Chiricahuas. They can tell all the stories they want about that fellow yonder, but he doesn't know what he's getting himself into."

The older man shook his head. "Maybe so, but I don't think he cares."

The stocky young lieutenant, as the Chief of Scouts had forewarned, refused the lending of one of his Apache scouts, or any Apache tracker for that matter. In fact, he seemed greatly irritated by Newt's arrival and made it plain that his help wasn't needed and that the recovery of the Redding boy was army business.

Newt left the agency within an hour of his arrival, and he turned in the saddle and looked back

once when he was a quarter mile from the camp.
Two Apache scouts, noticeable by the matching
red headbands they wore, were following him.
That West Point lieutenant intended to make sure
he left the reservation.

The Apache scouts, or policemen, or whatever
they were, hung back well behind, but they kept
him in sight. Sometimes they were far enough
back that he could only make out the dust clouds
their ponies stirred up, and sometimes they were
close enough for him to see them plainly with their
slumped riding posture and the Springfield rifles
draped across their ponies' withers.

Regardless of their continued presence, he
made camp in the mouth of a draw at the foot of a
bald, scrub brush hill. He built his fire at the back
of that draw against a boulder pile and made his
bed where he could see anyone coming to him.

It was well after dark when he heard horses
rattling over the rocks to his camp, and he threw
back his blanket and took up his rifle. He cracked
the Winchester's receiver open enough to make
sure there was a round in the chamber, then
closed it and waited for them, sitting against his
saddle for a backrest and the Winchester across
his lap. Shortly thereafter, two men dismounted
on the far side of his fire. One was an Apache and
one was the young white man he had talked to
back at the agency. Newt heard more rocks rolling
beyond them, and he assumed that there were
others out there.

"You got the lieutenant some agitated," the white

man said with his Adam's apple bobbing up and down in his skinny neck. "He doesn't like you causing trouble."

Newt put his thumb on the hammer of his Winchester. "Are you wanting some trouble of your own?"

Chapter Four

The white man said something to the Indian with him that must have been in the Apache tongue, and then hunkered down on his heels and took off his army campaign hat and began turning it by the brim in his hands, restless like. He wore the same cocky grin that he had given Newt back at the agency.

He was young enough to be cocky, maybe in his twenties, and tall—as tall as Newt but skinnier. His sandy hair was already thinning, regardless of his youth, and a wispy, narrow mustache shone on his upper lip. Those round, bright little eyes of his gleamed in the firelight on either side of a long, Roman nose.

The Apache with him was more on the edge, and he remained standing with a Springfield carbine resting in the crook of one elbow.

"Tell that Indian to sit down and put away his rifle, or I won't take him as friendly," Newt said.

The white man said something else in Apache, and the warrior squatted beside him without answering. He kept the rifle in the crook of his arm and stared back at Newt with a bland expression.

"He's only halfway there," Newt said.

"That's because he's only half a mind to do what you said," the white fellow answered. "He doesn't like giving up his gun. Says that was the first thing the reservation men asked him to do when he got here, and nothing's been good since."

"You're taking the long way around," Newt said. "Say what it is you've got to say. That West Point shavetail back there at the agency put me in a foul mood, and I'd just as soon sleep as talk to another of you government men."

"What I came here for is to see if you really got a hundred dollars of railroad money to pay a man to guide you."

Newt cocked the Winchester. "Kid, there's easier men to rob and easier ways to make a hundred dollars."

"You got it all wrong. You said you needed a tracker."

"Him?" Newt pointed at the Apache.

"Him and me. My name's Tom Horn, and this here is Pretty Buck."

"Pretty Buck? What kind of name is that?" Newt looked again at the Apache. The Apache was no older than Horn, maybe younger. And truly, he had a face that was so round and smooth and pretty as to be almost feminine.

"He doesn't like that name. It's what the soldiers gave him," Horn said. "But you couldn't pronounce his real name, so it will have to do."

"Can he be trusted?"

"He can. He's been scouting for Sieber and the army for three years. Went with us to Mexico the last time and served admirably."

"Sibby," Pretty Buck repeated Horn's words, as if that said everything that needed said.

"Ask him if he knows anything about the Redding boy."

"Already did. He says that the reservation gossip is that it was Chiricahuas who got the boy," Horn said. "There's one little band of the worst of the renegades that we didn't get rounded up this summer, and they are still roaming around Mexico raising hell."

"Does he know where we can find the boy?"

Horn twisted on his heels a little and made a wave of his hand toward the south. "Big country down there. Rough country. Boy could be anywhere if he's still alive, but he's got a few ideas. Knows the campgrounds they're liable to use."

"What kind of Apache is he?" Newt nodded at Pretty Buck.

"Nednhi. That's a band of the Chiricahua."

"And he's willing to help us go after his own people?"

"He's willing to hire on and take your money so he can buy a bolt of calico for a girl he's taken a shine to," Horn replied. "If you don't know anything about Apaches, the first thing you'd better learn is that they like nothing better than the prospect of a good fight. Doesn't matter who they're fighting."

"Hard to trust him when we'll be hunting his kin."

"Next thing you'd better remember is that there's hard feelings among the Apaches toward the broncos that won't settle down for peace. Every time there's a raid on a white farm, the reservation Apache get the blame just like the ones that really did the raiding," Horn said. "That, and scouting for the army is the only way a warrior can live like he admires and make him a name since we won't let them make war when they're of a mind to."

"What about you? You said that Sieber was the Chief of Scouts. I admit I've heard of him, but I don't know you from Adam. You some kind of Indian fighter yourself, or are you only wanting some money to buy a girl some calico?"

"I'm a scout sometimes but mostly a mule packer. Hunted Apaches with the army for a good while now, and I've covered a fair bit of country down in Mexico."

"You speak their language."

"A bit. You'll find that many of them speak Spanish, and I savvy that, too. I can ride and shoot and track some, and I can pack a mule like nobody's business. When things get hard you won't have to look around for me, 'cause I'll be right there with you."

"You say you've been to Mexico. Been there once myself. What did you think about it?"

Horn shrugged. "It can be a hard place to get back from. I don't necessarily care for it."

Newt nodded agreement. "If you had said anything else I would have known you were lying. I swore I wasn't ever going back there, but here I am."

"Man ought to be careful what he swears to."

"You're hired. You and this Apache, and any of his buddies that will come along that we can trust."

Horn rocked back on his heels and shook his head. "You're going to have to pay me three hundred dollars."

"You think highly of yourself."

"I speak their language and you don't. Might be that I can get us by the army if they give us flack, and you can't," Horn said. "I make a hundred dollars a month working for the army as it is, and you're going to have to bid higher if you want me to risk my neck with you."

"What about him?" Newt pointed at Pretty Buck. "Is he as proud of himself as you are?"

"A hundred will be just fine for him."

"What about his friends. The more the merrier, I say."

"You aren't getting any more Apache scouts. Him and me are both taking a big risk sneaking off the rez with you. The army might fire me for taking this little leave of absence, and they'll brand him a renegade if they find out he's slipped off from San Carlos. You try and take your own war party of scouts off the reservation and you'll have the whole army after us and treating it like an Apache outbreak."

"What about those Apache policemen I hear out there? Won't they tell?"

"No, they're good at keeping secrets. They would have shot you if the lieutenant had told them to. That's their sense of honor, but that don't mean they like the lieutenant better than one of their own. They'll cover for Pretty Buck as long as they can."

Newt got to his feet. "Well then, best I get saddled up."

"You aim to ride tonight?"

"The longer we wait, the less chance we have of finding that boy."

Horn cleared his throat and made a point to make sure Newt heard him.

"What is it now?" Newt asked.

"We want paid in advance."

"Like hell. You'll get paid when we're through."

"How do we know you've got the money?"

"You don't. You'll have to take my word on it, just like I'm taking you at your word."

"Pay us fifty dollars in advance so we know you're on the square."

"I'll pay you twenty dollars when we're in Mexico and you put me on the trail of the renegades we're after."

"You're a real hardass, Mister Jones."

"That's what they tell me."

"Well, you better be. Do you know what those

Chiricahuas will do to us if they catch us snooping around after them?"

"No worse than I aim to do to them if they won't give the boy up."

"You honestly think you're going to pull this off?"

"Got to try. That's what matters."

"I'll stick with you, Jones, but first time you play the fool and do something stupid that might get us killed, you can count me out. We've got to play it smart. I talked things over with Sieber the other day, and he thought there was a chance the army could trade for the boy if he's still alive. A slim chance, but maybe it will work."

Newt went to his horse and began saddling it.

"You hear me?" Horn asked. "We play it smart and try and trade for the boy. If that doesn't work we turn around and come back. Come back alive."

"Go get your horses." Newt was already throwing the packsaddle on the mule.

Horn and Pretty Buck left and soon returned mounted on their horses. Horn watched closely as Newt got in the saddle and gathered the lead rope of the pack mule.

"What worries me some, Jones, is that I'm beginning to think you don't believe you'll survive this trip."

"Wouldn't doubt it." Newt rode past them and started down the draw.

"Worries me more that you admit it and don't

seem to give a damn either way." Horn turned his horse around to follow and called after Newt.

"Worries like that is why I'm paying you three hundred dollars." From the sound of Newt's horse's hoof falls, he was already down on the flat and traveling at a trot.

Chapter Five

The trio rode southward, traveling fast and light. They skirted around Fort Grant, lest the soldiers there see them, and then pushed on to Hooker's ranch in Sulphur Springs Valley where they left Pretty Buck in the mountains while they rode down to purchase supplies. When they rejoined their Apache scout the pack mule's saddle panniers were loaded with a ten-pound sack of beans, three smoked hams, a dozen eggs, and a little coffee and flour and some other what-nots that the ranch was willing to spare.

They crossed the Southern Pacific tracks, camped at Dragoon Springs, and stayed east of Tombstone. The mining towns' denizens had always been a rough and ready bunch with no love for Indians, and the Apache wars and the summer's reservation outbreak had the rumor mill churning about supposed Apache raids and massacres. The last thing Newt wanted was to try to save Pretty Buck from a lynch mob, so they avoided the main roads where they could.

The morning of the sixth day they left the San Simon Valley and passed through the big dry wash called Skeleton Canyon, having come over two hundred miles as the crow flies. Pretty Buck said little on their journey, but Horn talked the whole way.

The mule packer had shaken his rope down when they left camp that morning, and although it was nearing noon, he hadn't once quit playing with it yet. He rode at the back of their procession and roped bushes and rocks, anything that provided a target. He spent the rest of his time twirling and flipping that thirty-foot-long grass rope and doing fancy rope tricks. All the while, he never stopped talking, chattering to himself about one thing for half an hour, and then moving abruptly to another subject without any prompting from either of his traveling companions, as if his mind was a grasshopper leaping from one thought to another in an erratic fashion that was hard to follow.

"Who gave you that mashed-up ear?" he asked once, calling ahead to Newt and pointing at the misshapen cauliflower ear that adorned one side of Newt's head.

Newt glanced briefly over his shoulder and scowled at Horn. "Nobody gave it to me. Fought some good, tough men, and they fought hard to mark me with it."

"That make it easier to wear an ear like that . . . knowing they were tough?"

Newt stared straight ahead. "I admit I wish I had a better ear, but at least I fought for the one I've got."

"You like fighting?"

"Puts some money in my pockets time to time when I'm between jobs."

"Who's the toughest man you ever fought? Boxing, I mean. Bet you wouldn't step in the ring with Sullivan or Ryan." Horn trotted closer and cast a heel loop and roped one of the pack mule's hind legs. He didn't take up his slack and let the loop fall, but the animal still shied and plunged past Newt, almost jerking the lead rope out of his hand.

"Put that rope away, you're scaring the mule."

Horn looked a little ashamed, but he grinned anyway. "That's a fancy pistol you're wearing. Where'd you get it?"

"Dead man gave it to me." Newt kicked up to a trot, hoping to avoid more conversation.

"How come him to give it to you?"

"He didn't say. He was dead."

Horn caught up to him. "My, but you're a dreary cuss. Makes the time pass easier if we talk some."

"Go talk to Pretty Buck."

"I've heard all his stories, and he's heard mine."

Newt looked to make sure the Apache was still with them. The young brave was three horse lengths behind them, taking the whole thing in with a grin of his own, as if he understood more English than he liked to let on. The first day on the trail he had packed away his pants and wore nothing but a heavy brown corduroy shirt and his breechcloth. His brown legs and moccasined heels thumped his pony's ribs with every stride, as if he feared the animal would stop if he quit urging it on.

"You prefer a short gun, or that big-bore Winchester you're carrying?" Horn asked.

"Kid, I'd prefer you to quit talking. Last time I went to Mexico I was weighted down with a chattering judge, and here I am stuck with you. Swore I was going to do better about the company I kept after that."

Horn seemed oblivious to what Newt had said and patted the buttstock of the rifle protruding out of its scabbard next to his saddle swells. He continued his former line of thought, as if Newt weren't still scowling at him. "Me, I prefer to keep any disagreements at a distance. Apaches got that right. Get you some high ground or good cover, and wait until they come in your rifle sights."

Newt gave an uninterested glance at Horn's rifle. It was a '76 Winchester like his own, but a plainer variation of the model. The only extra feature to it was a flip-up, tang-mounted peep sight behind the hammer.

"You hit a man with a pistol and he's liable to keep coming." Horn patted the rifle's buttstock again before he continued. "But put a .45-60 round in their brisket and you'll stop 'em in their tracks."

Newt didn't answer, and Horn took that as he disagreed. Horn straightened a little in the saddle and talked a little louder at the prospect of an argument. "Man with a name like yours probably favors a pistol, but if we have the bad luck to get cross with some of those bronco Apaches down there in Mexico you better forget that belly gun and lay hand to your rifle. The last thing you want is to let an Apache work close to you."

Once again, Newt didn't answer him.

It was Horn who scowled this time. "How'd you get that name? Widowmaker."

"Wasn't something I chose to pick up like you pick up a rock or any old thing. Some fool puts something like that on you, and there's nothing you can do about it if it sticks."

"You ought to take more of a shine to it. You know, wear it," Horn said. "I'll think on how you say it in Apache. That's a big medicine name. Might impress them."

"I'll wear my given name. Suits me well enough."

"No need to act all mad." Horn made an attempt to look put out, but he was too restless to try it long. "I was only trying to help you. That's what you're paying me for. Best you learn something about Apaches before we get any closer to those we're after."

"You and Pretty Buck do the tracking, and I'll do without the lessons."

"You ever ran across any wild Apaches? I bet you'd sing a different tune if you had."

"I did, once."

"What kind of Apaches were they?"

"They didn't say."

Horn snorted. "Let me guess, they were dead like the man that gave you that pistol."

"No they were plenty alive, but their horses were dead."

Horn studied Newt to try to tell if he was joking. "Dead horses, huh? Seems like things have a habit of dying when you're around."

Newt scoffed. "I like to think of myself as a friendly man, but Old Judge Roy said I had a talent for mayhem. You put it that way, maybe he was right."

"You, friendly? Man with a face like yours and a horse-killing disposition has got to put a little more effort into his friendliness. You know, talk a little and smile once in a while."

Newt turned his head to Horn, and a slow, strained smile spread across his mouth, showing too much of his teeth, and the muscles of his face moving so slow they should have creaked.

Horn gave a mock shiver and laughed. "That's damn right scary. Forget I said to do that. Reminds me of a corpse's grin. You just keep scowling and squinting and looking mean like you always do."

Newt pulled his horse up and took a deep breath before he spoke, as if gathering some patience. "Do you have to talk so much?"

Pretty Buck laughed and said something in his native language. All Newt could tell was that the words were aimed at Horn.

"What did he say?" Newt asked.

Horn gave Pretty Buck a displeased look. "He thinks he's funny."

Pretty Buck repeated the Apache phrase, followed by two English words he struggled with but managed to say clearly enough, "Talking Boy."

"That's because I'm an interpreter," Horn said while Newt and Pretty Buck laughed.

"Sounds like the Apaches knew you well when they gave you that name," Newt said.

"Laugh all you want to, but I'm the only man with the guts and the know-how to go on this fool trip with you," Horn replied.

Even Newt's spirits seemed to have been lifted by Pretty Buck's revelation, and he picked at Horn more. "Well for a man that claims to be such an Indian scout, it sure puzzles me how much noise you make and about why you'd wear a white shirt into Apache country."

Horn looked down at himself, as if noticing what he wore for the first time. The white shirt looked new, stainless and unblemished except for trail dust, and it was the second one he'd pulled from his saddlebags during their journey. A red silk neckerchief was draped around his neck. His brown, cotton ducking pants were equally new, although less clean, and they were tucked into a pair of tall-topped cowboy boots. A pair of Mexican spurs were attached at the heels with rowels the size of your palm, and they rattled and clanked with every step he or his horse took. He looked more like a cowboy than a scout.

For the first time, Horn looked seriously put out by something Newt had said, but he recovered quickly and sharpened one end of his mustache and straightened himself in the saddle. "Just because we're on the trail don't mean a man has to forgo his appearance."

"Well, maybe they'll see you first and shoot you while me and Pretty Buck are taking cover," Newt replied.

Newt rode on, and Horn decided to ride back beside Pretty Buck. It wasn't long before Newt could hear the young scout talking nonstop to the Apache scout. Pretty Buck replied rarely and usually with only a word or two.

No matter how much Newt scowled at Horn or poked fun of his attire, he saw that the young man knew how to handle himself on the trail. Horn knew wild country, he knew horses and mules, and if he was half as good with that rifle he was so proud of as he was with a rope, then there were far worse men Newt could have hired. And Horn had eyes like an eagle. Twice he spotted deer and other game animals moving in the distance that Newt or even Pretty Buck couldn't make out.

They had turned south out of Skeleton Canyon before it crossed into New Mexico Territory, and the way to the border lay through a maze of more canyons and wind-scoured passes that led into the San Bernardino Valley. That kind of terrain provided all kinds of ambush points, and the knowledge that they were in Apache country made Newt nervous traveling through it.

They rode some five miles, going no faster than a walk with Pretty Buck scouting well ahead of Newt and Horn. Often the Apache scout stopped, listening for sounds ahead, examining tracks, or sniffing the wind like a hunting hound, as if it, too, could tell him something about what lay ahead. Each time Pretty Buck stopped to decipher things, the two white men followed suit and waited until it was safe to move on.

Once, after a long stop, Pretty Buck called something back to them before he moved on down the trail.

"What did he say?" Newt asked.

"He said *enjuh*."

"What's that mean?"

"Can mean a couple of things, near as I can tell. Can mean it's good or it's done. I reckon he's telling us to ride on."

They passed out of the worst of the canyons an hour before sunup.

"*Enjuh*," Newt said when they hit the more open country.

Horn turned in the saddle and looked back at the way they had come. "Yeah, *enjuh*."

Come daylight, they stopped on a hillside within a mile of the old *presidio* and ranch at San Bernardino. The area was a popular campground for smugglers, raiding Indians, and other travelers passing through the country. Horn had a set of binoculars in his saddlebags, and they took turns glassing the area. No army camp was in sight.

When they rode down off the hill they did find

the sign that the army had been there—the ashpits of their fires and beaten shapes in the grass where their tents and horse pickets had stood. But according to Pretty Buck and Horn, the army had been gone for days, moving east into the Animas Valley. Not a single track showed that the soldiers had gone south of the border.

Newt squinted into the sun and studied the desert that ran south into Mexico, and then he started them toward it.

It was another day's journey through the canyon lands, weaving around islands of isolated mountains and tumbled country. They watered their horses and filled their canteens and waterbags at the numerous spring-fed tanks and basins dotting the drainages toward the Chihuahuan Desert to the southeast and the Bavispe River to the south. When nightfall came they avoided pitching their bedrolls near one of the waterholes, instead going on a little farther before making dry camp on a high mesa well off the trail and with a good view of the surrounding country. Any waterhole was bound to draw other travelers, and it was their wish to see such travelers before they were seen themselves. A cautious man lived longer in *Apacheria*, and all three were cautious men.

Coming to more open country, there was some argument as to whether to continue south or to veer eastward into Chihuahua. Pretty Buck insisted on the later.

"Why is he so bound and determined to go southeast?" Newt asked. "Everything you tell me is that we're most likely to find Apache camps in the big mountains to the south."

Horn nodded. "Maybe, but Apache are liable to be anywhere and Pretty Buck thinks that Juh and his band might be closer to Janos or Casas Grandes where there's good raiding and villages that will sometimes trade with them."

"Juh?" Newt repeated the Chiricahua chief's name that sounded like *whoa* to him.

"Juh's band is the main one we didn't get when we were down here two months ago. His bunch claimed they needed more time to gather the rest of the people hidden in the mountains, and they promised they would come back to the reservation when they found them," Horn answered. "You ask me, the real reason was that the old devil wanted more time to raid Mexicans and have a little fun."

Newt scanned the big country before him, realizing more than ever what a daunting task he had set himself to. Where did one begin to search for one little boy lost in the middle of such an expanse?

"Pretty Buck thinks we ought to work down the Janos River and then as far south as Casas Grandes. If we don't run across word of the boy or sign of Apaches by then, we'll cut west to the Bavispe and then on to El Tigre Mountain," Horn added.

"Then that's what we'll do."

Their plan was to question anyone they met as to whether they had seen Juh's band or sign of it, and especially to ask about any sighting of a white boy child. Given the chance, they could put the word out that they wanted to trade for the Redding boy. As warlike as they were, and as much trouble as they heaped on the Mexicans, the Chiricahua Apache were also known to trade with a few of the Sonora and Chihuahua villages.

Regardless of their hopes and intentions, not a strange soul did they see for another day's ride. Twice they passed remote, abandoned villages. There were irrigated cornfields left unharvested or picked clean by raiders, and the carcasses of slaughtered cattle and goats were littered throughout the countryside.

"Apaches ran them out. It's been a hard summer," was all that Horn said when they first came on such evidence of raiding.

When they did finally run across fellow humans on the high desert road, it was a party of Mexican woodcutters in some hills northwest of Janos. There were ten woodcutters and they rose up beside the road from where they had been taking a morning *siesta* in a mesquite thicket. Pretty Buck was riding in the lead, and at the sight of him the woodcutters took up arms and found cover in the thorny brush or behind their high-wheeled firewood carts. Newt waved to them, and Horn called out greetings in Spanish, but the woodcutters would not come out to talk. They cursed Pretty Buck and threatened him yet did not fire upon the travelers.

Not willing to hang around longer and risk a foolish fight, the trio pushed on to Janos, some six miles farther on. The town lay along the river on a high plain, broken only by gentle hills and consisting mostly of grasslands that were relatively free of the low brush and cacti that covered the Sierra Madre mountainsides on the western horizon. Scattered herds of cattle grazed shin-deep in grama grass, and intermixed with such rangeland were the fallow farm fields along the course of the river south of the town.

The trio entered town through an adobe archway that led into a plaza overlooked by the bell tower of a large church. The town lay at a crossroads between Chihuahua, Sonora, and El Paso, and the traffic and business the road delivered showed in the quality of the buildings surrounding the church.

The citizens on the streets did not panic at the sight of two strange and heavily armed *gringos* and one wild-looking Apache, but they did stare and whisper among themselves. Newt spoke enough Spanish to understand some of their murmurs and how the word of an Apache in town was spreading throughout Janos.

Outside the town's center were less well-built *jacales* and smaller adobe homes that belonged to the poor farmers and peasants, and it was there on the outskirts that the trio tied their horses to a goat pen fence next to a *cantina*. The *cantina* was only a tiny, single-room *jacale*, with a low roof and walls built from upright poles set in the ground and the cracks between the poles plastered over with adobe mud. The sign on the front of it marked it as a *cantina* and not a goat shed.

Newt ducked his way into the door, followed by Horn. Pretty Buck loafed well behind, reluctant to enter, but finally taking a stand one step inside the room.

A single bartender stood behind the hand-hewn slab of pine log that served as a bar, and three other men were leaning on that bar, nursing clay cups of liquor and taking careful note of the strangers who had walked in among them, especially Pretty Buck.

Newt ignored their stares and took a place at the bar. He gestured at the jugs resting on shelves behind the bar and then at the cups the other customers held. "*Tres bebidos, por favor.*"

Horn stood beside him, but Pretty Buck remained by the door even though Newt twice motioned him to join them. The bartender didn't answer Newt, nor did he pour the drinks.

"*Dame tres bebidos, por favor,*" Newt repeated, his tone not as friendly as it had been the first time.

The bartender nodded at Pretty Buck and looked a question at Newt.

"*Mi amigo,*" Newt said in answer to that look.

"Apache," the bartender said with a hiss, spitting after he spoke.

Newt rested his elbows on the bar and leaned closer to the bartender. So close that he could see in detail the beads of sweat dotting the bartender's face.

"*Dame tres bebidos,* ahora." Newt stressed that last word. *Now.*

The bartender looked to the three other patrons

of his establishment, but they said nothing to help. The bartender reached to the shelf behind him and took down two clay cups. He sat those cups in front of Newt and pulled the corncob stopper from a jug and poured the two drinks.

Newt took up neither of the proffered cups and stuck out a forearm and barred Horn from taking one, either. He held up his pointer finger to the bartender. "*Uno mas.*"

"You're pushing it, Jones," Horn said in a whisper.

One of the Mexicans down the bar said something to the bartender that Newt couldn't make out other than to tell it was about Pretty Buck and that the tone was not at all friendly. Horn rattled off a string of Spanish at the bartender, his tone pleasant and patient. The bartender shook his head and pointed at the two drinks he had poured.

Horn looked at Newt and shrugged. "He says he won't serve an Apache."

Newt strained to think of the words he needed, but he finally gave up on his limited Spanish skills and said to the bartender in clipped English, pausing often between the words to give them extra emphasis, "My friend here is a venerated warrior and a respected scout of the U.S. Army, and he has ridden a long way to your shithole of a town. You will pour him a drink."

The bartender must have understood the word "army," for that gave him a brief pause. But in the end, he remained unfazed and shook his head once more and pointed at the two cups, then at Newt and Horn.

"*Dos bebidos*," the bartender said.

Newt turned his head away for an instant and took a deep breath. He and Pretty Buck exchanged a brief look, and then Newt grabbed the bartender by the front of his coarse-spun cotton shirt. He jerked him halfway over the bar, and his other hand took hold of the back of his head and smashed his face down into the wood. He let go the instant the man's face resounded with a meaty thud against the hard surface, and the bartender teetered there for a short count with his nose flattened and bloody before he slumped to the floor.

The three Mexicans down the bar moved. Whether they intended to make issue with Newt's treatment of the bartender, or whether they were simply getting out of the way didn't matter. Horn snaked a long-barreled Colt revolver out of the flap holster on his left hip and pointed it in their direction. The Mexicans froze where they were, and the sound of the cocking hammer on Pretty Buck's Springfield carbine caused them to put their hands in the air.

Newt watched them while he reached across the bar and took down another cup from the shelf. "That's right. Keep those damned hands in the air."

He continued to watch them while he poured a third drink and motioned Pretty Buck over to him. The Apache scout took a place on his right, and Horn backed against the bar between Newt and the three Mexicans with his pistol still on them. He took up his cup with his free hand.

Newt motioned for Pretty Buck to do the same, and they lifted their cups and downed their drinks together. The liquor from the jug was only cheap *mezcal*, and nasty tasting and poorly made *mezcal* at that, but Newt smacked at the bite of it as if it were a fine drink.

He looked again at Pretty Buck. "*Enjuh.*"

Pretty Buck nodded and grinned back at him. "*Enjuh.*"

Horn slammed his empty cup down on the bar top hard enough to break it. "Damn right, *enjuh.*"

Newt stepped around Horn and went to the three Mexicans with their hands in the air. One of the weapons among them was a rusty Paterson revolver stashed in a younger man's belt. The model of the antique Colt pistol was so old and out of date that Newt had never seen its like. The other two men had no firearms, but they did carry large sheath knives. He yanked all three weapons free and pitched them in the far corner of the room.

He pointed at Pretty Buck. "*Mi amigo tenía sed.* He was thirsty, hear me?"

Whether the Mexicans understood him or not, they nodded anyway.

Pretty Buck started out the door first, followed by Horn. Newt was the last out and he almost ran into Horn's back. The young mule packer had stopped barely outside the door and was looking up at some Mexican soldiers sitting their horses facing the *cantina*. There were five of them in blue uniforms with red piping, and the one in the middle was an officer in some kind of silly plumed hat, gold shoulder braids, and wearing a silver embellished saber. He was a thin wasp of a man with a hard, pinched face. The look he was giving the *Americanos* was far from hospitable. What's more, the four cavalrymen with him already had their Remington carbines unsheathed and at the ready.

Chapter Six

"Who are you?" the Mexican officer asked in almost perfect English.

Horn spoke up before Newt could, and his answer was far different from what Newt would have given. In fact, Horn snapped his usually slumped spine straight and gave the officer a smart, lively salute. "American officers, Troop D, Second Company, Fourth Cavalry. I'm Lieutenant Horn, and this is Captain Jones. The Apache with us is our scout."

The officer gave them a more careful examination that bordered closely on disbelief, but his expression eventually wavered to some kind of reluctant acceptance when he noticed the army campaign hat and the flap holster Horn wore. "Where are your uniforms?"

"We've been two weeks in the field and we've found that blue uniforms don't work well for advanced reconnaissance."

"I am Colonel Herrera."

"*Buenos dias, Coronel.*"

"Are you aware that you are on Mexican soil?"

"We're in pursuit of Apache hostiles who have kidnapped an American child." Horn continued his lie without missing a beat.

"This is the second time this year that your army has entered my country without permission."

"We understand that your government and mine have an agreement."

Newt watched while Horn and the Colonel Herrera had a staring match. Horn was as bland faced and as fawning as a schoolboy.

"These Apache and this American child you seek," Herrera finally said, "what makes you think they are here?"

"We are merely scouting," Horn replied. "The rest of our company is camped at San Bernardino."

"I am aware of the American camp at El Rancho San Bernardino."

The look on Horn's face told Newt that the young packer had been counting on that army camp at San Bernardino to make his lie believable.

"You will find no Apache near Janos," the colonel continued. "I assure you that my men have been most diligent in seeking out and making war on such savages. We gave battle to the Apache in the mountains west of here not so long ago. It was a hard fight, but my soldiers were courageous and achieved a great victory. A victory, I remind you, that the Apache will be long forgetting, and a victory such as your American army was unable to accomplish despite your General Crook's bragging about his most recent campaign in those very same mountains."

"Still, you might have gotten word or heard a rumor about a small bunch of renegades and captive child with them," Horn said.

"I have heard of no such child, nor of Apache," the colonel answered. "It would seem that you have ridden a long way for nothing. This problem of Apaches, this is an American problem, I think, and it would be best for you to leave here and seek within your own country for the captors of this boy you speak of."

"The Apache raiding party we're after crossed into your country more than a week ago." Newt had heard enough of the colonel's talk, and he butted in before Horn could stop him.

"Once again I say, there is no Apache problem here. The only problem is one of your own making."

"What problem is that?" Newt asked.

"This trouble you bring with you." The colonel came close to an eye roll and tilted his head back and gave a sigh while he gestured with a lazy flip of his hand at Pretty Buck. "Your Apache tracker makes the citizens of this city nervous. Already many people have come to me reporting his presence. Should you remain longer, bad rumors will spread. This thing, this . . . *Cómo se dice?* How do you say it . . . ?"

Colonel Herrera waved a hand around in the air as if he could physically pluck the word he sought from it. "This fear, yes, this fear, this worrying will grow. One Apache will turn to many and to rumors of a raid. There is history, much history. Bad history. Apache history. This you do not know. You do not understand. People will be afraid to go into their fields to work, and instead they will have nothing to do but whisper to each other. Some will say that Colonel Herrera cannot keep Janos safe and that they should petition Chihuahua or Mexico City for assistance. We cannot have that."

"No, we couldn't have that." Horn put a hand to Newt's sleeve to start him toward their horses.

The three were barely mounted when the three customers from the *cantina* and the bloody-faced bartender came out the door and started complaining to the colonel in rapid-fire Spanish and pointing in the Americans' direction. Horn gave another less professional salute, and they spun their horses on their hocks and left Janos in a high lope before the good colonel had time to think more on the supposed U.S. Army officers he had so recently met.

They were nearing the river when a flock of crows lifted into the air in front of them, cawing and flapping their wings in protest. It wasn't the noisy birds that drew the trio's attention, but rather the perches that they had so recently roosted upon. There, at the edge of the road ahead of them, was a row of heads stabbed onto stakes set in the ground. Those heads had been there long enough that the sun and weather had all but mummified them, and the remaining skin had shriveled so much that the teeth on every one of them was revealed as if they were grinning at whomever should pass by. Some had been scalped, and others were missing ears. Even passing by the stakes at a lope, Newt could tell that they were Indian heads, and the sight of so many empty eye sockets and leering death grins made a cold shiver run up his spine and the hair on the back of his neck stand up.

After crossing the Janos River and riding out of sight of the settlement, they left the road and made three or four more miles cross-country before they stopped. The packsaddle on the mule had shifted, and they needed to readjust it and to let their horses have a blow.

"Do you always go around whacking bartenders when you're outnumbered in a foreign town?" Horn asked.

"A man that runs a tavern ought to have better manners," Newt replied.

Pretty Buck was watching Newt closely but said nothing.

Horn let out a low whistle and looked back the way they had come. "Well, those *pendejos* in that *cantina* don't worry me half as much as that Mexican colonel, or *acalde*, or whatever he was. I'd as soon we didn't see him and his Mexican regulars again. That was a hard man, if I don't miss my guess, and slippery as a snake."

"What did you think about the colonel's trophies we saw passing out of town?" Newt asked. "Looked mostly like women and a couple of children to me."

"Well, Herrera might have a different idea about a great victory. I was with the army and Colonel

Forsyth's column last spring when we came up after his fight," Horn said. "True, his Mexican regulars and militia put the ambush on old Loco's bunch and caught them flat-footed, but it was a massacre as much as it was a battle. When we looked over the battlefield the next day, the whole creek bottom was scattered with dead soldiers and Chiricahua. There was one washed-out hole in the ground where some of the Apaches had taken cover, and it was filled to the brim with their bodies. By the time we finished looking things over, we had counted better than sixty of Loco's people dead, and only about a dozen of them were warriors. The rest were squaws and children."

Newt grimaced as he visualized what Horn was telling him.

"And it isn't like those women and children got hit on accident in the heat of the fight. Herrera and his soldiers shot them down on purpose," Horn added.

"And then staked their heads on the edge of the road to brag a little to the public about what an Indian fighter he is," Newt said.

Horn nodded in agreement. "When we came up on him, he had a couple of dozen or so women captives and some children that he wouldn't turn over to us to take back to the reservation. We heard later that he gave seventy scalps to the governor at Chihuahua City as a token of his esteem, and he gave the children to some families in Bavispe for more political favors. The mothers and sisters and grown daughters he sent to the coast and sold as slaves. I imagine that money paid for that fancy sword he's wearing."

"Nasty business," Newt said.

"Some say the Apache are primitive savages," Horn said. "That may be. They're a hard people, for sure, but I guarantee you there are worse kinds of savage. And it never has anything to do with the color of a man's skin or what tribe he belongs to."

Once the horses had rested the three moved on, mere specks crawling across the windswept plain and working ever slowly to the southeast. Often, they checked their back trail for signs of Colonel Herrera's soldiers or some posse from Janos in pursuit. Pretty Buck scouted far ahead.

They reached the San Miguel River late in the day and rode past the earthen ruins of a massive pueblo. What remained of the clay mud walls were so ancient and desiccated as to be the color of pale buckskin, and with the setting sun behind them they shined on the flat desert like a beacon. Newt had seen other such ruins in his travels but never one that struck him as this one did. Without knowing why he did so, he veered from his course and rode closer to the ruined city.

Once upon a time there had been a great central plaza, ancient ball courts, pens for breeding exotic parrots from the jungles of Central America whose feathers could be sent along the trade roads to the north, shops for artisans and craftsmen, and a labyrinth of multi-storied homes and apartments rising up like a monument to power. Now there were not many walls left standing higher than a man's head on horseback, and pack rats scurried in the rubble.

He rode silently through the skeleton heart of the fossil that the old city had become. Chunks of adobe and fragile bits of bone crushed beneath his horse's hooves in clouds of red dust, carried away by the wind that blew through the ruin walls and howled like a banshee.

He knew nothing of the kind of people who might have built and ruled over such a place, but he understood the last stroke delivered at its end. The mark of war was there to see. The soot-blackened, charred timbers amid the collapsed rubble told a story of fire and conquest, of life given over to a bitter end. For an instant, that banshee wind might have been the wailing of the defenders as raiders and their torches finally breeched the pueblo's walls.

When he heard another crunch of his horse's hooves he stopped and leaned from the saddle and stared at the broken bits of an ornately painted piece of kiln-fired pottery. Parrot feathers that had been contained within that pot, so old that they were bleached of color, fell apart like ashes and drifted away on the wind.

Horn rode up while he leaned from the saddle. Ignoring him, Newt stared hard and long into the years and seasons beneath him, feeling a truth overwhelm him that he lacked the words for. Layers of earth upon layers of earth; city upon city; time stacked upon older times; bones and pottery shards lying upon more bones and pottery shards;

all the living and dying, and living and dying in the entirety of the world returned to dust from whence it came.

"What are you looking at?" Horn asked.

Newt straightened in the saddle, blinked at Horn as if he were surprised at his presence, then turned his horse away and shook his head. "The future."

Horn followed him toward the river. "What future? I don't see anything but an old dead town."

"Mine. Yours. We've all got it coming in the end. Some leave a mark, some don't."

"My, but ain't you a ray of sunshine," Horn said.

"It is what it is."

"Well, begging your pardon if I don't give up the ghost and fall over right this instant," Horn said. "I'd like to stick around a little longer, if you don't mind."

"Dying ain't hard. It's living that takes a man's measure."

"Is that your edge, Widowmaker? That you ain't scared of dying?" Horn asked.

"Edge? Kid, I don't have a clue what you're talking about."

A slight frown formed on Horn's mouth, but he shook it off. "Every man like you with a gun reputation has got him some kind of edge. They say Clay Allison is crazy in the head, Wild Bill never missed a shot, and Doc Holliday has enough nerve to sit down to breakfast with the Devil himself and tell the bastard to shut up and pass the biscuits."

"Kid, Hickok got himself shot in the back of the

head, and mark my words, those other two aren't headed for anything but an early grave. That's all your so-called edge will get you."

Horn's usual cocky, boyish expression disappeared, and all the playfulness drained out of him in an instant, until there was nothing but a strange stillness on his face and a cold look in his eyes. "Don't call me kid anymore. I don't like it."

Newt noticed the quaver of barely controlled anger in Horn's voice, and he realized other things then about Horn that he had misjudged. "All right, I won't call you kid."

Horn tried to bring back his usual lightheartedness, but there was still that intensity in his stare, as if he couldn't let it go, and is if something else and something older were eating at him. "My daddy beat me every chance he could because I was his kid and he could, so I run off from him and headed west. Ever' place I stopped along the way somebody was calling me kid, no matter that I've been living by my own wits and doing a grown man's work since I was fourteen. And they called me a shavetail when I first went to freighting and packing for the army. Every time I turned around there was somebody hacking on me, but I've come a far piece since then. And nobody is going to call me anything but my name."

"Take it easy. You're working yourself up over nothing."

"Maybe nothing to you. I guess you think me being willing to fight over something like that is silly," Horn said, the passion creeping back into his voice. "But I'll fight you for it, Jones. They say you're as tough as they come and maybe you look down on me, but I'll fight you just the same 'cause I think it's worth fighting over."

"Horn, you figure out what's worth fighting over and you've done more than most men. Might be that you'll leave a mark before you go."

Whatever else Horn might have said was interrupted by Pretty Buck running across the plain toward them. He was whipping his horse with a braided rawhide quirt and asking for all the speed it had.

"He's riding like his tail's on fire," Newt observed while he gathered his reins to hold his suddenly excited horse in place.

"Whatever it is ain't good." Horn stuck the spurs to his horse and slapped it across the top of its hips with his hat.

The Circle Dot horse squatted for a second on its hindquarters and then bolted after Horn's horse so hard that Newt was rocked backward in the saddle. At that same time a gun boomed.

It was less than two hundred yards to the river, and Pretty Buck swung in with them as they neared the flood bank. His long hair flew straight behind him and he was leaned low over his horse's neck. Another gunshot sounded as they spurred their horses off the high embankment and hit the river at a dead run. The water was chest deep to their mounts at midstream, and the horses crossed in high, slow lunges. Twice little dimpled burps of water appeared beside Newt, and it wasn't until the second one that he realized it was bullets striking the water beside him. He looked back behind him, but the ride was too wild and the confusion too great to make out who was doing the shooting.

Pretty Buck was the first to reach the far side, and he bailed from his horse and led it into a thicket behind a pile of driftwood. By the time Newt and Horn had dismounted, Pretty Buck was already kneeling behind a rotten cottonwood log with his Springfield carbine resting across it.

Newt threw a hasty wrap of rein around a mesquite limb, jerked his Winchester out of its boot, and ducked through the brush until he found a spot to belly down off the right end of the log Pretty Buck had taken a stand behind. Horn knelt on the opposite end. Another bullet smacked into the cottonwood log in front of them, showering them with bark and debris.

Newt raised his head up and searched the opposite side of the river. He could make out nothing in the failing light other than dust and the occasional flash of something moving behind it. He glanced to his side and saw Horn pushing the brim of his hat out of the way and up against the crown before he brought his rifle to his shoulder.

"Congratulations!" Horn said as he thumbed back his rifle hammer and pressed his cheek against the stock.

"For what?" Newt asked.

No sooner than he asked, an Indian appeared on foot out of the dust on the far side of the river. He was there and then he wasn't, running and then fading into the ground like he had never been there at all. And then another Indian appeared at a different point, making a quick dash and then dissolving into the sand like magic. Another bullet whined over their heads.

"For what?" Newt shouted again at Horn.

Horn's Winchester cracked and slammed against his shoulder, and he levered another round home before he took the time to look Newt's way. "You found your Apaches, Widowmaker. Real friendly, ain't they?"

Chapter Seven

Newt swung his rifle to the next Apache he saw moving across the river. It was two of them this time, moving in perfect tandem, as if they synchronized their assault some way for purposes of confusion. He chose the one on his right and tried to take aim.

As before, the warrior disappeared behind cover before he could fire, but he kept his rifle sights aimed at the place, waiting for his target to show himself again. To his dismay, when the warrior did move again he did not rise up from the same position where he went to ground, but rather from a point several yards away. Newt swung the muzzle of the Winchester and snapped a shot as the warrior was going to ground again, but he knew he was too hurried and had missed the instant he pulled the trigger. While he had been wasting a shot, another Apache took the opportunity to make a short rush forward.

Newt cursed his own foolishness and waited

for the Apache he had fired at to move again, trusting Horn and Pretty Buck to handle any others encroaching upon them. He thought he was beginning to understand the Apache tactics of closing with an enemy, and instead of holding on the spot where the Apache had disappeared, he moved his aim about three yards to the left. Some kind of long-stemmed agave plant or yucca bush offered a bit of cover there among a stretch of bare ground, and he guessed that the Apache might crawl toward it and use it to screen the beginnings of his next rush.

The Apache was patient, and he waited long before he moved again. Newt was beginning to doubt that he would appear at all, so it surprised him when the warrior finally lurched to his feet from behind the very bush he was watching. He pulled the trigger the instant he saw a flash of movement pass before his front sight, and was rewarded to hear a grunt of pain and to see the Apache fall awkwardly to the ground. Newt levered another round into the Winchester and fired a second bullet into the yucca. That follow-up shot must have come close, for it flushed the warrior from his hiding spot and he raced along the river-bank in a wild, weaving run and dove behind a hump of ground. Newt was disappointed that in three shots he had been unable to shoot truer, but he was pleased to note that the Apache appeared to have been limping.

Horn hadn't fired another shot since his first one, and he had dug the ground out a little with his sheath knife so that less of him was exposed above the log. The Apaches continued to fire an occasional shot their way, but none of them came close to hitting one of them, and that gunfire, too, soon slowed down.

A loud, shrill war cry sounded from across the river, and it was answered with another whoop by one of the Apaches.

Horn lowered his rifle from his shoulder and scratched at the back of his neck. "Something's wrong. Apaches usually fight quiet. They don't get loud until it's over or they're right on top of you and finishing you off."

As if to prove him wrong, another round of war cries went up on the far side of the river. This time it came from several of the Apaches over there. A couple of them were even laughing.

Horn said something to Pretty Buck, and the Apache scout seemed to agree with whatever it was. The Apaches across the river started laughing again and called out ribald challenges to them.

"I think they're drunk," Horn said. "That's what I think."

Newt reflected on how poorly the Apaches had shot, when any of the trio should have been easy pickings while crossing the river. And the laughter sounded odd. Nothing about a fight ought to be that funny.

One of the Apaches called out to them. Pretty Buck said something back, and there followed a long exchange in their native tongue. The firing from the Apache side ceased.

Newt listened and kept a close eye out for their attackers trying to crawl closer while Horn and Pretty Buck were distracted by all the talk.

"That's Juh's boys over there," Horn said. "They say they aren't drunk, but they've come from Casas Grandes. I guarantee you they stole them some *mezcal* or traded for some. They're so soused they can hardly talk."

The gray light of dusk had about given way to darkness. Newt squinted across the river. "What else are they saying?"

"I think old Juh himself is doing most of the talking. He wants us to come out and talk," Horn said. "Claims they thought we were Mexicans and this was all a mistake."

"You aim to talk to him, or do we wait it out and give them the slip when it's full dark?" Newt asked.

"He can talk all he wants from over there," Horn said with a scoff. "He's drunker than I think he is if he believes I'm going out in the open for a little powwow."

"Ask them about the boy."

"Done did. He ain't talking unless we come out face to face and show we've got good hearts."

"You told me it was him or some of his bunch that likely took the boy."

"If the boy made it to Mexico, Juh will know of him."

"You tell him I'm coming out."

Horn did a double take. "Do you hear what you're saying? Apaches are mean enough when they're sober. You give them too much *tiswin* or

Mexican firewater and they'll fight a buzz saw for the fun of it."

"Go ahead and tell him that we want to trade for the boy."

Horn called out across the river again. He paused often as if straining for the right words. Twice he stopped to speak with Pretty Buck in Spanish, and it was the Apache scout who relayed the last of their message. The Apaches across the river seemed to think on it some, for the brief answer they gave was a long time coming.

"He wants to know what you offer as ransom," Horn said.

"Tell him to name his price."

Horn started to say something else to the Apaches but pointed across the river instead. "You tell him yourself."

A gray horse was visible across the river, even in the poor light. All Newt could tell about it was that there was an Apache on its back. The Apache rider rode slowly down the riverbank and onto the gravel bar that made up the shallow shoals. Newt started to get to his feet.

"I'm telling you, don't go out there," Horn said.

Newt rose slowly behind the log, half expecting to be shot at. He passed behind Horn and Pretty Buck, then headed to meet the warrior on the gray horse.

"I'm telling you, this ain't a good idea," Horn said.

"Put that on my tombstone." Newt did not stop.

He carried his Winchester in the fold of his left elbow.

Pretty Buck surprised him and fell in behind him when he passed. The scout said nothing, and Newt couldn't ask why he was willing to come along. Horn remained behind the log, shaking his head in dismay and cursing under his breath.

It was only fifty yards to reach a point at the water's edge opposite of the Apache on horseback waiting for them, but the walk there seemed to Newt to take forever. Sounds that he had not noticed before suddenly became loud, like the sound of his own footsteps and the grind of gravel under the Apache's restless and stamping horse. A locust buzzed its wings and croaked and hummed somewhere in the night.

Only fifty yards separated Newt and Pretty Buck from the mounted Apache when they finally stopped—nothing but wide open space and a narrow strand of water between them. A three-quarter moon was already glowing overhead, and Newt knew that there was enough light reflected off the water for any of the Chiricahuas still hidden along the riverbank to see him good enough to try a shot.

The Apache on the horse said nothing, and Newt responded in the same manner. There seemed to be some waiting game that Newt did not understand beyond a faint intuition that he should not speak first. Pretty Buck stood beside him, and he, too, kept his silence.

The nearness and the wait gave Newt time to

study his adversary. He was unable to make out much detail, other than the warrior wore some kind of Mexican army coat, and the brass buttons on it gleamed faintly in the moonlight. The nervous movements of the Apache's horse also seemed to give him trouble, for he rocked and reeled on the horse's back.

The mounted Apache finally spoke, and Pretty Buck translated what he said into Spanish. "That is Juh. He asks who are you, and why you look for a white boy."

"Tell him that I am the boy's uncle."

Pretty Buck acted as if he knew that was a lie but went with it anyway. More words passed between the scout and the warrior across the river. Newt watched as the warrior rode his horse knee-deep into the river, moving that much closer to them. His words seemed to become more belligerent and agitated, and Newt noticed for the first time that his speech sounded somewhat slurred.

"He says that his people do not have such a boy, and he thinks you only come to make trouble for them," Pretty Buck translated again into Spanish.

Newt's Spanish was far from perfect, and he wasn't sure he was catching everything that Pretty Buck meant to tell him.

At that moment the warrior let his horse come a few steps closer. He shouted something and lifted an object in his right hand. Newt almost brought up his Winchester, ready for the Apache to charge at them brandishing a war club or a pistol. But he quickly saw that the object the warrior held was only a small clay jug. The warrior turned the jug up to his lips and shouted again once he lowered it again.

"He wants to fight you," Pretty Buck said.

Newt watched the warrior reeling on the back of the horse, obviously drunk as Horn had guessed. What's more, Newt could see him well enough then that he was pretty sure the warrior was an elderly man, not just by his shape and posture, but by the crackle in his voice.

"Tell him I didn't come here to fight him," Newt said. "I only want to trade for the boy."

Pretty Buck did as he asked, and the warrior across the river shouted something again and rode his horse in a wide circle. Newt heard a splash and soon saw the clay jug go floating along the current past them.

"Watch him, Jones," Horn called out.

"Surely that old Indian isn't serious," Newt said to Pretty Buck. "Tell him to sleep it off and we'll talk about things in the morning."

Pretty Buck said nothing. Either Newt's Spanish had failed him, or the scout's had.

"Tell him again that I don't want to fight," Newt said.

Pretty Buck didn't get the time to relay that, for the old warrior let out a war cry, and that cry was answered by some kind of cheers or other war cries from the other Chiricahua braves along the river. The old warrior gave his horse a kick to start it forward, tugging at something hanging beside his leg.

Newt put his free hand to the trigger guard

on his Winchester, but he did not shoulder the weapon. "Tell him what I said."

Pretty Buck turned and left him in a trot, saying something over his shoulder that Newt couldn't make out.

The warrior was coming across the river, still kicking his horse madly and having a great deal of trouble keeping the animal going in a straight line. He brandished a rifle in one hand.

Newt shouldered his Winchester when the Apache was at midstream. At that point the warrior's horse must have lost its footing, or else the warrior was so drunk that he pulled on its bridle too hard. The horse reared high on its hind legs, front hooves pawing at the air and with its mouth gaped open. At the same time the warrior's rifle went off, whether intentionally or by accident. Newt saw the streak of flame from its muzzle blaze into the night sky, and the roar of it must have startled the horse enough to put it over the edge. It teetered upright no longer and fell over backward, plunging the warrior into the river beneath its weight.

Newt kept his Winchester up and watched the thrashing animal try to roll over and get its legs back under it. When it was finally upright it came out of the river on his side, rider-less and trailing its bridle reins. It stopped and shook the water from it, and then trotted away toward the thicket where Newt's own stock was tied.

Newt thought he could make out the old warrior

floating in the river, and he watched that dark shape drift on the slow current. The old warrior did not move and floated facedown.

The other Apaches began moving. Newt heard the brush crack on the far bank and the whisper of their moccasins coming over the ground. He backed away with his Winchester kept at ready.

By the time he reached the log and his two companions, he could make out the forms of several more warriors on the far riverbank. The old warrior's body floated directly before them.

"Let them fetch him," Newt said to Horn and Pretty Buck.

Whether Horn and the Apache scout had intended to take advantage of the Chiricahuas' attempt to retrieve the body and open fire or not, they lowered their rifles and did as he asked. Pretty Buck called to the Apaches and must have told them what Newt had said, for it wasn't long before two of them waded into the river and drug the old warrior out of the water.

A half hour later and there was no sound from the Chiricahua raiding party.

"Well, Jones, you haven't been three days in Mexico and you're already a big man among the Chiracahuas," Horn said to break the silence.

"How's that?" Newt asked.

"They'll remember the man who killed Juh."

"I didn't kill him. Didn't even shoot. He fell off his horse; you saw it."

The three of them waited some more in silence.

"Any chance they'll talk to us now?" Newt asked later.

"Not likely, but I'll try," Horn said.

He explained what was desired to Pretty Buck. The scout called across the river several times but received no answer in return.

"They might take their chief and leave, or they might cross the river elsewhere and try and put the sneak on us from the side or behind," Horn said.

"I always heard that Apache won't fight in the dark," Newt said.

"Who'd you hear that from?" Horn asked. "Grant you, they don't favor it like a Comanche might, but they're always looking for an advantage."

"Think they'll charge us?"

"No, they won't charge three guns across open ground. Apaches don't go for the hero stuff like a lot of other Indians," Horn said. "They're crafty fighters, and what an Apache admires is winning and not getting yourself killed doing it."

"I'm guessing they've got us outnumbered three to one."

"They still won't try to rush us from all the way across the river. A Comanche might, or a Sioux might just to show his buddies how crazy brave he is, but Apaches don't go for that foolish stuff," Horn replied. "Now, what they may do is wade across the river a ways up or down it and put the slip on us. Stalking is more their style, and it won't be hard for them to work in on us in this brush."

"Any chance they've got the boy with them?"

"No, but he may be where they were going before they run on to us, or where they came from."

"Are you saying we pull out of here and see if we can trail them tomorrow?"

Horn folded down the brim of his hat. "That's what I'm saying."

"Then I guess there's no sense waiting."

Horn searched the brush on their side of the river, as if the Chiricahuas might already be surrounding them. He stood and moved in a stooped-over fashion toward the horses. Horn and Pretty Buck waited until he came out of the thicket leading their mounts before they rose up from behind the log.

Instead of mounting, they led the horses for the first half mile away from the river. They picked their way as best they could, careful not to crack any brush and avoiding rocky ground. Often, they stopped to listen for the sounds of the Apaches on their back trail, but there seemed to be no pursuit.

They were on the far side of a strip of dense oak and mesquite thicket and once more upon open ground before they got on their horses. Pretty Buck took the lead and headed west. It was too dark to see much of anything, and Newt had no idea where the scout was taking them.

Somewhere hours later they entered the foothills of the northern Sierra Madre with the black shadows of high mountains. Pretty Buck led them on a winding course and into a canyon that slashed between two of those rock-strewn hills. They followed a dry creek and made camp under a leaning cottonwood next to a few small potholes of stagnant water in the middle of the rocky stream-bed. They made no fire, and Pretty Buck went up on the side of the canyon to stand the first watch. Newt and Horn left their boots on when they lay down, kept their horses saddled, with each man keeping hold of a bridle rein.

Sometime later, Newt came awake. He was star-tled to find that he had slept so long, and light was already spreading across the sky. He sat up and shoved away his blanket and looked around him. The bottom of the canyon was a narrow strip of trees sloping upward toward a saddle connecting the two hills that confined it.

He looked through the stark, bony shadows of the trees toward that pass in the hills, and he searched up the nearly vertical walls of the canyon rising up a hundred feet above him, trying to orient himself. Horn still lay asleep under his blan-ket, but there was no sign of Pretty Buck.

The fact that Pretty Buck hadn't woken one of them earlier bothered Newt. He left his horse ground-tied alongside Horn's and went in search of the missing scout. A rocky point jutting slightly out into the canyon provided a route up the bluff and a vantage point to see down the canyon the way they had come. It was a natural place for Pretty Buck to have chosen to stand watch. Newt entered a thick clump of willows, intent on climbing up to that point. He had some inclination that Pretty Buck might have fallen asleep.

The willow thicket was dense, and it took some effort to push through the numerous limbs. He ducked under the last one to get free of the tangle, and he barely had time to recognize the high-topped Apache moccasins and several pairs of bare brown legs at eye level to him before a carbine butt struck him on the temple and drove him to the ground.

He was all but blinded by the force and pain of the blow, and he struggled to regain his faculties while his arms were gathered roughly behind him and his wrists were lashed together with rawhide thongs. He fought against them enough that, for a brief moment, he managed to roll onto his side. His right eyebrow was cut badly from the blow they had struck him, and he stared upward at his attacker through a bloody slit. An Apache warrior, his face seamed with tiny scars and creased with weather lines and his cheek bones smeared with war paint, leaned over and peered down at him. His dark eyes were sunk deep within his skull, and the hate and the intensity in them burned like living fire.

Newt drew up his knees and kicked at those trying to bind his ankles, but the Apache peering down at him lifted the Springfield rifle he held and drove the butt-plate downward into Newt's skull a second time.

Chapter Eight

There was blessed nothingness, and then the pain came back. Newt's skull felt like it had been cracked and was about to bust wide open from the inside. With every beat of his heart his head throbbed in unison, and the overwhelming misery and dizziness begged him to clench his eyes shut tight and simply lie down and curl into a ball and drool himself back into empty oblivion. But pain was not new to him, and pain made him mad. To give in to it was the same as admitting he had lost, and not to fight it was the same as proving he couldn't take it. There was a pure clarity to pain, and it brought with it a drive to lash out. Fanged and clawed animals knew that primal drive and single-mindedness. Some men knew it. Simple, animal emotion—beat the pain, then bite and slash back at those that caused it.

He forced his eyes open and took a deep, ragged breath. The world around him was a cloudy blur, but he did not need to see clearly to determine that he was sitting on the ground and bound with his back to a tree. His bonds were so tight that when the nausea overcame him he could only move his chin to one side and tilt his head enough to vomit on one of his legs instead of both of them. He wretched so hard that he expected to see blood.

When his guts were empty, he lifted his sagging head once more and found that he could see a little better. Seven Chiricahua warriors sat around a fire, all of them squatting with their arms resting on their bent knees and staring at him, and several of them smiling or laughing as if watching a man puke on himself was truly funny.

Seven Apaches—stone-cold warriors and blooded men of the kind only a desert could give birth to, all staring at him out of those brown flint eyes, the fierceness of their gazes exaggerated by the war paint smeared upon their faces. Their laughter and their guttural utterances were only a dull dream to him, washed over by the continual pounding in his skull.

Newt looked around for Pretty Buck, but the scout was nowhere to be seen. All the warnings given to him about trusting an Apache came back to him right then. Either Pretty Buck fled at the arrival of the war party without giving any warning to the two white men, or he had purposely sold them out.

One of the Apache warriors, the small one wearing the white cotton shirt with the sleeve garters and a breechcloth over pants of the same color tucked into the tops of his knee-high moccasins, reached into the fire and drug out a knife he had left in the coals. Half the blade was glowing cherry red when he pointed it at Newt, and he slung his long hair off one cheek and gave Newt a grin as wicked as the glowing carbon steel. Newt wasn't sure if it was his blurred vision tricking him, or if he could really see the waves of heat lifting off the blade. But the one thing he was sure of was that knife was meant for him.

Newt blinked and blinked again, trying to refocus his vision. The one with the knife was on his feet and moving around the fire. Newt tugged against the rope tied around his chest to secure him to the tree trunk he rested against, and he jerked so fiercely at the rawhide thongs that bound his hands behind him that they dug into his wrists and the blood began to flow. When the Apache neared, Newt stiffened and braced himself for the bite of hot knife and everything, real and imagined, that came with that.

And then the Apache went past him, followed by another of the warriors.

Newt knew that his hearing was coming back when he heard Horn scream. He knew that it was Horn's voice, even before he turned his head and saw the young packer tied in a similar fashion to a nearby tree. Horn screamed again and cursed at the top of his lungs. Newt couldn't help but hear, and he watched it all. That was what they wanted. They wanted him to see it happen to Horn and to know that the same or worse would soon happen to him.

The other warrior sat on Horn's outstretched

legs so that he couldn't move them while the
Apache with the knife dabbed the blistering steel
against the soles of Horn's bare feet. Newt looked
down at his own feet and realized that they had
taken off his boots, too.

There are storytellers who spin tales of brave
men who spit in their captors' eyes and laugh at
torture and fate. Horn was a brave man and he
was tough, but he didn't laugh. Oh, he did spit
some, but that was only the drool spraying while
he screamed his bravery like a wailing infant. He
cursed them in three tongues, sobbing those oaths
in a quavering crescendo of passion each time the
knife flicked out and seared his flesh. They burned
the sole of one foot, and they worked their way up
his leg, slitting one pants leg and leaving raw red
hickeys of wet flesh inside his calf muscle. Never
did they leave the knife blade against him long,
but long enough.

The knife eventually cooled, and they returned
to the fire and shoved it back in the coals. Newt
knew that his turn with the knife was next from the
way they watched him. He tried not to think about
all the stories he had heard about how long an
Apache could make such tortures last.

He watched the knife in the coals while the
seconds ticked away with each beat of his heart,
and the blade grew hotter. He tried to find some
morsel of willpower from deep within that could
see him through, and that could make things
better than they were. But it wouldn't come, as if
the usual force that bound him together had bled

out from his wounds or vomited forth from his guts. He only felt weak and weary, and for one of the few times in his adult life, he could also feel the fear creeping over him. And he hated that fear, and the more he feared the more he hated it and the more his anger rose. He grasped at that hate and fed it and mixed it with the fear. He glared back at the Apaches with gritted teeth, and he had understood why Horn had bawled profanity amid his screams of pain.

One of the warriors went behind Newt and began to untie the ropes securing him to the tree trunk, while four more of them put a loop from a lariat around his ankles. That they had other things in store for him was readily apparent when the sixth one of them led up Newt's pack mule.

The instant that they released him from the tree he fought them. He managed to kick one of them into the fire, and he give a glancing head-butt to another one, but there was only so much he could do with his hands still tied behind his back and five of them on him. They drug him by his heels to the one tall tree in the canyon, an ancient cottonwood with multiple trunks that towered above the rest of the low vegetation. One of the warriors tied a rock to the free end of the lariat and threw it over a high limb. The rock was removed and the rope was tied then to the mule's packsaddle, and Newt was hoisted into the air until he hung upside down with his head suspended some four feet off the ground.

The pain in Newt's head grew worse hanging

that way. From his upside-down point of view, he watched the Apaches bring tinder and firewood and lay the beginnings of a fire beneath him. They scooped up some coals from the other fire with the very same knife blade they had burned Horn with, then carried them over and lit the tinder. The new fire was slow to blaze, but smoke drifted upward in a choking cloud.

Newt saw the tickle of tiny flames growing larger within the kindling beneath the firewood, and he squirmed and tried to swing himself away from the heat and the smoke. The warriors seemed to find great fun in his antics, but their attention was drawn away when another warrior arrived from down the canyon leading Newt's horse. Apparently, the Circle Dot horse had spooked during the Apaches' arrival or wandered off.

The horse was led past Newt, and the warriors followed it to a point several yards away. They gestured at the gelding in some kind of argument and seemed especially interested in the brand on its hip. Soon, the warriors gathered around the horse.

Only one of the raiding party remained squatted before the fire beneath Newt's head, never once glancing at the Circle Dot horse, but instead keeping an intent watch on his captive. He appeared to be the oldest of them by far, a stocky, barrel-chested man, in a breechcloth and dark wool pants tucked into his knee-high moccasins. He wore a vest over a white cotton shirt, and some kind of Mexican silver necklace hung down to his chest. He had a broad face with a jutting chin, and the skin of his face was like old leather soaked in bourbon, with deep age lines and what looked to be a dimpled bullet scar below the outer corner of his left eye.

There was another scar on one knee that looked to be from a bullet, same as the one on his face, but it wasn't only the scars that marked the man. It was something in his gaze and the single-mindedness with which he watched Newt suffer. He sat quietly in front of that fire with his mouth set in a tight line while the other warriors argued over the horse. The flames grew higher, as if the intensity of the old warrior's watch fed them as much as the firewood.

Before him on the ground, the old warrior had Newt's saddlebags, and he finally tired of watching Newt's growing torment and opened one of the bags. While he pilfered through the contents he spilled on the ground, the twisting, creaking rope rotated Newt on his axis enough that he could see Horn.

"They think your horse is a spirit horse," Horn said in a surprisingly calm voice. "It's that brand on him. Medicine sign, they think."

Truly, the discussion among the warriors gathered around the horse had shifted from questions and discussion, to an argument of hushed but rising tones.

"A couple of them are hungry and want to eat him, but the others are afraid to and think it better to eat the mule," Horn added.

The old Apache in front of Newt paused in his examination of Newt's personal items long enough to feed a couple of larger sticks into the fire. Newt was already sweating profusely, and a drop of that sweat or blood from his head wound fell into the fire with a sizzling hiss. He bent at the waist and tried to elevate his torso higher and farther away from the heat, but it gave him little relief and he couldn't hold the pose long.

"Never thought I would go out like this," Horn said as if talking to himself.

The old Apache had found something of interest within the saddlebags, and he bent over and held the item close to his face, as if to see it better. By then, Newt's forehead was beginning to sting, and a gust of wind fanned the fire for a brief instant and he heard and felt the ends of his hair singe. In time, he knew they would build the fire higher or lower him closer to it.

The old Apache held up the thing for Newt to see. It was the cardboard-backed postcard with the Redding boy's photo on it, the one Matilda had given Newt. The old warrior asked a question of Newt in his native tongue, and then in Spanish.

Newt couldn't understand him, for the heat had grown to the point he could barely think. He gritted his teeth and slung his head to try to find some relief.

"He's asking you if you know the boy," Horn said.

Newt groaned and tried again to lift himself from the waist.

"Answer him," Horn said louder. "The boy, Jones. Answer him."

Newt managed only to nod.

The old warrior stuffed the photograph in Newt's vest pocket and stood and went to the mule and untied the lariat rope from the packsaddle. Newt immediately fell into the fire, and he rolled over twice in a frantic attempt to escape the burn. One shoulder of his shirt was on fire, and he ground that shoulder into the earth to put out the flames. When he finished, the old warrior was standing over him. The other warriors seemed to have finished their argument over the Circle Dot horse and came over and joined him. Newt couldn't understand what was said, but it was obvious they wanted to know why the old warrior had cut him down.

The talk turned to an argument worse than the one over the horse, but the old warrior must have had some clout or prestige among the group, for whatever he said caused them to drag Newt back to the tree he had been originally tied to. They secured him as they had the first time and left him there while they went to sit by the fire.

Sometime later, nearing midday, they killed the pack mule and cut away its loin and portions of one hindquarter. They cooked pieces of the mule meat over their fire on willow sticks or sotol stalks and talked among themselves while they wiped at the hot grease and blood juice on their chins and gestured often at the two white men.

The Circle Dot horse stood on the far side of the fire beyond them, tied by itself and away from the other horses belonging to the Chiricahua raiding party. The gelding stood resting with one hind leg cocked and its neck sagging. Once it turned its head, and Newt thought that it looked at him. The horse's usual, calm, bored expression somehow gave him hope. He couldn't say why or how, but it did.

Chapter Nine

"**A**paches sure do like their mule meat," Horn observed as he and Newt watched their captors' impromptu banquet. "Lots of Indians will eat a horse or a mule in a pinch, even a dog, but an Apache likes it. You and me? We ride a horse or mule until it's worn out, then we let it rest and wait until it can go again. An Apache, he'll ride that critter until it can't go anymore, coax it a little and beat on it some and go another ten miles, and then he'll eat it and run on foot until he can steal him something else to ride. Doesn't like to eat turkey and won't eat a fish or a bear to save his life, but mule? Now that's a delicacy."

Horn's observation was the first thing either of them had said in an hour. Their cramped muscles and swelling wrists made it too hard to think and talk, and as the temperature rose the flies came out and picked incessantly at their wounds.

The warriors said little that seemed to pertain to

their captives, rarely looking at them other than to occasionally come over and check that they were still tied securely. Most of their conversation seemed to be storytelling while they gorged on mule meat. Newt had never seen men able to eat so much, especially for men of such short stature and light weight. One of the warriors had removed his shirt as the afternoon heated up, and when he finally finished eating and lay down on the ground for a nap his belly was bloated and distended to extraordinary proportions.

"Eat like wolves," Horn said as if reading Newt's mind.

Newt agreed but didn't answer him. It was a long afternoon.

After sundown most of the warriors spread blankets and lay down beside the fire. Only the old warrior and one other remained awake. Of the two, the other left the fire to go down the canyon, probably to stand some kind of guard or to check on their horses tied in the willow thicket. The old warrior remained. He swiveled his head and those sly, twinkling, obsidian eyes watched Newt like they had when Newt was hanging upside down over that fire.

The Apache brought out the photograph of the Redding boy again, and he held it up in the firelight for Newt to see. "*Lo conoces?*"

"He's asking if you know the boy," Horn said.

Newt had understood the Apache plainly. The

old warrior's Spanish was good, and better than
Newt's own skill in that language.

"He is the son of a friend," Newt replied in hesitant Spanish, unsure if he got the words right.

"The son of a friend, a revered woman," Horn
added in the same tongue, going into more detail
than Newt had. He talked passionately and long,
and emphasized the part about a revered woman.
The words rolled off Horn's tongue like music,
despite his miserable state—*mujer viejo, mujer sabio,
abuela querides*, and *amada*—as if those terms had
great importance to an Apache.

The old warrior nodded and said something
that Newt couldn't follow. He tried to ask but jum-
bled it and grew frustrated and looked to Horn.
"Ask him if he has seen the boy."

Horn asked and the old warrior nodded again
and spoke.

"He said the boy was in their camp, but he is no
longer," Horn translated when the old warrior was
finished.

Horn and the old warrior talked more, sometimes in Chiricahua, and sometimes in Spanish.
Regardless of what Horn had claimed about his
prowess with Apache dialects, he was obviously far
better with Spanish.

"Their camp was attacked a week ago, and several
women and the boy and some other children were
taken," Horn finally said.

"Taken by who?" Newt asked.

"*El Sacha Sangrienta.*"

Newt only recognized something about blood.

Horn saw his look of confusion and added, "The Bloody Hatchet. Only man down here with a name meaner than yours, Jones. Surprised you haven't heard of him. They say he's hell on wheels with a pistol. Killed twenty men, if you listen to those Mexican guitar pickers singing their *corridas* in every *cantina* between Nogales and Chihuahua City."

"Never heard of him."

"Rufus Clagg's his name, but most down here call him the Hatchet, or worse," Horn continued. "He's one part Shawnee Injun, one part Mexican, one part white, and the rest of him is pure unadulterated killer and treacherous son of a bitch.

"He and those that ride with him are leftovers of old James Kirker's scalp-hunting gang, or Rufus was sired by one of them or something. The songs never tell it the same. Bunch of bad-egg Mexican *banditos*, half-breed renegades, and *gringo* dry-gulchers who got run out of the States with a price on their heads. Rufus and them raid where they please, trade whiskey and guns with the Indians, and rustle stolen Mexican stock over to the American side of the border. I reckon now he's taking to stealing children to round out his sins."

"What would he want with a bunch of Apache kids?" Newt asked. "And why would he risk traveling with them and letting them slow him down with the Apaches bound to come after them?"

"Who knows? They say Rufus is a bold one, and I've never met a bandit with what you would call an overabundance of caution or one I could think like. Maybe he intends to sell them off to the copper mines west of here or haul them down the Yaqui River to Guaymas and sell them off as slaves to whatever boat captain wants them."

"If all this is true, how come they're here, instead of running down this Hatchet and getting their kids back?" Newt asked and gestured at the old warrior and the rest of the war party. That sly look in the old warrior's eyes made Newt skeptical of the story. The Apache could be merely making it up to cover for the fact that the boy was dead.

What little Newt knew about the Apache was that they often kept captive women and children— Mexican, white, and those from other tribes—to make wives or adopt as their own. Many known men among the Apache had Mexican mothers or grandmothers, and one of the warriors then lying beside the fire appeared to be more Mexican than Apache from his mustache and chin whiskers and other things about his look. And Newt had even seen a redheaded Apache scout while at San Carlos, obviously not of pure Apache lineage. The various bands that made up the Apache peoples had never been as numerous as other tribes, for it was a harsh land that they called home. Adopting such child captives and taking stolen wives was a way of keeping up their numbers with the constant warfare and hard living that was their lifestyle.

But not all women and children who suffered an Apache raid lived to become Apache themselves. Not by far, for just as often the warriors killed them on the spot, by whim, or especially when a raiding party needed to cover ground quickly.

When a captive was taken alive, it was no guarantee that they would stay that way. Their head might be bashed in with a rifle stock or a rock if they made too much noise or if they didn't have the endurance to stand the physical trials of such a life. Or simply when in some way they displeased their captors somewhere down the trail. Not a pleasant thing, but the way it was. Never once, since Newt had set out after the boy, had he forgotten that William Redding Jr. could have been dead even before Newt had gotten word of the kidnapping and massacre and before he had made one step toward Mexico to retrieve him.

The old warrior was saying something else to Horn while Newt had been distracted with his own thoughts.

Horn translated. "Their little band has more troubles than the Hatchet. They've had both the Mexican and American armies after them for almost a year now. Colonel Herrera and his soldiers are looking all over for them, along with *Rurale* and militia companies from several villages. Near as I can tell, the Apache and Mexicans have been killing each other for almost two hundred years or better, and every Mexican in Sonora and Chihuahua would like nothing better than to wipe them out.

"The Apache are a dying breed, even if they're too tough and stubborn to admit it. Oh, they're hanging on to what they can down here and avoiding the reservation for a while. But they're running and hiding to do it, and they can't get time to feed themselves other than raiding. That's half the reason why Chihuahua and Loco surrendered to Crook this summer, and old Gok here and these other bucks with him are feeling the pressure. Gok or none of the renegades he runs with will admit it, but they're worn down. All they want is to gather up all the livestock and plunder they can steal from the Mexicans and get back across the border to the reservation and lick their wounds."

Horn had pointed at the old warrior when he first said that name, but Newt didn't quite catch it. He nodded his head at the old warrior. "What'd you say his name was?"

Horn repeated the old warrior's name in Chiricahua.

"Gok," was the closest to it that Newt could understand or pronounce.

"Seems like one of the little girls that Rufus stole was Gok's niece," Horn added.

Newt looked at the old warrior again, Gok, and couldn't imagine a man like that sitting there doing nothing when his little niece was taken captive and being hauled across the mountain to God knows where. Something still seemed fishy, and the crafty look about Gok made Newt more suspicious.

There was a long silence. Newt was learning that an Apache spent as much of a conversation in silence as they did speaking, and took more time to listen and ponder on what was said. That was something he admired, no matter how annoying it was at the moment.

Gok finally spoke again. His question was to Horn, but he was looking at Newt when he asked it.

Horn replied to Gok and then turned to Newt. "He wants to know about you, and I told him you were a great warrior among my people."

"Horn, your ability for tall tales is starting to worry me," Newt said.

"Apaches set a big store by a man's reputation. He says he sees that you are a warrior by your scars."

"Scars don't have to mean anything," Newt said.

Horn looked at Gok. "*Cicatrices*," was all he said.

"*Cicatrices*," Gok repeated the Spanish word for scars as if he held reverence for it. He then touched the bullet dimple on his cheek, the one above his knee, another that looked like a saber cut below one knee, then his side and then one forearm, and several other locations on his body supposedly bearing the marks of war and battle.

"He also wants to know if you are a medicine man," Horn said.

"What?" Newt asked.

"He's known as man who has big medicine himself, and he wonders if you are, too," Horn said.

"What makes him think that?"

"He saw how you caused that horse to rear and fall on his friend at the river," Horn said. "The other Apaches first thought it was you who fired and spooked the horse, but he was closer to the crossing and saw that you did not even try to shoot because you didn't need to."

"Is Juh dead?" Newt asked.

Horn looked stricken, and he glanced quickly at

Gok and then back to Newt. "Don't say his name. Apaches don't speak the names of the dead. It's bad medicine, you know?"

Gok spoke more, pausing often. Newt caught some of the parts in Spanish, but he looked to Horn for clarification and to fill in any holes in what the old warrior had said.

Horn let out a low whistle while he eased his wounded foot to a more comfortable position. "Never would have thought that."

"Thought what?" Newt said. "What did he say? All I caught was something about the children and going after them."

"Listen, Jones, and listen close. You play this right."

"Play what?"

"He'll let us go if we'll help him go after the Hatchet."

Newt had never looked away from Gok while he was talking to Horn, still trying to plumb what was hidden behind that wily expression of Gok's. "You tell him what you need to tell him to get us loose."

Horn shook his head, and his voice went quieter. "Don't bank on him not knowing any English."

"He's got six warriors with him, and he's obviously some kind of bigshot with them," Newt said. "He doesn't need two white men to help him."

"He used to be a big man," Horn said. "But he says his people have turned away from him. They blame him for the loss of the women and children, and they blame him for other things lately."

"So those young bucks won't go with him?"

"They want to play with us some, and when we're dead they'll divide up our guns and horses and go back to gather their people and head for the border. They've been raiding into Chihuahua for two weeks. They aren't sure if the Mexicans haven't already attacked their stronghold while they were gone, and that worries them. I'm thinking Colonel Herrera has hit them hard recently."

"Just us and him to go after those kids?"

"That's right."

"We'd have him outnumbered."

"He says that he thinks you are a man of honor, because only such a man would come so far after a boy that isn't his own," Horn said. "You give him your word that you will help him try to get the children back and he will let us go."

"He says those others won't go with him or listen to him anymore," Newt said. "Are they going to let us go?"

"He says they will. He has argued much with them about it, and they have agreed, whether they like it or not. That horse of yours helped things. Gok agrees with them that it's big medicine, and maybe a spirit horse. Says that brand is a Tarahumara mark. Says those Indians aren't good fighters, only swift runners, but there was a time when they had powerful medicine men among them."

Newt glanced again at the Circle Dot horse, still standing on three legs asleep. Trust that horse to rest any time he got the chance, and trust that horse not to know what kind of predicament his master was in. He thought on how he had come by the horse, and the stories a certain Mexican don had told him about the gelding's history and the odd brand.

"Tell him he has my word," Newt said.

Horn did.

Gok woke the other warriors, relayed the state of things to them, and one of them went behind Horn and untied him once they had time to get good and awake. They saved Newt for last. Gok stood in front of him while another went behind him. The other warriors took up their weapons and stood in a semi-circle facing him beyond the fire.

Newt felt the ropes slack and then the rawhide on his wrists being slashed with a knife. He almost fell over but righted himself. His hands were too numb to function properly or at all, and with the back of one forearm he dug clumsily at the dried blood almost matting one of his eyes shut. He wasn't sure he could get up, and he wasn't sure that those warriors weren't going to kill him if he did.

The life slowly began to come back into his hands, blood circulating where the rawhide thongs had shut it off. His hands began to tingle and then to burn with a pain that was almost as bad as sticking them in flames. He waited and gritted his teeth, all the while never taking his eyes off Gok standing before him.

When, after a long while, he stood, more than one of the Chiricahuas readied their rifles for trouble. Gok was wearing a gunbelt decorated with silver Mexican *pesos* hammered and engraved into *conchos* and with other fancy silverwork. An ivory-handled Colt pistol and a Bowie knife rode on opposite hips, and the holster and the sheath were decorated much the same as the gunbelt. Gok made no move to put his hand near either of the weapons. He simply waited and watched with that unreadable, stoic expression.

Newt held out one hand, palm up and open. "*Dame mi pistola.*"

Gok didn't flinch. Newt kept his open palm waiting.

"I ought to kill you," Newt said.

Horn was up on one foot, balanced against the tree they had tied him to. He looked frantic the instant Newt said that.

Either Gok didn't understand any English, or he was that confident, for he reached behind the small of his back and drew out Newt's pistol with the blue crosses in the grips. He put the pistol in Newt's hand.

Newt holstered it. His breathing was slow and heavy. Gok was a powerful man, but Newt towered over him many inches. Yet Gok held his ground, waiting for something that he did not say.

"When do we start?" Newt asked.

Horn repeated the question, and Gok answered.

"First light," Horn said.

Gok watched Horn translate, and it was plain that he wanted some kind of confirmation from Newt.

Newt took a deep breath and let it out. "*Enjuh.*"

For the first time, Gok smiled, or almost, and nodded. "*Enjuh.*"

With that, Gok turned and walked back to the fire and lay down on his blanket. The other warriors were slower to relax any at all, but they eventually hunkered down by the fire, closely watching the two white men. Newt and Horn were wondering what to do next.

"Did you ask him about Pretty Buck?" Newt asked Horn.

"I told you, don't say the names of the dead," Horn said.

"They killed him?"

Horn looked up at the point of the mountain where Newt had thought to go and look for Pretty Buck. That look said it all. Pretty Buck wouldn't be riding with them west.

Horn sat back down against the tree and gingerly began to examine his burns. The sole of that damaged foot looked terrible. Great blisters were already formed; the pale white of the stretched skin and fluid pockets stood out starkly in the firelight and against the soot-black and charred skin surrounding the blisters.

It was a while before he seemed to notice that Newt was still standing and hadn't moved at all. "What are you looking at?"

Newt gestured at Gok. The old warrior seemed to already be asleep.

"Let's wait until morning," Horn said. "We ain't out of the woods, yet. Not by a long shot."

Newt spat a bloody wad of phlegm at the fire and kept his gaze on the sleeping Gok. "You tell him I want my damned boots back."

Horn started to protest.

"And you tell them not to eat my horse."

Chapter Ten

"You never did pay me that twenty dollars you promised me when we got to the border." Horn was riding his horse with his bad foot bare and out of the stirrup on that side. He had rigged a crude bandage out of the sleeve of a spare shirt, and there was something pitiful in the ragged spectacle of him slouched in the saddle and letting his horse make its own way along the narrow eyebrow of a mountain trail they traveled. He squirmed in the saddle often, probably because the burns on his inner calf were rubbing against the fender of his saddle.

Gok was several yards in the lead. Newt watched the old warrior's broad back, thinking things, but mostly wondering why the Apache was so confident that they wouldn't kill him in revenge for what he had done to them.

"I was talking about that twenty dollars," Horn said. "Didn't you hear me?"

"What good would it do you now?" Newt answered. "You said this morning that our chances of surviving this were looking slimmer by the minute."

"It's the principle of the matter. It would remind me why I came with you."

Newt thought about the wallet of cash in his saddlebags and wished he had trusted Horn more and earlier, and gone ahead and paid him. "Nothing to spend it on out here anyway."

"I could hold it in my hands. Help pass the time, you know, thinking on how I could spend it."

"We've got plenty to think about. You want to carry the money, you can."

"How much money have you got?" Horn looked at the saddlebags. "If you've got enough we could ride back to the border and hire us some fools to come back down here and get that kid and get their feet burned."

Newt leaned in the saddle and looked down at the mountainside dropping in an almost vertical descent several hundred feet below them. He guessed them already well over five thousand feet of elevation, and the trail they rode on was barely wide enough for a horse. In no place was it good enough or smooth enough to let a rider on it quit thinking about that fall.

"You know any fellows fool enough to go after the boy?" Horn asked.

"Only two," Newt said. Then he thought about Pretty Buck and regretted saying it. He hadn't really known the Apache scout, but he had seemed a good sort. Too good of a sort to go under so young and the way he had.

Gok disappeared ahead of them when the trail dipped sharply downward into pine forest. With the trail becoming less challenging, he kicked his pony to a trot. For a seasoned Chiricahua warrior, Gok surprised Newt how careless and unworried he traveled. Or perhaps Gok knew they were nowhere close to the Hatchet's gang, and that the terrain was too rough to worry about Mexican regulars.

Newt had asked Gok early that morning about his lack of caution. Horn had translated where he needed to, and the gist of it was that Gok claimed he would be able to sense when enemies were around, long before they arrived. Gok had said nothing since.

Newt placed little stock in Gok's supposed "medicine" powers and figured the old warrior knew this ground intimately and had reason to suspect there was no danger. Newt also suspected that Gok's friends might be trailing them. He often checked his back trail for signs of them.

A small black bear flushed from the timber a hundred yards in front of them, and Newt's hand went reflexively to the buttstock of his Winchester in its rifle boot on his saddle before he realized it was only a bear. Still, he was glad to have his weapons back.

The Apache had risen from their blankets an hour before daylight. They ate more of the mule meat, and then without a word to either Gok or the white men, they mounted their horses and rode away to the south. Newt's and Horn's weapons and other belongings were left in a pile beside the fire. Knowing how short of guns and ammunition the renegade Apache were, Newt hadn't expected that.

When they went over the dip in the trail, they found Gok stopped in the middle of it at the edge of the pines. He seemed concerned.

"What's the matter?" Newt asked.

Gok obviously didn't understand him, or was too intent on something ahead to answer.

"*Que pasa?*" Newt repeated.

Newt then realized that Gok was watching the little black bear running fearfully at high speed down the mountainside. Gok remained where he was, even after the bear was long out of sight.

"Just a bear," Newt said.

Gok said something. Said much in fact while he sat his horse and refused to move ahead.

"That bear has him spooked," Horn said.

"Only a bear," Newt repeated.

"Apaches think bears are special. Most of them won't eat one, and those that kill one don't want to touch it. They think that the spirits of wicked people sometimes become bears and that to touch one or eat of its flesh will let that bad spirit possess them. Some Apaches feel the same about owls and coyotes."

Gok said more.

"He says he had the bear sickness once." Horn asked Gok to retell a part of it, then continued his translation when Gok was finished. "Says that when the bear heart took over his own that he foamed at the mouth and could not sleep. When he did sleep after many days, he had bad dreams."

"*No bueno,*" Gok said when Horn was finished. He didn't so much as gesture at the way the bear had gone, as if he feared to do that much. Only his gaze showed where the bear had gone.

"Just a bear," Newt said for a third time.

Gok changed back to speaking Apache. Newt looked to Horn and saw that Horn was again having a hard time understanding Gok.

"He says you should not laugh at the bear sickness, and that even a good man can be overcome with the bear heart," Horn said.

"I've been worse things than a bear," Newt replied.

"He says that when you think you are well from the bear sickness, you will still never be the same," Horn added. "Always, a bit of the bear's heart will live in you. You will do things that you would not do without it. That's the bear and the bad spirit acting out."

Newt motioned at the trail ahead of them, impatient to be moving. When Gok finally kicked his horse forward he turned from the trail and went up the mountain, as if afraid to go near where the bear had crossed their path or its tracks.

"Superstition," Newt said, more disgusted with the detour than Gok's beliefs.

"Gok's got magic," Horn said. "All the Chiricahua say that about him. There was a time when all the young braves wanted to follow him on raids. They said he could tell when the Mexicans or the Americans were coming long before they ever showed. Lozen was like that, too. When they wanted her to use her magic she would go up on a hill and spread her arms out until her palms tingled and told her which way they should go or where the enemy was."

"She?"

"Woman, but a warrior. Not unheard of, but rare," Horn said. "And one of the prettiest women I ever saw, but too mean and hated white men too much for me to spark her."

"I wish we had got that bear," Newt said. "We could use the meat."

Horn looked less sure, and Newt noticed that.

"Don't tell me you're scared of bear spirits, too?"

"I don't know. Maybe not, but you spend long enough with the Apache you get to thinking things that you didn't consider before. I stayed with old Pedro in his camp for most of a winter once. I saw a medicine man in that camp predict when we were going to have company three days before the guests arrived."

"Not shocking that the rumor spread about somebody coming."

"No, nobody knew. And he predicted how many were coming and whether they would be man or woman and what band they belonged to. I'm only saying . . ."

Gok called back to them over his shoulder.

"What did he say?" Newt was getting tired of having to get Horn to translate everything, and his head still hurt. Those two things were both in his tone and the growling way he talked.

"*Shush Bijii*," Horn said. "He says you have the Bear Heart. The sickness is gone, but he can see the bear in you. And the bear spirit will come and go in you, and it worries him that maybe he cannot trust you as he once thought."

"Never ate a bear in my life."

"Never once? From your accent I would have guessed you from east Tennessee, or parts nearby. Kentucky or Arkansas, maybe. You've got the mountains in your talk," Horn said.

"Tennessee, right enough."

"And a hill boy like you never ate bear?"

"Only bear I was ever around, I watched him drink a beer."

"You're kidding."

"Nope."

"What kind of bear drinks a beer?"

"A Langtry, Texas, bear. Belonged to that judge I told you about."

"What were you doing in Langtry?"

"I was fixing to ride to Mexico."

"See? Maybe there's something to what Gok says. How'd that trip turn out?"

"Wonderful."

The look on Newt's face made Horn think he

was lying. "Mexico ain't so bad. I reckon there are worse places. You can say that about it, don't you think?"

"You can say that about anywhere."

"Well, maybe we ought to rethink Mexico and consider the good things."

Newt frowned at him as he was wont to do. "Too much talking."

"But you haven't talked no more than a few sentences since we broke camp this morning," Horn called after Newt as the big man kicked up to a trot and pulled ahead of him. "I tell you, Jones, we've got to work on those social skills."

Chapter Eleven

They followed trails that only an Apache would know of, and perhaps saw places that none but an Apache had ever seen. They stayed north of where the peaks of the Sierra Madre began to really touch the sky, skirting those looming crags and following a winding way through narrow passes and over some of the steepest, roughest terrain Newt had ever ridden a horse over.

Always, they kept a westward course, and sometimes their way grew so rough that they had to dismount and lead the horses over boulder-strewn cuts and shale bank slides where one false step and a quick fall could cripple or kill man or beast. Gok seemed to think nothing of the bad country they traversed, but Apache were more at home on foot than on horseback, and it appeared that he thought a horse could go anywhere a man on his own legs could go without using his hands. Maybe he was right, but once during the day Horn's horse fell off the trail and ended up in the bottom of a gully on its back with all four legs sticking straight up. They were an hour righting it and half again that time finding a way for it to climb back up to the trail.

They made one night's camp in a glade cut in between two mountain peaks. It was nothing but a scooped-out hole in the mountains with a little running water coursing down its middle, but as pretty as a manicured city park to Newt and a place he would never have imagined existed until he stumbled upon it. Horn said the Apache knew of lots of such places and made them their strongholds and summer camping spots.

Newt said nothing to either Gok or Horn. He simply unsaddled and brushed down the Circle Dot horse and hobbled it to graze on the mountain grass, and then he lay down after wolfing down a cold supper of leftover bacon he carried in his pocket. He was asleep long before Horn had the coffee ready. Horn and Gok sat up long into the night telling stories and theorizing about the big man with them.

Again, an hour or more before sunup they were riding west. Horn was quiet for once and appeared as if he hadn't slept at all.

Newt pointed at Horn's bandaged foot. "Bothering you? You look rough."

"Naaa." Horn shook his head. "Bit sleepy, I guess."

"That's what you get for sitting up all night working your jaws."

Horn scoffed. "That's what I like about Apaches. You take an Apache man. He'll stay up all night telling stories and sharing his *tiswin* with you."

"*Tiswin?*"

"Apache beer." Horn looked a little put out at being interrupted, but went on. "Like I said, he'll stay up all night enjoying good company, then he'll lay down and sleep 'til noon or so while his women get the place revved up and his meal ready. He'll get his belly full, then smoke him some tobacco and tell a few more stories. Then he'll get up and go hunting or maybe go visit somebody else's lodge. Now tell me that ain't living easy like."

Newt ignored him. Gok was leading them down a last, long decline, and a mesquite-choked flat was visible a mile or more below them, with the ribbons of two rivers coming together on that flat.

They were halfway down to the flat when Newt thought he saw dust rising up from along one of those rivers. Gok apparently saw it, too. Their chosen path down a canyon led them out of sight of the river. When they once more could see the flat, Gok dismounted in a pile of boulders that had tumbled down from above in the far-flung past. He motioned for Newt and Horn to dismount, and they did so and left their horses and followed the old warrior to a vantage point where they could study that dust cloud without revealing themselves.

Newt peered at the dust and said as if to himself, "Passel of men on horses."

Gok must have recognized the English word for horse, because he nodded and then said, "*Rurales.*"

"Yep," Horn agreed. "Those do look like *Rurales.*"

Newt wasn't sure how they could tell who was making that dust cloud, unless their vision was twice as good as his. But they seemed sure.

"Country lawmen," Horn said in case Newt didn't know what a *Rurale* was. "Kind of like roving police or those Texas Rangers. There are companies of them stationed all over this country. Most of them are ill-equipped, and some of them are little better than highwaymen with a badge, but I bet that's old Pablo Chavez's bunch. If it is, they're nobody to mess with."

"We'll let them pass, and then we'll cross behind them," Newt said. "No problem."

Horn hobbled over to a rock and took a seat. He propped his game foot up on his other knee and picked at something on the bottom of it.

"Cactus sticker," he said. "I sure miss wearing my boot. We never appreciate our feet like we should."

"We should have ridden into Casas Grandes like I said and left you there," Newt scolded. "You're in no shape for this."

"I'll keep up. Let's just sit here a while and let those *Rurales* pass. A little rest will do my foot good, and I'll be right as rain. You watch."

"You barely made it every time we got off and led the horses."

"Yeah, but I made it. And I'll keep making it. Mama Horn didn't raise no sissies."

"How come you to come with me? And don't tell me it was for the money."

Horn smiled that smile of his. "How come you're down here?"

"That boy's grandmother is my friend—"

Horn cut him off. "Yeah, you've already said that. A man doesn't come down here doing what you're trying to do for no kind of friend, woman or not."

"I don't have many friends."

"I can believe that." Horn laughed but did it quietly. "Tell me the real reason, Jones. How come you're trying to get yourself killed doing something that you don't have a fart's chance in the wind of getting done?"

Newt started to say something but stopped short.

"Don't have the words for it, do you?" Horn asked.

"No, I don't. Half my life I've been doing things that I can't explain or I probably wouldn't do again."

"Well me, neither. Maybe I was bored, or maybe I'm out to make me a mark like you said back there at that old city on the San Miguel."

"When those *Rurales* have passed we're going to ride, and ride fast," Newt said. "That Hatchet is way ahead of us, and it's time we made up some ground."

"I'll be with you."

"You better be, or I'll leave you."

Newt went back to the place he'd left Gok, but Gok was gone. Careful searching of the canyon below him led Newt to finally spot the Chiricahua. The old warrior had slipped a hundred yards farther down the mountain and was down on his belly with that Long Tom Springfield infantry rifle he packed along rested across a rock. Newt noticed then that the *Rurales* were almost directly below Gok, following a course between the river and the foot of the mountain.

The *Rurales* were close enough by then—still a long rifle shot—that even Newt could make them out plainly for what they were. There were a dozen men in the *Rurale* company. He could see the big, sugarloaf brims of their *sombreros*. The number of guns they were carrying and the way they dressed like some kind of *vaquero* or Mexican cowboy gave them away.

He knew what Gok was about to do, but there was no way that he could get down there fast enough to stop him or call out to him without giving their position away. All he could do was watch and wait for the roar of Gok's gun.

He didn't have to wait long. That long-barreled Springfield cracked and smoked, and one of the *Rurales* in the front of the line, the one on the yellow horse and with the red shirt on, tipped off his horse like a hammer had struck him in the head. It was an incredible shot, maybe two hundred yards or better, and the *Rurale* had been riding at a trot and through the mesquite brush.

The other *Rurales* looked up the mountain while Gok reloaded his trapdoor single-shot. By the time he was aiming again, the *Rurales* were off their horses and climbing up through the rocks. One of their bullets spanged off the canyon between Newt and Gok with an angry whine.

Gok never fired again, and by the time Newt had Horn on his horse the old warrior was already coming at a run and almost to his own horse.

"What the hell were you thinking?" Newt asked in English, regardless of whether or not Gok could understand him.

"*Enjuh*," Gok said, as if that made everything better.

And then he leaped on his horse in one smooth swing of his leg and the hand not holding his rifle grabbing a handful of the horse's mane. It was the move of a young man, not a man of Gok's apparent age. Newt would have guessed him somewhere north of fifty or so.

Newt got on the Circle Dot horse and followed Gok back up the canyon until they hit another canyon leading into it and sloping down to the river on the other side of the point of the mountain where they had left the *Rurales*.

"That was a damned fool stunt he pulled. What was he thinking back there?" Newt asked Horn.

Perhaps it was pure chance, but at that very moment Gok looked at Newt and said in surprising and perfect English, as if it explained it all, "Damned Mexicans."

Gok moved ahead of them again, guiding them down the new canyon.

"Do the Apaches hate all Mexicans like he does?"
Newt asked Horn while he checked their back trail.
The *Rurales* were going to be a long time working
their way up that mountain, but they were mad
enough to do it faster than they had any right to.

"Mostly, and the Mexicans hate them about the
same," Horn said. "Lots of years and bad things
between them. Lots of good folks on both sides
gone under."

Newt nodded that he understood, as he had
heard much the same his first time in Mexico.
However, he found no pleasure in that understanding. "Bad blood and too late to do anything
about it, I reckon."

"The way I hear it, Gok's got more grudge than
most when it comes to Mexicans, and they like him
even less," Horn said.

Newt noticed that Horn was breathing harder
than he should. His blistered foot must have been
bothering him worse than he let on. "What about
Gok?"

Horn seemed to find something funny about
the way Newt said the old warrior's name, but he
let it go and said nothing about it. "You ask him
sometime, and maybe he'll tell you the straight of
it if he wants to. Or maybe he won't."

The side canyon choked down so narrow and
was so rough that they could barely get their horses
down the rugged chasm. Newt wasn't happy that
they were going down on the flats. He would have
much preferred to stay up on the mountain and

take advantage of the terrain. Even outnumbered like the *Rurales* had them, the Mexican lawmen would have a hard time flushing them out or over-running three men with good rifles and plenty of cover and the high ground. But Gok's plan seemed to be to cross the river and outrun the *Rurales* to the mountains on the other side of the river bottom.

The last hundred yards down the canyon was a slide of loose ground and eroded debris, and their horses had to go fast to keep from falling. They hit level ground at a run and were soon in the cover of a dense mesquite thicket. Ahead of them, rising up above the shorter mesquites, Newt could see the green line of cottonwoods along the river. That green line was only a short ride away.

But instead of going toward the river, Gok pulled up and looked back at the mountain behind them. He turned and pointed at the river, then at them, and the river again. It was plain he wanted them to go on while he remained behind. What he intended, Newt didn't know, whether it was to wait for the *Rurales* and kill another one while getting himself killed, or something else. Newt didn't care.

He slapped Horn's horse on the hip and the two of them tore through the thicket toward the river. Gok remained behind.

Recent fall rains had swollen the Bavispe River where it made its big turn to the south, and it took Newt longer busting brush to find a more suitable place to cross. Even that wasn't a good crossing, but it would do in an emergency.

Newt gave Horn a concerned look. "You up to this?"

Instead of speaking, Horn answered him by spurring his horse into the river. Newt was right behind him, and they hit swimming water not ten feet out. Horn was lighter and remained in the saddle, but although the Circle Dot horse was a strong swimmer and swam high in the water, Newt wanted to lighten his strain where he could. He slipped from his back and let the horse drag him along by the saddle horn. The river was wide there, and he alternated his attention from the near bank to the far one. It wouldn't do to be caught in midstream by the *Rurales*. He tried not to think anymore about that and hung on and let his horse swim.

Once they were out on the far bank, they got into cover of the brush and trees and turned back and kept watch on the way they had come. Newt hadn't a single bit of dry cloth to wipe his guns down, but he did the best he could with leaves. He unloaded both weapons and attempted to dry the cartridges, too. He would be sure to clean and oil both his rifle and the Smith pistol when he had the chance.

Horn remained on his horse, as if he lacked the energy to get down. Newt thought that was best, anyway. If they had to run it would be better not to have to help the kid on his horse again. He wondered about Horn's foot. He couldn't see how bad it was with the bandage on it.

They waited until the sun was well down behind them and had almost given Gok up for good when he came riding through the brush to them. He seemed no worse for his wear, and Newt had no idea where the old warrior had crossed the river. It was obviously a better crossing, for Gok was only wet up to his moccasin tops. What's more, Gok was leading two strange horses with Mexican Charro saddles on them, the kind with the big wooden saddle horns.

Gok gestured for them to go, and he led off to the west before Newt could ask any questions. But Newt wasn't about to let it go. He kicked the Circle Dot horse up until he was close to Horn and Gok.

"How'd you get those horses?" He knew good and well that Gok had ridden around the point of the mountain and slipped up behind the *Rurales* and raided their horses while they were up on the mountain looking for him. He knew it but wanted to hear it.

"*Enjuh*," Gok twisted around on his pony and said with a grin that made him seem years younger than he was, as if the whole afternoon had been a normal day.

Newt was trying to understand how one old man who was scared of bears and who snored like a freight train in his sleep and was so stiff kneed in the cool mountain mornings that it took him half an hour to get moving right could sneak up on a whole company of *Rurales* and get away without their horse guard spotting him.

It was then that Newt saw the fresh scalp hanging from Gok's gunbelt.

Gok saw him looking at the scalp and his grin changed to something more like a smirk.

"Those *Rurales* never did anything to us," Newt said. "That was cold-blooded murder what you did back there."

Horn didn't translate, either because he was too out of it, or simply because he didn't want to.

Newt tried to find the words in Spanish but gave up for he knew it would do no good, whatever he said to Gok. All he could think of was to say again in English, "You could have gotten us killed."

"Damned Mexicans. *No bueno*," Gok said.

Newt wanted to lay hands on the Apache right then, and he wanted to get free of him. But he needed Gok's tracking skills and he needed his knowledge of the land. And that made him madder, that he needed such a killer to help him. He tried to tell himself that the Apache and the Mexican people had been at war for generations, and that it was no wonder they shot each other on sight. But that didn't soothe him.

It came to him that he hadn't heard Gok shoot since he had shot the first *Rurale* from the mountain. No matter, the old warrior had done for two *Rurales* by himself and hadn't gotten a single scratch in the process. Everything he had guessed about Gok from the instant he first laid eyes on him was true. He tried not to think about how he had known that instinctively, but he did.

Was he a killer, same as Gok? Wasn't that why

Matilda Redding had wanted him to go after the boy? Oh, she said it in a nicer way—that bit about being a man with the bark on. She wanted him to go after the boy not because she trusted him but probably saw him for what he was the instant she first met him back on the Pecos. Did she think of him as he thought of Gok? He tried to imagine how she saw him—just a raggedy man who hadn't made anything of himself in better than thirty years. A violent man with a past no gentleman would claim. Nothing but the scars he had received and the ones he had given to tell his story. Nothing to his name other than a dead man's gun and a horse even an Apache wouldn't eat.

For years, Newt had told himself that he was going to amount to something one day, all the while hating the name he had somehow earned, like it or not. Always going to change and always putting that off with every bad excuse life kept offering him. And here he was again, fighting and clawing, and with nothing to offer anyone but his gun and his fists. And no one who would miss him when he was gone. It was an ugly truth, but one he couldn't deny. He had known it for a long time and had been reminded of it when he rode through the ruins of that ancient city. A man like him was never headed for anything but a hard end.

Gok and Horn had pulled too far ahead of him, and Newt sped up his horse. Horn was listing a little to one side in the saddle, and Newt thought he might have to prop him up. Damned fool kid, coming down to Mexico with him. He was young enough, yet, to learn and change his ways and find something different. Maybe go back to the States and find that pretty Apache woman he had talked about, or one of those Mexican *señoritas* with the flashing brown eyes. A kid like him had a chance to change before it was too late. Smart kid and a fine talker. He would make a politician or a lawyer or such if someone pointed him that way.

The Smith pistol on Newt's hip had shifted, and righting it to a more comfortable spot and the feel of those grips against his palm put his mind back to task. No sense whining about the way things were, and no since thinking too much. They said the Widowmaker was a hardcase, and they would say it when he was gone. Let them say what they wanted to. He was going to get the boy back if he was still alive. Matilda was counting on him, for one reason or another. Let the cards fall where they would, and pity those who got in his way.

Another set of mountains loomed up to the west, and Gok was leading them that way. Newt rode alongside Horn and put a hand on the kid's shoulder to brace him. Horn was so sick and hurting that he didn't know that Newt was helping him.

Chapter Twelve

They turned south and followed the Bavispe once they reached the foot of the mountains they had seen to the west. On the day after crossing the Bavispe Gok sped them up, as if he knew something that he had not shared. Twice, Newt had seen sets of horse tracks but knew not who made them. The tracks could have been the *Rurales* they had left the day before, or they could have been made by any riders. The Hatchet had such a lead on them that the tracks were too recent to be his or his men's.

Horn was better after a night's rest. Newt had lanced the blisters on Horn's foot, and Gok had rubbed cool mud from the river on them before they rigged up another crude bandage. Although Horn was better, Newt feared that the poison would set in Horn's foot, no matter how much they attempted to doctor it. And then Horn would die or they would have to cut off that foot. Either way, if the rot set in Horn was dead. Newt kept a watch ahead, hoping he would see a village or town in the distance. Maybe they could find a doctor if they passed upon a settlement.

Gok didn't seem concerned about Horn's foot, as if he had seen such wounds before and thought them nothing to worry about. Or he simply didn't care.

Newt noticed for the first time that the front sight on Gok's rifle was missing. It was amazing that Gok had made such a long shot on the *Rurale* with the gun missing its sight. Most Indians Newt knew weren't much of a rifle shot, but then again, he hadn't met many Apache and he was sure that Gok was unusual, even among them—an efficient killing machine.

They came upon the burned-out Apache *rancheria* late in the morning. The fall days were getting steadily cooler and the wind whipped up the length of the narrow valley, whistled through the open rib bones of several cow carcasses strewn about, and flapped a piece of scorched steer hide serving as a partial roof over the pole frames of one of the handful of brush wickiups in the ruined remains of the Apache camp. There had been three lodges, and Newt didn't need to wait for Gok to come back from looking over the tracks and other sign around and in the camp to know what had happened. Somebody had hit the village and hit it hard. There were two bodies that Newt could see from where he sat on his horse and watched Gok work over the signs. A man and a woman, both old, both now dead with their scalps taken and

other things done to them. Whoever had done it
had set fire to the lodges before they rode away.

When Gok rode up, Newt knew who had attacked
the Apache camp before Gok said anything. Horn
did, too. The look on Gok's face said it all, and
then he went ahead and said it, anyway, "*La Sacha
Sangrienta.*"

The Hatchet had done this.

Horn translated as Gok filled in the details.
Eight men, maybe more, had hit the Apache camp
a day or two before—men with shod horses, and
men who scalped old men and women and cut off
their ears. *Piezas*, those ears were called in that
country and time, trophies again like the Apache
heads Colonel Herrera had spiked along the road
to Janos. There had been a time when the state of
Chihuahua had offered a bounty for scalps and
pairs of ears.

"He says the Hatchet and his men got two more
children here," Horn said.

There were no bodies of children, so Newt knew
that it was more slaves for the Hatchet to sell.

"How does he know it wasn't *Rurales* or Herrera's soldiers that did this?" Newt asked.

Horn led him over to the body of the old woman.
She lay flat on her back with a large, ragged split
of busted bone in her forehead.

"He carries a hatchet for his nasty work. That's
how he got his name," Horn said.

Truly, it looked as if a hatchet or an ax blade
had busted the old woman's skull. Newt looked
away, sick at the sight of that old woman's scalped

and mutilated head, and her eyes staring wide open up at him and the sky. He waited a moment and then got down off his horse and pushed her eyelids closed with his hand. There was no time for burying them, but he could at least do that much.

Gok seemed uneasy that he had touched the dead and rode on without them. Newt and Horn followed but lagged well behind him on purpose.

"How far behind him are we?" Newt asked.

"You heard Gok. Maybe two days. Maybe a little less," Horn said. "Those kids should slow them down."

"You know of any towns downriver that they might be heading for?"

"Never been down this way, but Gok says that there's a village called Opata about two more days south. Some other tiny Indian villages in the mountains closer, but I can't remember their names."

"How's the foot?"

"Better."

Newt couldn't tell if Horn was lying or not. "You up for this? We might run on to them any time. It won't be easy."

"Like I told you, I'll be right there with you."

"Good, I'm counting on you."

"That back there"—Horn pointed behind them at the Apache *rancheria* they had left—"I've seen Apaches do things as bad or worse, but just the same, men who could do that don't deserve to live."

"We'll do our best to get the children back."

"I'm not talking about only getting those kids

back. I'm talking about killing those that did it. Setting things right."

Newt started to tell him that killing never set anything right, and he wondered if Horn had ever killed a man. But it didn't really matter. He knew what Horn was feeling. It didn't matter if the need for such revenge was wrong. He kept thinking about that Apache woman with her head caved in. First, they had to get the kids back, but if the Hatchet and his men got in the way he would do for them like the rabid wolves they were. He had done plenty of hard things and had plenty of guilt already weighing down his conscious. What would one more thing hurt?

Hardcase, that Widowmaker, that's what some said about him. Newt chuckled with little joy in it, and the sound came out of him as icy as a north wind in December. He put a hand to his Smith .44 and made sure it was still there, ready to hand, and he watched the trail of the Hatchet's men marked plainly in the sandy ground of the valley—tracks headed southward, and tracks headed to a reckoning.

Chapter Thirteen

There was a Mexican village not far downriver. They found it on the second day after leaving the burned Apache camp. It was really no village at all but a few simple huts and *jacales* gathered together in a mountain hamlet, only existing so far from anywhere by some stubborn persistence on the part of the few inhabitants who called it home and irrigated their cornfields from the potholes of water in the nearby creek. Newt and his party never would have found it if the riverbed hadn't tightened down into a steep, high-sided canyon with no room to keep following its course. For miles the river ran through such chasms, and they, like the Hatchet and his men, swung west into the big mountains once more.

The Hatchet hadn't found the village, or he had no interest in it. Newt and his party, on the other hand, needed food, as the chase hadn't afforded them time or ability to hunt or to detour to some place where they could obtain supplies. And they hoped to find a *curandero* to check out Horn's wounded foot. Many villages had such a folk healer. Aside from the more questionable practices of the *curanderos* that often centered around superstition and magic, many of them had some basic doctoring skills learned by necessity or passed down from previous generations of their profession. Certainly such a healer would be far better at treating Horn's wounds than Newt and Gok.

At first the villagers had hid in their homes, afraid to come out at the sight of Gok and the two rough-looking white men with him. But Horn spoke to them and eventually coaxed them forth. They were a kind, friendly people. Timid, but hospitable even to a hard crew like Newt and his two companions. The women wore brightly colored dresses, and the men plain white and coarse spun cotton pants and shirts seen over much of Mexico among the peons, with braided grass belts and homemade, low-crowned straw hats. There was not a cobbler in the village, and both men and women wore low moccasins made from deerskin. The hat making was the Mexican side of their heritage, and the moccasins a leftover skill from their native Opata ancestry.

Unfortunately there was no *curandero* in this village, but they were able to trade for some corn, a gourd-shaped chunk of cheese, and a hindquarter of fresh killed venison.

Gok and Newt lounged under the roof of a brush arbor, while one of the women of the village did her best to clean and tend to Horn's foot.

When the woman was through with him, Horn limped over and sat down with them. He was carrying a pair of Apache-style moccasins, and he didn't say where he had gotten them from. He sat on a stool and studied his foot as if he were dreading what he was about to do. It took him three times to get one of the moccasins on his bad foot, and he was panting by the time he got it done. Once the worst of the pain was over, he tightened and tied that moccasin and donned the other one.

He stood up and tested his new footwear and crippled foot, hobbling a few steps away from them and back. "There, good as new."

Hardly, but Newt didn't say so.

Horn took his boots and disappeared into the village. When he came back the boots were gone, and the same for his big spurs strapped to them.

"That was a good pair of boots, and I paid twenty dollars for those spurs," Horn said.

"You traded them for those moccasins?" Newt asked.

Horn nodded and looked down at his newly clad toes. "Got three pair of them in trade. There wasn't any way I could get my foot in those boots, but I'm going to miss those spurs."

Newt had no idea what one of the villagers would want with a pair of silver-mounted, big-roweled spurs, for there wasn't a single horse to be seen in the whole village, the only livestock being a few burros and a pair of oxen.

The women of the village cooked for them, grilling the meat on a grate inside a beehive oven, and making a dish of corn, chili, and the cheese. The three men ate all of the venison on the spot, along with everything else served to them. When they rode out of the village they were less hungry, but they only had a sack of dried ear corn in their saddlebags and three canteens filled with goat milk the villagers gave them in parting. Their salt was gone, their coffee was gone, and they had no prospects for resupplying those things in the near future.

Horn wanted to hunt, but game was scarce and they needed to travel fast. Gok had suggested the day before that they eat one of the spare horses, but Newt had thought they might trade it or sell it to buy supplies should they come across a town proper. The poor villagers in that mountain hamlet couldn't afford the price of a horse, and Horn had paid a single silver dollar and traded a handful of Horn's .45 Long Colt cartridges as payment for the food. The villagers hadn't asked to be paid, giving what they could spare freely, but they especially appreciated the cartridges. They only had one gun in the entire village and hadn't had any cartridges for it in more than a year. Newt couldn't imagine living in the middle of Apache country and roving slave traders without a single gun to defend themselves with. Gentle people with friendly ways, but they were tough, all right.

Gok thought that they would catch up to the Hatchet at any time, but the outlaw somehow kept ahead of them, towing along a dozen plus children, or not. Gok read the tracks like some men read books, and said that the Hatchet had the children tied in a line, neck to neck, walking until their moccasins wore out and their little feet began to bleed while his men rode. The last two days the Hatchet had made at least ten miles per day, and those kids had walked it all.

Horn may have claimed he was getting better, but he had talked little as of late. Sometimes he slept in the saddle, and sometimes he stared at the countryside ahead through red-rimmed eyes. But he stayed on horseback and he kept going without complaint. Newt didn't say so, but he admired that. The only thing Horn seemed to take pleasure in was sipping on the goat milk in his canteen. His upper lip was crusted with dried milk, and he smacked every time he took another swig.

The kid's cavalry hat was smashed and crumpled and had lost its shape, and his clothes were ragged. His white shirt, once so bright and clean back at the border, was soiled and torn and threadbare at the elbows. He had sewn the leg of his canvas pants that the Chiricahua had slit with bits of yucca leaves looped through the fabric and tied into knots to hold the knife slash closed. His crude seam didn't hold, and that pants leg flapped and flopped in the wind.

Newt knew that he looked no better. The travel and the miles were wearing on their clothes and gear like it was wearing on their minds. Goat milk or not, it needed to end.

* * *

The day after they left the village, the trio came in sight of the river again where it passed out of the tight confines of the canyon it ran through, and the country opened up into a narrow valley choked with brush and cactus. That meant more thorns and things to cut and stab you, and more things to tear your clothes and keep you from seeing too far ahead when you were lost in the brush.

Often, they rode to the top of hills or ridges, trying to get above the brush and find a good view of what lay ahead. It was on the top of one of those hills that they spied the smoke in the distance, maybe two miles ahead and near the river. It was an hour until sundown.

"Reckon that's them?" Horn asked.

"Maybe," Newt said.

"The Hatchet?" Horn asked the old warrior.

Gok nodded.

They rode cautiously toward that finger of smoke drifting upward in the distance and left their horses hobbled in a gully when they were still a quarter of a mile away. Horn remained with the horses, while Gok and Newt moved out on foot. Newt immediately wished he had a pair of moccasins like the other two wore instead of his boots. The Apache moved as quietly as a cat, and it wasn't only because of those moccasins. It was years of practice. He was at home in such a place, doing what they were doing, hunting and stalking men. Several times, Gok gave him dirty looks when he stumbled or made too much noise.

Later, Gok stopped and smelled the air. Newt had heard that an Apache could smell a man smoking a cigarette from a good distance away, or smell where one had been smoked as keenly as a bloodhound. It was hard to believe that a human's senses could be so keen.

And then Newt smelled it when the breeze shifted a little. Wood smoke. Faint, but wood smoke it was. They were very close.

When they eased up to the top of the next sharp-combed ridge, the camp was visible below them on the far side. It was dusk, but there was light enough to see what they wanted. It was the Hatchet's camp.

They waited for true nightfall, counting the Hatchet's men passing back and forth in the firelight. There were ten of them. They were loud and they were unworried. Only a single guard did they have out, and he looked half asleep where he sat near their horses. The only way they could make him out was by the glow of his cigarette ash every time he took a drag on it. That was a fool thing to do in Apache country.

Newt and Gok slipped closer, until they could see the shadows of the children sitting before the fire. They were still roped together, and one of the Hatchet's men was doling out bowls of some kind of stew or broth to them. The children drank from the bowls in silence.

Newt could see little detail about the children beyond that. It was too dark and their heads were down. Even if he had been closer he might not have been able to tell if one of them was the Redding boy. He wanted to move down the ridge to the very edge of the camp, but Gok saw what he was about to do and stopped him. Newt, after some thought and grumbling, decided it was too risky, and they moved back toward where they had left Horn and the horses.

Ten men against three—the odds weren't in their favor. But they had seen two things that might give them a chance. The Hatchet's guard was careless, and those outlaws had three bottles of tequila with them that they were imbibing freely from.

Newt looked up at the night sky when they got back to Horn and the horses. The moon was almost full. Good light to move among the brush quietly, and a good night for raiding.

But there were two problems that worried Newt, and that he couldn't figure his way around. One was how to move the children if they managed to regain them. There were eighteen of the kids, and they had no horses to mount them on other than the two spares Gok had taken from the *Rurales.* Eighteen kids, only five horses, and a week's hard run to the border while likely being pursued. That wasn't something pleasant to think on.

The other problem, the main problem, was how to defeat ten professional murderers and thieves without getting the children harmed in the fight. If they went in on the sneak and were discovered, there was going to be a fight. Surprise and shock would be on their side if they went in fast and hard, but again, they would risk the kids getting hurt. Neither option was acceptable except in the direst of straits. All he had thought of since leaving San Antonio was finding the boy. Now that he was finally there, he had no clue how to follow through with the rest of it. And time wasn't on his side. Every day he waited, the closer the Hatchet came to the larger towns and the coast. If the Hatchet made the Yaqui River with the children, he might load them on a boat to go downriver, and Newt would lose all chance of catching him.

They rode farther away from the Hatchet's camp before making camp, fearing the outlaws would hear it if one of their horses were to nicker. Newt was still thinking on how to get the kids back when they spread their blankets on the ground with no fire. The Hatchet's men were most likely to be sleeping soundly under the influence of that tequila, and maybe there was some way he could turn that to his advantage. The waiting and the doubt frustrated him greatly.

It was the wee hours of the morning before Newt's mental wrestling finally yielded an idea. It was chancy, but less chancy than anything he had thought of thus far. Odds were it wouldn't work, but maybe, just maybe . . .

He couldn't sleep, even after his plan was formed and the night was slowly turning toward day. He kept working that plan over and over in his mind. Horn seemed restless as well, tossing under his blanket and mumbling in his sleep.

But Gok had no problem sleeping, not since the

instant he first lay down on his blanket. Newt could tell by his snoring and wished he had thought to camp them farther away from the Hatchet's camp than he had. The old Apache's snoring could wake the dead.

Chapter Fourteen

"**A**re you ready for this?" Newt asked Horn.

"Let's get it done," Horn answered.

The sun was already an hour in the sky, and Gok was glaring at Newt, still unhappy that they hadn't attacked the Hatchet's camp in the twilight before dawn. Regardless of how calm the old warrior had been the day before and how contentedly he had slept through the night, he seemed unusually agitated that morning. There was a set to his mouth and something in those devilish eyes of his that Newt hadn't seen since Gok had sat and watched him hovering over that torture fire. Newt guessed that it was the nervousness of being so close to the children, yet not having them in hand.

And to make matters worse, Gok had slipped off before dawn to have one more look at the Hatchet's camp, returning with the news that his niece was among the captives.

And he had another thing to tell.

"*Y has visto un güerito tiene dias anos?*" Newt asked

him. Had he seen a ten-year-old white boy among the captives?

"*Sí,*" Gok said, and then he held two fingers up. "*Dos chicos Americano. Dos güeritos.*"

"*Dos chicos?*"

"*Sí, es verdad,*" Gok replied.

Newt went to his saddlebags and pulled out the photograph of Billy Redding and brought it back to show Gok. He tapped the photograph with his finger and asked, "*Este chico?*"

"*Sí,*" Gok said, and nodded adamantly.

Two *gringo* boys, and one of them was Billy Redding.

"We'd better get moving," Horn said.

Gok went against the impatience and seething anger he had been showing all morning and held them up by disappearing into the brush. They thought they heard him chanting or praying, but they could not be sure. When Gok returned a short time later, his face was painted for war— three horizontal lines drawn with his fingers where he had drug them across his eyes and the upper part of his face, two black lines and one white line that crossed over the bridge of his nose.

"What was he chanting about?" Newt asked.

"He was making medicine for war," Horn replied.

They rode five miles, stopping only once to survey the remains of the Hatchet's camp. The renegades had left early and their trail heading south was plain to see. Newt and his party circled wide to the east and did not swing back to the west until they were sure they were well past and ahead of the Hatchet. They rode on, looking behind them often, until they struck a road. Gok knew the road but not its name, and he could only say that it went down the Bavispe to Granados and then on to the silver mining camp of Soyopa on the Rio Yaqui.

Newt wondered if the mines at Soyopa were where the Hatchet intended to sell the children. Slavery had long been outlawed in Mexico, but it still went on, regardless of whatever laws were on the books.

The road passed between the river on the west, and a low mesa to the east with a tower of red sandstone rising up on top of it like the crown of a hat rising up from a hat brim. Horn dismounted and took his rifle out of its saddle scabbard.

"My mouth's dry," he said.

"That's because you're nervous," Newt said.

Newt was aware that Horn had been eyeing one of his two canteens hanging from his saddle all along, and the complaint about a dry mouth was probably a ploy.

"Mind if I have a swig of your goat milk before I go," Horn asked Newt. "I drank the last of mine yesterday, and I've got a pure craving for another taste of it."

Newt looked at the canteen containing the milk. There was only about a third of it left. "You don't want it."

"I wouldn't have asked you for it if I didn't want some," Horn said. "Here I am likely to die because of this damned plan of yours, and you're going to deny me a swig of milk that you haven't hardly touched since those Mexicans gave it to us. I'd say that's stingy."

"Go ahead if you've got to. I don't want it."

Horn unscrewed the cap on the canteen and turned the spout up to his lips. Just as quickly, he spat the milk out and began to gag. "It's spoiled!"

"That's why I let you have it."

Horn hung the canteen back on Newt's saddle horn and tried to spit the bad taste out of his mouth while he stared at Newt like he wanted to fight. "You're going to learn to appreciate me one of these days."

He gave Newt one sullen last look and left the road and headed up the side of the little mesa. Newt got off his horse and pulled his Winchester free. He opened the flap of one of his saddlebags and took out a box of cartridges that he stuffed in his coat pocket.

Gok rode his horse closer to Newt's and reached out and took up the canteen that held the spoiled milk. Newt started to say something, but didn't. Gok seemed to take that silence to mean that the milk was his, and rotten or not, he turned up the canteen and drank greedily and so long that he drained it dry. When he was finished he hung the canteen back on Newt's saddle horn, licked his lips, and gave a great belch.

"*Muy bueno*," he said when he looked at Newt again.

Newt didn't know what to think, but nothing Gok did should have surprised him. The hint of a wry smile formed on Gok's mouth and then was gone. He obviously enjoyed showing him how weak a white man was that couldn't drink blinky milk when they hadn't had a real meal since leaving the village upriver.

"You know what to do," Newt said in English.

It didn't matter that Gok couldn't understand him, for the old warrior knew what to do without being told. They had discussed it all in detail with Horn playing the translator, and kept discussing until they found the kind of spot along the road that Newt was looking for.

Newt took a stand in the timber and brush along the river not fifty yards from the road. Gok went on down the road with their horses and tied them in a thicket past the point where the road was pinched between that hat-shaped mesa and the river. He rode his own horse back toward their ambush site, and when he was at the place they had chosen he stopped and waited.

Newt watched Gok from behind a cottonwood trunk on the riverbank and wondered if he could pull it off. Horn had said that the Apache were crafty fighters and admired nothing more than a smartly laid trap. Well Gok was about to get his chance to show how crafty he was.

It was a cool fall day, but Gok had stripped to nothing but his breechcloth, his moccasins, and that silver-mounted gunbelt. A wide cloth headband held back his hair from his forehead. He had left his sightless Springfield rifle back with the other horses. Instead of the rifle, he held only an empty glass tequila bottle in his hand—a bottle he had found in the Hatchet's camp.

When Gok saw the Hatchet's dust cloud coming from the north he took up the blanket lying across his horse's withers and draped it over his head and shoulders. Sometime later, when the lead riders from the Hatchet's gang were in sight, he slumped on his horse's back and bowed his head enough that his face was hidden from view. The empty tequila bottle hung at the end of one arm as if he were about to drop it. To all intents and purposes he looked like he was drunk and had fallen asleep in the middle of the road.

And that's how he was supposed to look.

The Hatchet had four of his men riding point as a vanguard. They drew up when they saw Gok. They were at first cautious, but soon they yelled out to him. Gok did not answer but remained slumped on his horse.

The lead riders came on, with the rest of their party lagging a little behind out of caution. The Hatchet's procession was now close enough that Newt could make them all out, from the riders to either side, to the ones riding rear guard, and the line of children sandwiched in the middle and walking in single-file. Those children were yoked neck to neck with rope and some kind of collars around their necks, exactly as Gok had predicted from the tracks he read days earlier. There were eighteen children, and from the size of them, their ages ranged from maybe six to twelve or so, both boys and girls. Most of them had literally walked right out of their moccasins, and their raw feet shuffled through the road dust while their filthy faces stared ahead of them blankly and hopelessly.

The point riders stopped once more, this time a little more than a hundred yards from Gok. Again, he did not answer their calls.

Two more riders left their positions riding to either side of the children and joined the point riders. The rest of the renegades remained behind. Newt looked for the one called the Hatchet, but either the outlaw did not come forward, or Newt was unable to recognize him from the stories Horn had told.

The Hatchet's gang was a mixed lot of *gringos*, Mexicans, and Indians and half-breeds. Several of them wore bandoliers of cartridges across their chests, and all manner of weapons were draped upon their persons and saddles. A Mexican in a big felt *sombrero* called out for Gok to clear the road.

When the Apache didn't respond, a white man with a red beard and a potbelly bulging out from between his suspenders rode a little forward of the others. He had a falling block, single-shot Remington-Hepburn sporting rifle propped upright on one thigh.

He shouldered the weapon and took a long time aiming, making a show of it for his friends, but his bullet only struck the road well beyond Gok when he finally fired. He was either an exceptionally poor shot or had been merely trying to scare Gok off. Knowing the kind of men they were,

Newt guessed that he was a poor shot, long-range fancy gun or not.

Gok kept his nerve and did not run away, but he took advantage of his horse shying from the ricocheting bullet. He let the animal spin around and made like he almost fell off its back and had a hard time getting things under control. Once the horse was still, he took a mock slug from the empty bottle and looked up at the outlaws as if seeing them for the first time.

"You missed," one of the outlaws said, and the other men laughed.

"Just trying to scare him," the man with the red beard growled.

"Drunk-ass Indian doesn't have sense enough to get gone. Bet you can't shoot that whiskey bottle out of his hand."

The one with the red beard ejected his empty shell case and was thumbing in another cartridge and getting his Hepburn ready. Gok wasn't about to risk sitting there and letting them shoot at him again, no matter how badly that one shot. He took another fake slug from his empty bottle and let out a drunken, crazy war cry that sounded somewhere between a squalling tomcat and sick rooster. He kicked his horse up to a trot and aimed directly for the renegades at the front of the line. He made sure to totter from one side of the horse to the other with his head wobbling as if his neck were made of red India rubber.

The renegades' concern had shifted to hilarity, and instead of shooting Gok they let him come closer, offering bets as to whether the drunk Indian would fall off his horse or not before he got to them.

A tall man on a pale gray horse rode forward to join the men in the front. Or maybe he wasn't so tall as he seemed. It could have been how rail thin and long limbed he was that made him seem that way. He wore a white felt *sombrero* on his head, and a belted red wool poncho or *serape* covered his torso. But his likeness to the Mexicans in his gang ended there. He was a different creature by far, as if you had slung bits and pieces of three or four different kinds of men together. He wore his hair in two long braids, one hanging over either shoulder Indian-style. The tallest pair of boots that Newt had ever seen was on his feet, and the tops came well past his knees. Such boots were usually only seen in antique oil paintings of dashing cavalry officers from the Continent.

The newcomer tilted his head back to get the brim of his *sombrero* out of the way, and the sun flashed on his face. It took Newt a moment to realize the man was wearing some kind of spectacles with strange orange lenses. The tall man coughed and then said something to those gathered beside him that made them laugh.

Gok pulled his horse up barely twenty yards from them. He hurled the bottle at them and managed to strike the tall man's gray horse on the end of the nose. The horse crabbed backward on its haunches and slung its head and reared up.

While the tall one in the funny glasses was trying

to stay on his frightened horse, Gok let out another war cry and reined his pony around and lit out of there in a run.

For a wonder, none of them fired on him in that instant. They were cursing him and shouting all kinds of vile threats, but nobody shot until he was already well away and leaning low over his pony's neck. The frantic horse belonging to the man in the orange glasses was creating such a storm that they crashed into each other's horses and jostled each other in an attempt to get a shot at Gok.

Seeing that he was rapidly putting distance on them and in a fury, all six of them chased after him, with only the tall man in the orange glasses and three others left behind with the captive children. The Mexican who had first called out to Gok had the fastest horse among them, and he rapidly took the lead. He had drawn a machete from a saddle scabbard and was pointing it forward like he was leading some cavalry charge and not simply a bad man full of bloodlust to hack one poor drunk Indian to pieces.

Gok let his pony run, but he held back on his reins enough to keep them feeling like they had a chance to catch him. They were only a long stone's throw behind him when he passed through the narrowest point between the hat-shaped mesa and the river. A couple of the pursuers lost patience in ever running Gok down and laying hands on him, and fired at him. But shooting a pistol from the back of a running horse was no easy thing, and they missed. Bullets whipped the air all around the Apache.

Gok let the blanket fly from his shoulders, and it spread out like a kite and sailed directly into the Mexican, tangling his machete in it and covering his horse's head. The horse immediately propped on its front legs and came to a jarring halt and began bucking. The Mexican *bandito* was no bronc rider, and he was thrown to the ground.

Horn's rifle bellowed from up on the mesa in that very same instant, and another of the Hatchet's men reeled in the saddle and his horse went wild off the road. Newt leaned out around the cottonwood tree and shot another of the renegades, knocking him from the saddle.

It took that second shot for the Hatchet's men to realize they had ridden into a trap, but it took them moments that they didn't have to get their horses stopped and headed back the other way. Again Horn's rifle boomed, and Newt worked the lever on his Winchester as rapidly as he could, shooting into the milling men in the road. Loose horses were running everywhere.

Two of the renegades rode into the brush between the road and the foot of the mesa. They had spotted Newt and fired at him from cover. A bullet slapped the tree trunk at belly button level not six inches from Newt. He flinched and ducked behind the tree as other bullets cut through the thicket around him. But the renegades in the brush on the far side had not spotted Horn up on the mesa, and they were easy pickings for him from that high vantage point. He shot the first one, and the impact of his bullet striking the man between the shoulder blades slammed him over the front of his saddle.

Horn fired a second time and missed, but he did manage to flush the other renegade back out into the road. Newt leaned out around the cotton-wood trunk again and shot at him. The outlaw screamed and clutched at his leg, and his horse broke into a run. Though hit hard, he stayed in the saddle and whipped his horse toward those of his gang who had remained behind. Both Horn and Newt missed shots at him.

And then Gok was coming back at a dead run, and he slowed little before he bailed off his horse on the fly. The momentum of that dismount gave him foot speed, and he charged toward the Mexi-can with the machete who was then getting to his feet. Gok had his knife in one hand and his pistol in the other. The Mexican saw him too late. He raised that machete over his head intending to chop down on Gok and split him in two, but the Apache had already closed with him and was inside the reach of that long blade. Gok plunged his knife into the Mexican bandit's right armpit and stuck his pistol in his belly and pulled the trig-ger at the same time. Gok had withdrawn the knife and was leaping off the road and into the brush before the Mexican bandit's body hit the ground.

The first of the Hatchet's men that Horn had shot had his horse parked on the edge of the road and was so wounded that he couldn't sit upright in the saddle. Gok sped out of the brush at his side as if he had never once quit running and leaped at him. He landed astride the horse behind the renegade's saddle and pressed his pistol into the renegade's side and pulled the trigger two times. Then he shoved the renegade's limp body to the ground and took his place in the saddle and rode back into the brush.

It was a good time to take cover, for the remaining men in the Hatchet's gang were firing upon them from up the road. They had spotted both Newt and Horn, and they sent a hailstorm of bullets their way. All Newt could do was to hunker down behind the cottonwood, but Horn had the high ground and was farther away from the gang. He shifted positions often on the mesa, taking advantage of the rough terrain and taking potshots at the gang. Gok fired from somewhere in the brush between the road and Horn's position, and the combined firepower of he and Horn drove the remaining outlaws farther up the road. Soon the gunfire slackened until it was nothing at all.

Chapter Fifteen

The outlaw bunch was caught in a bad position. They were on low ground and out in the open, and they had no idea how many men they faced. They most likely thought it was an Apache war party that had ambushed them, exactly as Newt had intended. They could take to the brush on one side of the road or find cover along the riverbank on the other and fight it out, but the last thing any man but a fool wanted was to have an Apache war party able to use that same cover to close on them.

Newt watched it all and knew this was the gamble he had taken. There was no way they were going to get all of the gang, and his plan had been to separate the Hatchet's forces and weaken him to the point that he would leave the children behind. Sounded good when you said it, but he wasn't sure if the whole damned thing wasn't about to backfire on him.

The Hatchet's men had disappeared to the

sides of the road, whether intending to fight from there or simply getting out of sight of Horn's rifle while they talked things over, Newt didn't know. The children remained in the road. Maybe they were too scared to move, or their captors wouldn't let them leave it. And that was one more problem. It was going to be hard to smoke that gang out for fear of hitting the kids.

Newt began to work his way along the riverbank toward the children. It was slow going, and despite the dense cover provided by the vegetation along the river, he expected any second for one of the outlaws to spot him and take a shot at him.

It took him the better part of half an hour to work his way upriver, moving low and sometimes on hands and knees. All the while, the children remained in the road. Some of them were even sitting on the ground. Horn fired a shot from the mesa, purposely aiming high at the riverbank side of the road opposite the children. His shot wasn't returned.

Newt was barely ten yards from the children. He saw something move on the far side of the road, closer to the children, and immediately assumed it was some of the slave-trading trash who had stolen them. He raised his rifle and waited.

Gok appeared from the brush and knelt beside one of the children, a girl. The Apache was tense and constantly scanning around him while he spoke to the little girl. She was obviously Chirica-hua or some other kind of Apache, for Newt could hear enough of their murmuring to tell the sounds of the dialect.

Gok whispered orders to the rest of the children while he tried to pull the girl to her feet. Frightened and confused, the children were slow to respond. Some of them smiled at the sight of Gok, but most of the others only gave him blank expressions or cringed from him. The rope linking them together made it hard to get them on their feet and coordinated.

Newt scanned the road beyond them and to either side of it. He expected Gok to be gunned down at any minute, but no shot came. Either the Hatchet's men had retreated, or they were waiting to draw out more of the Apache they thought were with Gok. Not a saddle horse was in sight, nor was the handful of pack mules that the slave traders had used to carry their gear.

Taking a chance, Newt stepped out onto the road. He kept his back to the children when he reached them, still looking for signs of the enemy. He kept shifting his attention from one face to another, looking for the Redding boy.

There were both Mexican and Indian children among the captives, but it was hard to tell one from the other. They all looked the same in both condition and misery.

Many of them were half naked, but so filthy with grime and road dust and burned by the sun and weather that they were almost identical in skin color. They carried blankets and scraps of blankets to cover them, or bits of buckskin and filthy cotton rags that were the last remains of what they had been wearing when they were captured. Some wore nothing but outsized adult shirts hanging nearly to their knees and the sleeves flopping past their hands like scarecrows.

A flash of a bit of grimy, pale face caught Newt's attention near the end of the line. He went closer and took hold of the boy and rubbed away the filth with his thumb and saw that it was indeed a white boy. Tears were streaming out of the boy's eyes and leaving streaks down his grubby cheeks while his mouth trembled.

"Billy? Are you Billy Redding?" Newt asked.

The boy didn't answer him and tried to look down at the ground. Newt grabbed his chin and forced his head back.

"Billy Redding," Newt said again.

The boy blinked and another flood of tears poured forth.

It was the boy he sought, Newt was sure of it. In the photograph the boy was sitting in an upholstered chair in some parlor, wearing a suit and with his dark hair oiled and combed—clean and unafraid, with a sack of hard rock candy on his lap that his mother and father had probably bribed him with to sit still for the camera. Now his hair was tangled and matted, and he was wearing one of those men's shirts five times too big for him. He immediately looked down at his bare toes sticking out from under the tail of the shirt when Newt released his chin. A tiny boy for his age, and too scared to talk, but Newt was sure it was the Redding boy.

Gok hissed something at Newt to get his attention and then motioned him off the road. Together, they hustled the children into the brush. Gok led them on a winding course until they found a relatively bare spot in the midst of a dense thicket.

Gok signaled for the children to sit down while Newt knelt and watched their back trail. He could see only glimpses of the road through the brush.

"*Se fueron,*" Gok said.

Newt did not understand Gok's Spanish.

Gok pointed in the direction of the road and gave a wave of one hand to the north. Then he made a walking motion with two fingers and pointed again in the same direction. "*Se fueron.*"

From the hand signs Newt understood that Gok believed that what was left of the Hatchet's men had fled upriver. That fit with what Newt had already come to believe.

They remained hidden, waiting. Horn could see a large swath of country from the mesa, and they would trust to him to let them know when it was safe. If they heard him shoot they could work deeper into the brush and try to elude pursuit that way.

Newt heard horses walking up the rode from the south an hour later, and then Horn called out to them. Gok got the children on their feet, and Newt led them back to the road.

Horn was leading their own horses and driving several more in front of him. He stopped when he saw Newt emerge from the brush.

"I kept watch to make sure they went on, then it took me a while to round up all the horses I could," Horn said.

The collars on the kids' necks were made of a strap of leather fastened with a single rivet, much like a dog collar. There was also a harness ring to run the rope through to string them together. Gok and Newt cut the collars off with their knives. Some of the collars were loose enough to make it easy to slip a blade between the collar and the child's neck, but others were tighter. Regardless, it was a painful process for all of them. The children's necks were chafed and red-raw from the collars.

Most of the Apache children took the pain without complaint, and usually without so much as flinching. Billy Redding, on the other hand, cried and whimpered and squirmed when Newt tried to remove his collar. Newt had his hands full trying not to cut him while holding him still at the same time. He was busy with such when somebody said something behind him.

"I'm sure glad to see you, mister." It was a kid's voice.

Newt finished cutting the Redding boy's collar free before he looked around. It was another small boy. It took Newt a moment to realize he was a *gringo* child. The kid was stockier than Billy Redding with a sharp nose, big eyes, and chin like a little barroom brawler. He looked up at Newt with something akin to anger written all over his face. He wore a crude sack shirt that hung to his thighs, a breechcloth, and what was left of a pair of Apache-style moccasins. Instead of an Apache headband, he had found a castoff rag and used it to cover his head in place of a hat. Had the boy stood on the deck of a sailing ship he could have passed for a tiny pirate. Wisps of red hair stuck out from under that pirate rag.

"They were going to sell us," the boy said.

"I reckon they were," Newt answered.

The boy spit as a sign of disgust. "I tried to run away from them twice, but they caught me every time."

"What's your name?"

"Charlie. Charlie McComas."

"What'd you say, boy?" Horn asked, having overheard him.

"Charlie McComas."

The name seemed to have some impact on Horn, but he didn't elaborate. Instead, he busied himself with catching horses and getting the kids up on their backs.

There were eighteen kids, and Horn had managed to round up four of the outlaws' horses. Those four horses, plus the two spares that Gok had taken from the *Rurales*, made six. Most of the children were small, so they mounted them double and triple as needed, putting the older or stronger children at the back to help keep the younger ones calm and in place.

Gok was already on his horse with the little Apache girl he had been talking to earlier behind him. Newt thought to do the same with Billy Redding, but the boy fought him, whether because he didn't want to get on the horse or because there had been too many hands on him during his captivity, Newt didn't know.

"Let me help," Charlie McComas said.

Charlie took hold of one of Billy's arms. "We got to go now."

Billy calmed somewhat, but still stared at Newt with big, scared eyes.

"Your daddy sent me to get you," Newt said to Billy.

"Papa?" That was the first word the boy had spoken.

"And your grandma Matilda," Newt added.

Billy began to tear up again, but Charlie soothed him. Instead of mounting Billy behind him, Newt put him in front of Charlie on one of Gok's horses. Billy clutched the big Charro saddle horn with both hands and never said another word or looked at Newt again. His mouth hadn't stopped trembling. Charlie McComas reached around him and took the reins.

"You two stick close to me," Newt said.

"You think they're up there somewhere waiting to waylay us?" Charlie asked.

Newt understood that Charlie was asking about the Hatchet's men. He looked to Horn. "Did you see that Hatchet fellow with them?"

"I saw him, and you did, too," Horn said.

Newt looked down the road behind him at the bodies lying there.

Horn saw him looking and shook his head. "We didn't get him, if that's what you're asking."

Newt considered that, thinking aloud. "Couldn't be but four or five of them left, and you hit one of them."

"Yeah but the Hatchet ain't one to go forgetting what we did to him today."

"He's real mean," Charlie butted in.

"Which one was he?" Newt asked, but he had a good idea already.

"Ain't no man I ever saw dresses like him," Horn said.

"Let me guess," Newt said. "The man in the orange glasses."

"That's him."

"Give me gun, mister, and I'll help you fight him," said Charlie. "I'd rather be whipped with a switch twice a day than let him take me again. You didn't see what he did to an Apache woman with that hatchet of his."

"I saw it, boy," Newt said, and it pained his heart to think that such a little boy had to see such things.

Gok had started north, and the children fell in behind him, with Horn and Newt riding in the rear. Newt kept close watch on Billy and Charlie.

They left the road in a short while, and Gok led them through a mesquite-choked valley and over the top of a low ridge. Once over the ridge he turned north once more, paralleling the road most times, but with the ridge keeping them out of sight of it and anyone on it. Without asking, Newt knew that Gok thought there was a likely chance that the Hatchet could be lying in wait somewhere on that road.

Horn's foot must have been better, for he was more his usual self, talking to the children to try to lift their spirits, or simply talking because he loved to talk. Newt knew that Horn thought the worst of it was over, and that had as much to do with his good mood as his healing wounds. Horn thought they were done and on the downhill stretch, with nothing left except to ride back to the States and hand the boy over to his family and listen to everyone call them heroes.

Newt knew better. It never was that easy. He looked to the north at the way ahead and saw nothing but mountains and mile after mile of scrub brush and nothing. And more nothing, as far as the eye could see, all the way to tomorrow and on to the rest of the days to come. That out there was danger. You didn't measure that kind of journey in miles. You took its measure by surviving it. You survived it by winning any way you could, and you won by surviving.

It wasn't over by a long shot. Wouldn't be over until he took the boy back to Matilda, and there were a million things besides the Hatchet that could stop them. Trouble around the bend, waiting to see if they could take it. Newt could feel it in his bones. Like his dear departed ma had always said, the Devil never rests, and he rides some men more than others. If it wasn't one thing it would be something else. There was always trouble, since the day he was born.

Gok's laughter drew Newt back into the here and now. It was quiet laughter because Gok was too much of a warrior to risk an enemy hearing him when he was running and hiding, but it was laughter just the same. And it was Horn that made him laugh.

Newt listened to the rest of the story Horn was telling, and listened to them all chuckle when the punch line came, even many of the children who had nothing much to laugh about in a long, long time. Horn didn't know it, but his story caused even Newt to crack a smile. Newt would have laughed with them, but he held it in because that was his habit. He would have told Horn thanks, but Horn wouldn't understand what he was thanking him for.

Newt looked to the north, toward the border again. To hell with trouble, and to hell with the Hatchet or anybody else that thought they could stop him. Three hundred miles wasn't all that far. If the Devil was going to ride him, well, he better take a deep seat and a faraway look, because it was going to be a long hard ride.

Chapter Sixteen

Gok changed directions the morning of their second day with the children. Instead of continuing northward he led them to the east into the big mountains again. The Bavispe River's course was in the shape of a "U," flowing northward from its source on the Chihuahua line until it made a great bend around the northern end of the Sierra Madre sixty miles short of the border. It flowed southward from there, down the other side of those great mountains on its long journey to merge into the Yaqui River. They had recovered the children on the western side, and Gok intended to cross over and rejoin the river and then follow that valley to the border.

His thinking was that it would be harder for anyone to track them in the rough breaks of the high country, and they were less likely to run across Mexican army patrols or any other enemies that might be more than glad to find so many

Apache children with only one warrior and two worn-out white men to protect them.

Newt was concerned that they would lose some of the horses in the high country, if his last trip over those mountains was any indication, or have to abandon them completely. But Gok insisted. He said that his people would be gathering soon to go back to the reservation, and if they hurried they could catch up to them and ride with them back to the border to meet the American army waiting to escort them back to their final destination. He also said that there were many villages and towns along that leg of the river, and that Newt or Horn might go to one of them and buy supplies. Newt didn't know the country, and there was merit in Gok's plan, regardless of Newt's concerns about the horses and being put afoot so far away from the border.

So into the mountains it was, climbing and always climbing. Horses or not, it was so rough at times that they had to dismount and lead the horses. Soon, all was forgotten but the demands of putting one foot in front of the other. After a day of such travel the horses, men, and children were worn out. They made camp in a wide-bottomed swag between two knobs sloping up to a bald granite peak, not because it was a good camping place, but because they could go no farther. Newt guessed the camp was somewhere above four or five thousand feet of elevation.

The children collapsed to the ground almost as

soon as they slid from the horses' backs and their
feet touched the ground. Newt went to each of
them in turn.

"Drink, boy," Newt said. "You need to drink."

Billy Redding turned up the half cupful of water
Newt had been holding out for him and took a sip.
Not the whole cupful, but a sip. All of the other
children had practically snatched the cup away
from him and sucked down their portion with
greedy gulps.

Billy hadn't said anything since those few words
he had spoken when Newt had informed him that
his father had sent him after Billy. Some of the
other children were traumatized to the point they
were a bit shaky and probably not as they had been
before being taken captive, but Billy was the worst
of them. Newt guessed that maybe the boy had
been treated more roughly than the others, or
maybe the change from being a rich man's son to
an Apache captive, to being stolen once more by
slave traders was too much for him. In Newt's
experience, most people could only take so much.

The kid seemed to be free of any major injuries,
and he didn't seem sick, yet he wouldn't eat unless
made to, and now he didn't want to drink. They
had ridden a dry trail for almost two days with
nothing but four canteens and two canvas water
bags to water that many horses, eighteen kids, and
three men. The men did without, the kids got a
ration of a half-cup of water occasionally, and the

gaunt horses drank the rest. All of them, men and beasts, were thirsty, except for Billy.

The oldest child among the rescued captives was a Mexican girl wearing what had once been a pretty blue dress. The bottom of it had been torn off, and Newt realized that it was the same fabric as what covered Charlie McComas's head. Her face was bruised and she walked with a severe limp, and looked as if she had seen some rough treatment from the Hatchet's men. That being said, she and the McComas boy seemed to have weathered their ordeal better than the others. She took the cup from Newt and continued giving the rest of the children their ration of water.

Newt looked back to Billy Redding and saw that the boy had lain down on the ground and curled up into a ball on his side with both arms around his knees.

"He thinks he's dead," Horn said from where he was building a fire. "Seen it before, but maybe he'll snap out of it."

"Give him time," Newt said. "They've been through a lot."

Charlie McComas was helping Gok unsaddle the horses.

"Now that's a tough one," Horn said.

"That he is."

"You know who he is, don't you?"

"He didn't say."

Horn gave an ironical grunt. "All those licks on the head you've taken in the boxing ring must have rattled your noggin. That there is Charlie McComas, Judge McComas's boy. Everybody thought he was dead."

"Reckon that judge will be glad to get him back."

"No, the judge is really dead. Chatto's Chiricahuas killed him and the boy's mother last spring and ran off with the boy," Horn said. "Judge McComas had plenty of political connections, and his wife's brother is a Kansas senator or some such. That boy there is the main reason the army come down here last spring."

"Well, there he is in the flesh."

"Old Nantan Lupan will have a conniption fit when he finds out we got Charlie. The newspapers and the politicians gave him hell for coming back without the boy," Horn said.

"Hard to find anything down here, much less keep it. Who's Nantan Lupan?"

"That's what the Apaches call General Crook. Means chief wolf, or the big bad boss wolf, or something like that."

Newt saw Gok's head turn at the mention of that name, and he noticed the flash of anger it caused.

"The general didn't try all that hard to find the boy, maybe because he didn't believe we would ever find him, or because he had other things on his mind. But we asked about Charlie after we got the Apaches to surrender," Horn said. "One of the squaws claimed that the boy had been alive and well up to the point we hit Chatto's camp right before the surrender. Most of the Apaches got away from us that day, and we never even knew that the boy was in the camp. But he was, only he didn't get far before one of the warriors running from us stopped long enough to smash in his head with a rock. You see, our White Mountain scouts got trigger happy and shot a squaw during that fight, and the warrior killed the boy in retaliation."

Newt thought about the freshly healed scar at the edge of Charlie's hairline that he had seen the first time the boy removed his pirate rag. It was about the size of what a big rock would make.

"The McComas family put up a big reward for the boy," Horn added. "We stand to make a tidy profit if they'll still pay."

"We've got a long ways to go yet."

"What are they paying you to bring the Redding boy back?"

Instead of answering, Newt walked over to help Charlie and Gok finish with the horses.

"Know'd it. They're paying you a king's ransom, ain't they? That's why you come down here," Horn called after him. "I should have asked you for five hundred dollars instead of three, but I wasn't sure you could afford it, and I never thought it would go this far. Thought I would guide you down below the border for a few days and you would see that it was no use and want to go back to the States and say what a big try you had made to get the boy back. Sounded like easy money then."

Newt pitched a saddle on the ground and looked at him without saying anything.

"Some kind of hero, ain't I?" Horn clucked his tongue and shook his head.

"Think what stories you'll have to tell when you get back," Newt said.

The mention of stories caused Horn to break into a long and rambling tale about his boyhood on a Missouri farm and a favorite dog of his. Newt only caught parts of the story because he was watching the children. They had lain down close to the little fire Horn had built. It was cold at night that high up and that late in the year, and instead of sleeping separately the children had piled together like a litter of puppies and covered themselves with blankets. Newt wondered whether it was the cold or the captivity they had shared that made them sleep that way.

Gok sat on the ground close to them with his niece on his lap. The little girl was asleep with her head resting on his chest and her arms around his neck. He was stroking her hair, lost in thought.

"*Enjuh*," he said when he saw Newt watching him.

The next morning they were rigging makeshift blanket ponchos for the children when Charlie McComas came into camp carrying a stick in one hand and six dead pack rats in the other. The boy pitched them on the ground beside the fire and went and got Newt's skillet out of the saddlebags.

Newt finished cutting a slit in the middle of the blanket he was working on and slid it over Billy's head. He pointed at the rats. "What you got there, Charlie?"

"Breakfast."

Horn saw the way Newt responded to that and laughed. "Never ate rat, Jones?"

"No."

"Apaches favor it."

"Apaches like mule, too, and I don't think they're one to recommend what I eat."

"You'll eat it if you're hungry as I am." Horn stepped closer to watch the boy work.

Charlie raked some coals out of the fire and set the skillet on them. He held out a hand to Newt. "I don't have a knife."

Newt gave him his. "Be careful, it's sharp."

Charlie wrinkled his nose as if that was a foolish thing to say, then he forgot about Newt and began to skin and gut the rats like he had done it many times before. He put the cleaned carcasses of the little rodents in the skillet and squatted down to tend to his cooking. He was so tiny and so intent on his work, with his tongue sticking out of one corner of his mouth, that it caused Newt to chuckle.

Horn walked over to Newt. "He's an independent little scamp. Hunts and takes care of himself like an Apache boy. Guess he's already learned some things living with them."

Once the rat meat was done, Charlie supervised the distribution of the portions to each child. He was obviously proud of his accomplishment.

Some got legs and some got ribs and back. None of the children seemed to have any qualms about eating rat. The smell of the cooked meat even gave Billy an appetite. Gok and Horn were next, and they attacked their share with equal gusto, sucking the bones after they had stripped the meat off, then sucking the juice from their fingers to savor the flavor as long as they could.

"Only problem with that is there ain't enough of it," Horn said.

Charlie held out a fat hind rat leg to Newt.

"You eat it, or give it to one of the other kids," Newt said.

"Eat," Charlie said. "It's good."

All of the children, as well as Gok and Horn, were watching him. Newt was as hungry as any of them, but there was little to go around. He would rather one of the kids get a little more but knew that he was going to lose face in front of Gok and the Apache children if they saw that he thought he was too good to eat a rat.

He bit into the hot little morsel and then ate some more. Newt had eaten many things during hard times, and once he had lived on nothing but rattlesnake for days. Never had he eaten rat, but it was surprisingly good. The rat leg was reduced to nothing but a slick bone almost as quickly as the children had cleaned up their shares.

"Not bad, huh?" Horn asked.

"Not at all, but I'd guess you'd have to call it

something else on the menu if you were ever going to serve it in a restaurant," Newt replied.

"It's better if you can boil them in a pot," Charlie said.

Newt looked at Charlie and nodded at him. "You'll do to ride the river with, boy. You'll do."

After their scanty meal, they gave the children another ration of water, finishing off the last of it. They mounted the children and started up the mountain, as usual with Gok leading the way as if he were half mountain goat.

Two hours later they found water, and at midday they crossed over the mountain and below them lay the valley near the headwaters of the Rio Bavispe. They could see for miles and miles from their vantage point, and of great interest were the adobe walls of a good-size village on the bank of the river. Of even more interest was the sound of a cavalry bugle carrying clear and far in the thin air.

Chapter Seventeen

There was Mexican cavalry down there, but they needed supplies and they needed to turn over the six Mexican children to someone. It was decided that Newt would go down the mountain with those children, while Horn and Gok remained hidden in the mountains and guarded the rest of them.

Gok didn't especially like the idea. For one, Newt suspected that he would have liked to keep all the children to take back among his Apache friends and family. And the other reason was that Gok feared the children would talk and put the army on the lookout for him. The latter was a concern that Newt had himself.

And Gok wasn't the only one who was upset about the plan. Although young Billy had shown little interest in Newt to that point, he came and clung to Newt's leg the instant it became apparent that the big man was leaving.

Newt pried him loose and held him at arm's

length by both shoulders. Charlie had come to help with Billy, but he stopped and stared at them both.

"You boys listen to me," Newt said. "You stick close to the fire and stay warm, and mind what Mr. Horn tells you."

"You won't come back." Billy sniffled and rubbed at his freckled nose.

Newt was somewhat shocked that the boy had actually spoken and uncomfortable with the way Billy was looking at him. "Don't you worry, I'll be back by nightfall."

Charlie put a hand on Billy's arm.

"Don't go," Billy pleaded.

"Got to," Newt said. "Now you boys do like I said."

Charlie pried Billy away and guided him back a few steps. "Don't worry. We'll be right here."

"All right, Charlie. I'm trusting you to kind of look out for Billy."

"Can I have a gun?"

"No, you get Mr. Horn to do any shooting you need."

Charlie's little chin jutted out. "I'm big enough."

Newt unbuckled his gunbelt and slid his knife scabbard off of it. He handed Charlie the knife. "Might be that you need to skin some more rats. Take care you don't cut yourself."

Charlie nodded and his face lit up like a kid at a candy counter.

Uncomfortable with the way both of the boys

were looking at him, Newt mounted the Circle Dot horse and rode over to Horn and Gok. "You get gone fast if I'm not back by nightfall."

He went down off the mountain, with him leading the Circle Dot horse and letting the six Mexican children take turns on its back. They reached the outskirts of the town of Bacerac under a gray sky, with the clouds overhead forming a marble ceiling that made it appear that the sky went no farther than the tops of the mountains. It was nearing the end of the monsoon season, and Newt thought it might rain.

He was met at the edge of the town by a troop of Mexican cavalry, and after a few questions that he struggled to answer he was escorted to the central plaza. Within minutes, it seemed as if half the town had crowded around him. Again, he struggled with his Spanish, but the children told most of the story for him. Women tried to reach up and hug his waist, and the men wanted to shake his hands. The people were especially happy that two of the children belonged to families from that town. The parents of the children were called for, and when they arrived they wept and crossed themselves in the Catholic way and lifted their arms to the sky in thanks. And they hugged their children and smiled teary-eyed smiles at Newt and called him Don Valiente. Others in the crowd took up that name.

"*Gracias a Dios por Don Valiente!*" they called out. Thank the Lord for brave gentlemen. Newt grunted and scoffed at that. He tried to slip from the crowd and avoid answering more of the soldiers' questions, and he was almost out of the plaza when he saw Colonel Herrera leaning against a support post under the *ramada* of a large adobe building.

"*Buenos tardes, Capitán,*" the colonel said.

There was no sense in Newt acting like he hadn't seen or heard the colonel, so Newt went over to him. But he didn't have the gall to salute the colonel like Horn had back in Janos. "*Buenos tardes, Coronel.*"

Colonel Herrera pointed over Newt's shoulder at the crowd in the plaza still celebrating and making over the children. "It appears that you are a hero."

"Not by a long shot."

"Ah, such modesty." The colonel clucked his tongue and shook his head as if he didn't believe Newt. He bent at the waist slightly in a mock bow, and there was equal mockery in his voice. "*Te saludo, Don Valiente.*"

"It wasn't that big of a deal."

The colonel nodded again, as if that was something he did agree with. "And where did you find these children, if I may ask?"

Newt had already prepared the lie. He gestured vaguely to the southeast. "I ran on to a little camp of Apaches and traded for the children."

"What did you trade?"

"Huh?"

"I said, what did you trade?"

"Money, horses, some tequila . . ." Newt said. "And a few trinkets and such. You know."

The colonel clucked his tongue again. "No, I do not know. This is why I ask you. How is this that you bring back these children?"

"Luck, I guess."

"Yes, much luck you have." Newt started to leave, but the colonel refused to let it go. "I don't believe you. These people . . . these silly people may believe you, but I do not."

"You believe what you want to," Newt said. "It was you that told me you didn't have an Apache problem."

The colonel's eyes narrowed slightly, and Newt saw what he had seen before in the colonel—that he was quick to anger and a petty, prideful man. "The Apache are no problem for me, I assure you. Everyone knows this."

"Well, I'll leave you to it."

The colonel held up a hand to stop him. "What of your friends, Lieutenant Horn and your Apache scout?"

"Lieutenant Horn was called back to the border, and the scout went with him." So much lying was beginning to grate on Newt, and he realized that he was holding his breath before he spoke.

"I would ask you more, far more, *Capitán Jones*, but these people think you are a different man than what we both know," the colonel said in a lowered voice as a priest and several of the children passed by. "I don't think you are an officer at all.

Comprende? Me entiendas? I think you are . . . how do you say . . . *un impostor? Un bandito?*"

"You think what you want to think."

"There is this barman you beat in Janos, and now you bring these children and say how you rescue them and do this miraculous thing all by yourself. Maybe you took these children and bring them back and think the town will pay you some ransom or reward. Maybe you think we all say what a brave and good man you are. Maybe you come down here to make me look bad. No? Maybe this is how you think. *Que no? Es verdad? Usted cree que puede hacer esto a mi? Ah, como se dice* . . . You think you can do this, and I will not be bothered? You think this is your country to do as you will?"

"Seems like you're doing all the thinking."

"This is no *gringo* country. You do not belong here," the colonel said. "Some men like you, I always show them that they cannot do these things. Ask the people, they will tell you this is true. Colonel Herrera, he is no man to trifle with."

Newt had pushed his luck further than he wanted to, and he walked away while he still could. He had noticed several of the colonel's cavalrymen watching them while he and the colonel talked.

The crowd had mostly moved to the church, and he had no trouble retrieving his horse. He rode it to a low, long adobe building with a sign proclaiming it a general store. He left the Circle Dot horse at a hitching rail and went inside.

The shelves in the store were far from full, and

there were few shelves. The only way to bring in
supplies was via cart or wagon from El Paso or
Juarez, or by a mule train crossing of the mountains from Chihuahua City or up from Hermosillo.
The storekeeper had little to offer him beyond the
basic staples, a few dry goods and hardware, a
small collection of patent medicine, and other
trinkets. The rest of the things in the store were
from the area: handmade boots, sausages and dried
peppers hanging from the rafters, homespun
cotton clothing, and knives made from salvaged
wagon springs and other cast-off scrap steel. The
store even carried a keg of black powder, lead
ingots, bullet molds, and percussion caps. The
muzzleloaders, breech loaders, and cap-and-ball
revolvers and such had long since been a thing of
old in the States, but Newt could see how someone
in that faraway place would want to be able to roll
their own ammunition.

Newt purchased a sack of flour, a sack of beans,
half a dozen home-canned jars of hominy, two
sides of bacon, some chili peppers, a box of
matches, and the last pound of coffee in the store.
He considered the pile on the counter before him
and then considered how much money he had left
in the wallet Matilda Redding had given him.

He paid the storekeeper and took the flour and
bean sacks outside while the man bundled some of
the smaller items together and wrapped them in
brown paper that he tied with twine. Newt lashed
the sack tops together and hung them behind his
saddle to let them hang down on either side of

his horse like *mochilas,* what the Mexicans called their long saddlebags.

He went back into the store to get the rest of his purchases and was coming back out the door to his horse when he saw the man in the orange glasses riding up the street toward him.

Chapter Eighteen

Newt rolled his package inside his rain slicker and tied it behind his saddle, and he stuffed the jars of hominy in his saddlebags while he watched the Hatchet coming nearer. When the outlaw was close to him, Newt leaned down to pick up the sides of bacon, not so coincidentally causing his horse to block him from the Hatchet's view as he passed. The Hatchet twisted in the saddle when he had ridden on by, but all he saw was Newt's back as Newt tied the cured meat to his saddle horn.

The Hatchet stopped some fifty yards up the street and parked his horse in front of a *cantina*. He was alone, and Newt watched as he disappeared inside.

Newt took off his hat and scratched his head, debating the two things whirling around and around inside his brain like angry bees. One was the smart thing to do, and the other was not so smart.

"To hell with it." Newt put his hat back on and went up the street to the *cantina*.

The Hatchet stood at the bar on the left-hand side of the room, already nursing a glass of tequila when Newt stepped through the door. Newt went to the end of the bar nearest the front door. The Hatchet had turned slightly toward him and stayed that way, watching him carefully.

The bar was far better stocked than the store had been, proving, possibly, some of the citizens' priorities. Newt ordered a glass of whiskey and a beer. He tried to appear nonchalant and make as if he was studying his glass of whiskey. The first time he looked up at the mirror behind the bar he saw the Hatchet looking back at him. The outlaw's eyes were barely visible behind those orange lenses.

Newt didn't look away, each man measuring the other in the mirror. The Hatchet was dressed exactly the same as he had been before, only Newt was close enough this time to see the thin, groomed mustache that covered his upper lip, and an equally thin vertical strip of whiskers centered below his mouth. And he saw that the man wore two Model 1878 Colt double-action revolvers, one on each hip, and the buckle on his gunbelt was made of a huge, hammered silver *concho*. Not near so fancy or shiny as that belt buckle or his tall-topped boots was the rusty hatchet whose long wooden handle was shoved behind his belt in the center of his belly—dull except for the sharpened edge of it, and as rust-brown and blotched as old blood.

The Hatchet took a sip of his tequila and re-shaped the tips of his wet mustache, all the while watching Newt.

Newt downed his whiskey in a single pull, then followed with his mug of beer, which he drank almost as quickly. He wiped the beer foam from his mouth with the back of his forearm, and like the Hatchet, he never let his gaze waver from the mirror.

"You are very thirsty," the Hatchet said.

Newt merely shrugged.

"For a man with such a thirst you must have come far to get here."

"Not so far. How about you?" Newt wondered why the outlaw kept his peculiar glasses on in the dim light and shadows of the room.

One corner of the Hatchet's mouth moved upward. "As you say, not so far."

"Would have thought from the look of you that you'd had a long ride." The instant Newt said it he was wishing he hadn't. But something in the way the Hatchet was looking at him made him want to antagonize him, and the thought of the dead squaw with the cracked-open forehead kept coming back. "You look all tuckered out."

The Hatchet sucked at one of his eyeteeth and played with one of his black braids of hair, obviously annoyed. "Me? I'm fresh as a daisy."

Newt motioned with his empty beer mug for a refill. "Well, maybe you just had a bad day or something. I'm sure things will be better tomorrow."

The Hatchet sensed that there was something more to Newt's banter. And so did the bartender. He found an excuse to go to the back room, leaving the two men in the bar alone.

"Do I know you?" the Hatchet asked.

"Nope."

The Hatchet sharpened one end of his mustache again. "I don't recall your face."

"No, I figure you never saw me." Newt looked directly at the Hatchet and gave him his most bland and innocent expression. "Reckon you'd forget a face like this?"

"No, I can't say I would." The Hatchet laughed, but there was no humor in it. He reached for his tequila with his right hand and used that motion to draw attention away from his left hand dropping off the bar to hang by his pistol on that hip.

Newt noticed it but kept that same dumb, lazy look on his face. "Have you been down here long? Mexico, I mean."

"I get down here from time to time," the Hatchet said. "How about you?"

"Couple of weeks."

"Like it?"

"Nope; it's entirely too rough on a gentleman like me. Can't even travel the roads without worrying about somebody trying to waylay you," Newt said. "But I got what I came after, and I'm heading back to the States."

It was the Hatchet's turn to quit the mirror and look straight at Newt. He was older than Newt had assumed he would be, but it was hard to tell with that bright red *serape* and those tall boots covering most of him, and the tinted glasses hiding that much of his face. His nose and jawline suggested a hint of Indian blood, as Horn had claimed, but his accent could have been from Texas.

"I didn't catch your name." The Hatchet let go of his tequila glass and tapped the forefinger of that hand on the bar top. His other hand moved to touch the bottom of his holster.

"Newt Jones. And you?"

"Rufus Clagg." The Hatchet said it like he expected it to have an impact on Newt, and he was ready for it with that hand so close to his pistol.

It was plain to Newt that the Hatchet was worried that he was some kind of lawman. There was probably a price on his head. He also took note that the Hatchet seemed confident with his left hand. There weren't many two-gun men, and even fewer could use both hands—a tricky thing, and one that bore remembering.

"Are you a woodcutter, Mr. Hag?" Newt lifted a slow hand and pointed at the hatchet in the outlaw's belt.

"My name's Clagg." The Hatchet tapped his finger on the bar again.

"Begging your pardon."

"I chop other things."

"I bet you do," Newt said in a voice so quiet it barely made it across the length of the bar.

"What's that?"

Newt heard something rubbing against the front of the *cantina* and turned and saw the Circle Dot horse with its head sticking inside the doorway and staring at Newt with its usual lazy eyes and bored expression. The horse was rubbing his saddle and side against the doorjamb to scratch itself, and that's what Newt had heard.

"Is that your horse?"

"No, he thinks I'm his."

"Does he always do that?"

"What?"

"Walk into saloons?"

"Only when he's thirsty." Newt took a look to make sure the bartender wasn't seeing the horse mangling his plastered wall and dropping a pile of manure under his porch roof.

"You ought to do a better job of tying him."

"He won't stay tied," Newt said. "He's got a rebellious nature."

Newt looked out the window and saw more men tying their horses up to a corral fence down the street and closer to the plaza. There were four of them, three Mexicans and an Indian, and the Indian had a bandage above his knee. Newt recognized them as what was left of the Hatchet's gang.

Newt downed the last of his beer and went to his horse and picked up the trailing rein. The gelding was halfway into the doorway by then.

Newt pointed again at the hatchet in the outlaw's belt. "You be careful with that wood chopping. You might cut on the wrong tree and it fall on you."

"I'm always careful," the Hatchet said, realizing like he had all along that there was some byplay going on that he couldn't quite get a handle on. "And I'm always good."

Newt tried to back the Circle Dot horse up, but it refused to budge.

"Got to make this difficult, don't you?" Newt said.

He led the horse the rest of the way through the doorway, and his saddle fender scraped so hard against the doorjamb that Newt feared it was going to tear apart. He was turning the horse around in the tight confines of the room when the bartender came back from wherever he had gone. He stopped and looked at the horse as if he wasn't quite sure he was seeing what he was seeing.

Newt bent the brim of his hat to the bartender. "Begging your pardon. This here is a peculiar beast."

Newt led the horse back outside before the bartender could manage an answer. The rest of the Hatchet's gang was still at the corral messing around with their horses. Seeing that he had a little more time, he turned around and stood in the doorway.

"Hey there, Mr. Sag," he said.

"Clagg."

"Oh, ain't that what I said? Anyways, I just wanted to tell that, speaking of horses, you might ought to get rid of that gray horse you're riding. Mind you, I'm no expert on horseflesh"—Newt jerked a thumb over his shoulder at the Circle Dot horse behind him—"but he looks like he might be a little too high strung. Nervous, you know. Never can tell when a horse like that might throw him a fit."

Newt left before that had time to soak in. He readjusted his supplies on his saddle and swung up on his horse. He was well down the street and almost at the edge of town when he looked back one last time at the *cantina*.

The Hatchet was standing outside the door watching Newt, and Colonel Herrera was standing beside the Hatchet talking to him.

Newt faced forward in the saddle again and looked down at the Circle Dot horse's head. "Now, we've got to get this straight. Just because I go in a saloon doesn't mean you get to. You could get a bad reputation hanging around such places."

Chapter Nineteen

There was no one in sight when Newt rode his lathered horse into camp. Before he had a chance to become too worried, the children began slipping out of the timber and coming back to the campfire. Horn followed them, carrying his rifle nonchalantly in the crook of his elbow.

Gok came up from behind Newt, and Charlie McComas was with him. He was mimicking Gok's walk and trying to match strides with him. Newt thought then how much the boy already acted like a little Apache.

"Put that fire out," Newt said.

Horn took in Newt's hard-used horse and heard his tense tone for what it was. He quickly scattered the fire and began to kick dirt on it, and the children helped him. "I don't know what kind of trouble you got into, but how far is it behind you?"

Newt told him what had happened, and Horn interrupted him often to translate what was said for Gok.

"You should have killed him while you had the chance," Horn said. "You could have saved us a lot of trouble and done the world a favor."

"You weren't the one standing there in the saloon with him. That Clagg is a rough one. I don't think anybody is gonna put lead in him without taking some back," Newt said. "It could have gone either way."

"True, but the thought of what he's done, and him still breathing and maybe doing it again, is a hard one to take. Old Sieber always says to stomp your snakes when you get the chance."

"It galls me as much as you, but I promised I would get Billy Redding back to his family, and I can't do that if I'm lying back yonder dead," Newt said. "Clagg'll get his one of these days. His kind always does. If I never see him again, then I can live with that."

"You think he'll come after us?"

"I do. You can bet he knows by now about me bringing those children back, and that's gonna be a hard rock for him to get past his craw."

"You say that all calm-like, but you come running your horse into camp like the hounds were nipping at your heels."

"You let me do the worrying."

Horn gave a nervous chuckle. "You being worried, well, that worries me. What about you seeing the Hatchet and Colonel Herrera? Something stinks to high heaven there. You'd think the colonel would arrest him on the spot. The Hatchet's a wanted man, and putting him down would be a fine feather in the colonel's hat."

"I've got ideas about that."

"You mean you think the Hatchet might be in cahoots with the colonel?"

"Wasn't it you that told me about Colonel Herrera once selling those Apache women?"

"You think he's gone full slaver and partnered up with the Hatchet?"

"If you were a strutting, mean little peacock like Colonel Herrera, what would you do with the Indian children you wound up with while you're playing politics trying to wipe out every last Apache in Mexico? Maybe Clagg's paying the colonel off, or maybe he's handling shipments for him."

Horn grimaced. "If that's true, we're likely to have the Hatchet and his boys, *and* the Mexican cavalry after us," Horn said.

"I'd say that's likely if the colonel is slaving."

"Gonna be hard to hide from them, and harder to outfight them. Herrera's regulars have been fighting Apaches for years with him. They know this country, and they're tough and they're seasoned. And he can get militia and *Rurale* help from here to the border."

"I don't intend to hide from him or fight him," Newt said.

"What do you intend?"

"I'm counting on out-running his sorry ass," Newt said. "And when I get back to the States I'm going to get drunk and then sleep for a week."

"I'm glad you set reasonable goals." Horn began

to count off the things on his fingers: "Run like hell. Home. Get drunk. Sleep."

"You got it."

"Sounds easy enough. When do we start?"

Newt looked back down the mountain the way he had come and toward Bacerac. "I thought I saw dust on my back trail, and I'm also pretty sure I heard that bugle again. I'm guessing right now would be a good time."

They stuck to the mountains as they worked northward toward a stronghold of the Apache where Gok believed that others of his people would be camped. Twice they came across the tracks of Mexican soldiers, and once they hid up high and, through Horn's binoculars, watched a troop of cavalry in the river valley below.

They traveled slowly due to the terrain and the children, and the constant need to be on the lookout. The wind shifted out of the north, and it turned cold in a matter of hours. They wrapped themselves in whatever they could, and all of them suffered.

Two days out of Bacerac they reached the Apache camp Gok had been guiding them toward. The first thing they saw were three dead horses, and then beyond that were several burned wickiups and scattered personal items.

And bodies.

Gok read the tracks and the signs of the battle, and pointed them out to Newt and Horn. The

Mexican soldiers, thirty or more of them, had caught the camp unaware and driven the Apaches up the canyon. Two scalped and mutilated Apache women and an old man lay not far past the edge of the camp. Surprised or not, it appeared that the Apaches had put up a good fight, despite their losses. There were also three fresh graves, and Gok surmised that they contained the bodies of soldiers killed in the fight.

Farther up toward the head of the little valley, they came upon low parapets of stacked rock that the Apaches had hastily erected to fight behind while they bought time for their women and children to escape. Spent brass cartridge cases littered the ground behind those little rock piles.

Gok left the others behind and went up a trail that climbed out of the valley. When he returned, he told them that most of his people had gotten away and managed somehow to keep many of their horses. He thought they were one day ahead of them and that they would move as fast as they could toward the border and see if they could turn themselves over to the army or sneak back onto the reservation.

Horn helped Gok carry the Apache dead to a crevice in some rocks to bury them there. Newt saw the look on Billy Redding's face as he looked upon those bodies and the rest of the destruction of the camp. The other children sat their horses beside him, watching the same thing. Newt cursed himself for not taking them away from the camp and out of sight of such horror.

He motioned the children back down to the far end of the mountain glade and led them out of sight of the destroyed camp. He dismounted and walked over to stand beside the horse Billy and Charlie rode.

He reached up a hand on Billy's shoulder. "Steady, boy."

Billy didn't answer, but he did manage to nod at Newt, which was an improvement and a positive sign that he might be getting better. But Newt worried that the boy was too traumatized by what had happened to him and might not ever totally be himself again.

Charlie leaned around Billy and said, "Don't lie to him. Bad stuff happens, and if it's bad enough nobody can help you."

Newt was as concerned with Charlie's attitude as he was with Billy's inability to snap out of whatever place he had retreated to. Charlie was a strong little boy, but maybe too strong. "We came and got you boys, didn't we?"

Charlie didn't sound like a child when he asked, "You think you saved me, Mr. Jones?"

"When we get back . . ."

"Back to where?"

"Back to the States. Back home with your family."

"Father is gone, and so is Mother." Charlie looked straight at Newt with no tears in his eyes and with his expression and tone so matter-of-fact.

Newt heard the emptiness and the hurt in the little boy that he was trying to hide inside a tough shell. "I'm sorry."

"You didn't have anything to do with it, and nobody can fix it."

"How old are you, Charlie?"

"Seven."

"It's all right to be scared, you know."

"I cried some at first," Charlie said. "Didn't do any good, and they whipped me for it. You got to be quiet. Don't make any noise and don't fuss. They told us that, but Billy cried anyway."

"Billy's not the same as you."

"He still cries and he pees himself sometimes."

"That's because he's got wounds."

"Wounds? You're hurt and you don't cry."

"Not hurts on the outside, Charlie, but hurts on the inside. That's what I'm telling you. You've got hurts, too, always will have them. You know how you get a cut finger and sometimes the best thing to do is to take off the bandage and let that cut get a little air so it can heal?"

"Yeah."

"Well maybe Billy's letting his hurts air out so they'll heal. Maybe if he has time enough those hurts won't have to show so much."

"That's not what the Apache say. They say that a warrior ought to be tough."

"They told you that? You speak Apache?"

"No, but I've watched them," Charlie said. "Someday I'm going to be tougher than them or anybody."

"Oh, you are?"

Newt wanted to say more to Charlie, but he couldn't think of what that should be. And Gok was coming his way. The old warrior let out a long, shrill whistle, then did it a second time. It wasn't long before his horse came trotting to him.

"How do you teach them to do that?" Newt asked, impressed, although he had seen Gok do that many times.

Gok didn't understand the words, but he saw that Newt was impressed. He patted his horse on the neck and then swung onto its back.

Newt looked at Gok and then at the Circle Dot horse. He puckered his lips and did his best imitation of the whistle sound Gok had used. The Circle Dot horse's expression never changed, and it didn't so much as perk its ears at the sound. Instead, the animal yawned, stuck out its tongue, and shook its head so that those ears flopped.

Newt whistled again, but he had even less success. The horse turned and walked a few steps farther away and lowered its head and picked at a clump of dead grass. Newt looked at Gok again, and the old warrior said nothing.

Newt walked over and caught his horse, and as he was picking up his reins he said, "Why can't you be a good horse? I should have given you back to that Mexican Don that time. He tried to tell me that you were nothing but trouble and bad luck."

When Newt was back in the saddle, Gok pointed with his rifle at the trail the Apaches from the camp had fled along.

"*Vámonos*," he said.

And go they went, down the mountain toward

the lower country, and always working toward the border.

By the tracks Horn and Gok found, the Apaches had split into smaller bunches in an attempt to confuse their pursuers and to lose them. Gok said the Apaches would rejoin each other at some point they had agreed upon before parting. Sure enough, the Mexican soldiers soon gave up tracking the refugees or feared to follow them into a possible ambush. What's more, Gok seemed certain he knew where the next place where his people were headed. And he increased their pace because of that.

The temperature dropped even further as the day neared sundown, and Newt noticed Billy and Charlie shivering in the saddle beneath their crude and inadequate blanket ponchos. Newt took off his coat and slung it over Charlie's shoulders. The garment was big enough that it wrapped around them both, and Billy clutched it closed in front of him.

Newt shivered as a cold gust blew through his thin shirt, and he took his rubber slicker from behind his saddle and put it on. The slicker wasn't much for keeping a man warm, but it would do a fine job of blocking the wind.

Gok became anxious before they had gone another mile. Newt guessed that Gok believed they were getting close to his people. Maybe that's why he let his guard down, and maybe that's why the three protectors weren't more cautious about riding into the canyon ahead instead of looking for a way around it or scouting it more closely before they entered.

The canyon was a knife-edged cut through the middle of a flat-topped tableland with a dry creek running down its course. It was more like a giant crack in the earth or gully with almost vertical sides, and it sloped gradually downhill for several miles and was cut with many other side canyons and eroded draws that ran into it. At the bottom of that maze of cracks Newt could see where the ground leveled off into a gentle hump of scattered oaks and grassland.

They were only a little ways into the canyon and Newt was thinking about how pretty those oak trees were when a bullet thumped into one of his saddlebags and gunshots rang out and echoed off the canyon walls.

Chapter Twenty

Another bullet whipped through a fold in Newt's slicker, and another one spanged off a slab of stone so close to him that he was struck in the side of the face by chunks of rock and grit. The Circle Dot horse bolted ahead, and Newt fell from the saddle.

Half-stunned and hatless, he fought to his feet. Gok was charging on down the canyon, and the children and Newt's horse raced behind him. Newt caught hold of Horn's horse's tail as it passed him and hung on. He was drug along behind it in a stumbling, lunging run until he could keep up no longer and finally lost his balance and hit the ground again.

When he got to his feet for a second time, Horn was coming back to him in a run. Newt shook free of the tangle of his slicker, dropping it as he reached up and caught the arm that Horn held out to him. There was more gunfire from the canyon walls above them. Newt heard the sickening

thump of a bullet striking Horn's horse and felt
the animal shudder from the impact and the pain
in the moment he swung up behind Horn.

Horn turned the horse and started after Gok
and the children. His Colt was in his hand and he
thumbed shots at the puffs of powder smoke that
appeared on the left-hand side of the canyon walls
as they fled down it. Newt could do nothing but
hang on.

The canyon was long, and to continue along its
course was to be wide-open to whoever was firing
at them from above. Gok and the children turned
into a side canyon to the left, and Newt and Horn
followed them.

The side canyon was really no more than a large
eroded gully coming down off the high edge of
the tableland above them, and it ended in a steep
slide of powdery earth and loose scree. No horse
was going to climb that, and to turn back meant
coming under their attackers' guns again. One of
the children's horses had also been hit, and it was
down on its side struggling and thrashing. Horn's
horse faltered and stumbled on weak knees, and
they bailed from it.

Horn was getting the children into a clump of
brush and boulders on one side of the little canyon,
while Gok went back to the entrance and knelt
with his rifle shouldered, ready to fend off pursuit or an attack from that way. Newt looked up at
the canyon sides some fifty feet above them in
sheer walls, and he knew that the instant their

attackers looked down from those heights they were going to be easy pickings.

Only the talus slide at the head of the tiny canyon provided a way up, but even it looked almost too steep to climb. Newt ran to it, knowing he needed to get up to the top before it was too late. Horn must have been thinking the same thing and followed as fast as his injured foot would let him.

The bottom of the slide was so loose that Newt sunk to his ankles and twisted his knee, but he lunged forward, time after time. The higher he went the steeper it became, and the loose rocks under his feet shifted and slid and pitched him on his face twice. Each time he got up and struggled upward. The last thirty feet was so steep that he was almost on his hands and knees. He gained ground, and then he slid back, sometimes well below where he had started.

He fell forward over the rim rock lip of the canyon with his chest heaving and his heart pounding madly. As he landed on his belly he saw men coming at a run toward him. Some were on horses and some were on foot, and all of them were the Hatchet's men.

The high ground was flat like the top of a mesa, and his attackers were all spread out in front of him. There were five of them, and the closest to him was barely fifty yards away.

Newt's cheek found the rifle stock and he squeezed off a shot at the nearest man racing down the edge of the big canyon. That man staggered three more wild steps forward, hunched over, holding his belly with both hands, and then he toppled into the canyon below with a wild scream.

Another rifle boomed right beside Newt, and out of the corner of his eye he saw that Horn was sitting beside him with his knees up in front of him. His own Winchester was propped on one of those knees as he squinted at his rifle sights.

Horn's gun boomed and a Mexican pulled up his horse hard and sagged over the front of his saddle. Horn worked the lever on his Winchester and fired again, and that shot struck the same bandit's horse and knocked it down.

The Hatchet was the farthest away. Newt's vision was drawn to him out of the others by the brightness of the red *serape* he wore and that gray horse he rode. The Hatchet saw what was happening and veered to one side. He ran his horse parallel to Newt and Horn's position, firing his pistol on a dead run. Newt worked the lever on his Winchester and racked a fresh round home. He swung his rifle and tried a shot at him, but the Hatchet was moving too fast and Newt missed.

Before he could fire again he heard gunfire from down in the canyon behind him, and he twisted around in time to see Gok fighting hand to hand with another of the outlaws at the foot of the slide. The outlaw struck Gok a blow to the head with his rifle barrel that knocked Gok down. He was about to deliver another such blow before Gok kicked his legs out from under him and drove a knife into his throat when he hit the ground.

By the time Newt turned back around, the Hatchet and the other remaining outlaws with him were running away across the tableland. Newt tried to aim at them, but they were already too far away. He lifted his head from his rifle stock, but saw that Horn was going to try a long shot.

Horn methodically flipped up the tang peep sight on his Winchester and turned the dial elevator on it until he was satisfied. He tucked his cheek tight to the rifle stock once more and took a deep breath, as if he had all day and as if nothing in the world could hurry him. The Hatchet and the other outlaw were three hundred yards away by then and gaining.

Horn let out a part of that deep breath, and after a long count of two or so he squeezed the trigger. The outlaw fleeing beside the Hatchet leaned to the rear with his back suddenly arched and his *sombrero* bobbing and slapping between his shoulder blades. A few more strides of his horse, and his arms dropped to his sides and he tumbled from the saddle over the back of his horse's hips.

The Hatchet kept running until he dropped off of the rise and out of sight in the distance.

Newt looked at Horn and found him looking back.

"Not bad," Newt said.

Horn lowered his rifle and patted the stock affectionately. "When this old smoke pole talks, the bad men listen."

They waited longer, scanning the ground before

them in case there was more of the Hatchet's gang out there.

"Wish we had got the Hatchet," Horn said while they waited. "He was weaving his horse back and forth and too low in the saddle to get a bead on him."

"Well, we put him out of a gang. We ought to be well across the border in another day or so, and I don't think he's going to bother us anymore."

"You said yourself, he doesn't seem like one to give up on a thing. There's talk that a *Rurale* once killed a buddy of his and cut his head off and put it in a jar in his office. The Hatchet walked into that *Rurale* headquarters in broad daylight by himself, shot two of them, and carried his friend's head out of there."

"Tough or not, three of us can handle him, but I don't think we'll ever have to worry about seeing him again. Not if we keep moving. It can't be more than sixty or seventy miles to the border, and in another day we can be in a settlement on the American side. The Hatchet is going to be a while gathering new recruits, even if he doesn't want to quit."

"You thought about him riding to Colonel Herrera?"

Newt frowned. "I ever tell you that sometimes I wish you wouldn't talk?"

No other attacker showed himself, and after a long wait Newt became convinced that they had gotten them all or the rest of them had fled with the Hatchet.

Gok was at the bottom of the scree slide when they went back down into the side canyon. He was kneeling over the man he had killed, and when he rose up he had his knife in one hand and a bloody scalp in the other. He merely glanced at his two companions and then turned away.

Newt looked down at the mutilated head of the Mexican bad man and then saw the children peering at the dead body from their hiding spot. None of them said anything.

"Bloody savages," Newt said.

Horn looked to Gok and then back to Newt with a wry twinkle of his eyes and one corner of his mouth upturned. "You talking about him or us?"

"Him."

"Apaches don't take scalps as much as a lot of other tribes," Horn said. "Some warriors do, some don't. From what I've seen, the ones that do tend to save it for enemies they especially hate. And Gok there, he doesn't like Mexicans not one damned bit, and that man he scalped was one of them that took his niece and these other Apache children."

"I don't know that he likes anyone. I think he enjoys this."

"Well, be damned glad he's on our side."

Newt limped over to where the children had taken cover and coaxed them out of hiding and checked them over for wounds. None of them seemed worse for the wear, although they were frightened. He and Horn mounted them on their horses while Gok went up the scree slide and disappeared over the rim rock. And he did it much more nimbly than Newt had managed the feat.

Horn's horse had died while they were fighting off the Hatchet's men, and that made them two horses short counting the other one. They now had twelve children and four horses to mount them on. Newt took the gear off the dead horses and transferred what of it that they needed and could carry to the remaining horses. He remounted the children in pairs, leaving Billy, Charlie, Gok's niece, and the older Apache girl on foot for the moment.

Gok came back down into the canyon. Newt had assumed the worst and expected Gok to be carrying more scalps, but the old warrior only had two gunbelts slung over his shoulder, some canteens by their straps over the other, and three rifles held in the bends of his arms. He tied the rifles under the saddle fenders of the horses the children rode, then slung the canteens from their saddle horns. He said something to Horn that Newt didn't understand.

"Said his people are always short of guns and ammunition to fight with," Horn said.

The Circle Dot horse had run into the canyon with the rest of the horses during their flight, and Newt put Billy and Charlie both on the gelding's back and then got up in the saddle himself. Horn followed suit and put the older Apache girl behind him. That only left Gok's niece, and as Newt thought he would, Gok took her on his horse.

They went out of the side canyon cautiously, and

the rest of them waited at its mouth while Newt
rode up the big canyon to where they had originally
been fired upon. He had Charlie get down and
fetch his hat, for his knee was aching and slowly
stiffening from where he had wrenched it running
up the scree slide, and it was too difficult to get
down himself with the two kids behind him.

Newt examined the black hat while Charlie
went after his rain slicker lying nearby. Billy looked
at the hat as if he wondered why they had come
back for it.

"I'm partial to this hat," Newt said.

Charlie handed him the slicker, and while he
was trying to climb up behind the saddle Newt
examined the garment. There were two bullet
holes through the tail of it, and he realized how
close he had come to being shot. He slipped back
into the slicker and turned the horse around.

They joined back up with the rest of their group
and headed down the canyon toward a belt of oaks
visible a couple of miles away. It was Horn that
scouted ahead this time, and Newt and Gok rode
beside each other at the back of the rest of the
children.

Newt watched Gok playing with his niece and
telling her things that made her laugh. And then
Newt saw the scalp hanging from Gok's belt.

Newt turned his attention to checking their back
trail and to trying to get his shirt to quit rubbing
his neck. The rocks from the bullet ricochet had
stung him fiercely. He could see some blood on
that collarbone, but he couldn't see the wound to

tell how bad it looked. He was sure that he was not hurt badly, but it burned and stung. Gok saw him tugging at the neck of his shirt and motioned for Newt to show him the wound.

Newt pulled the neck of the shirt down so that Gok could see. The old warrior made a face and waved at Newt as if it were no big deal. Gok didn't appear to have received so much as a scratch in the fight, the same result the first time they fought the Hatchet's gang.

Horn came riding back and saw Newt looking at Gok. "What are you thinking?"

"Did you ever see anyone fight so wildly?"

"I told you, these Apache are fierce folks."

"I thought you said Apaches don't like to take chances they don't have to, but Gok doesn't seem to think that way."

Horn started a conversation with Gok that lasted a good while. When it was finished Horn translated for Newt.

"I asked him why he fights that way sometimes, and if he has no fear," Horn said.

"And what did he say?"

"He says he cannot tell us the source of his magic or he won't have it anymore."

Gok said something else, making signs and motions with his hands as if that would help them understand him. As usual, Newt couldn't make out much of what he said.

"He says that when the Mexicans at Janos killed his first wife and children and his mother, he cut his hair in mourning and sat with them for a long time," Horn said. "And while he was mourning a spirit voice told him the secret of his power."

"What secret?" Newt asked.

"That he can only be wounded and that no gun can ever kill him. He says that it will be a blade or some other weapon that will be the end of him, but no gun."

"If he truly has such magic, why did he just tell us of it and risk losing it?"

Horn asked Gok that, and Gok rode silently for several strides of his horse before he answered.

"He says that he is ready to die and does not fear death anymore."

It would have been impolite for Newt to scoff at such beliefs, so he didn't. And what did he know? Superstition or not, many soldiers before battle had their rituals and charms. They might wear a certain piece of clothing or jewelry, do seemingly trivial things the same way every time, eat a certain meal, or any number of things. And no doubt, a man came to believe more in them when he survived after practicing them. Such confidence could make a man braver or make him move faster and stronger instead of locking up with fear or being hesitant.

Horn seemed to have been thinking a similar thing. "Me and you may think all that medicine stuff is silly, but to an Apache it's no different than one of our preachers praying to God for his divine help."

"That's something to think on."

"Doesn't matter if it's true or not. They believe

it's true," Horn said. "An Apache warrior going on a raid has war names for all his weapons and will not call them by their normal names until he is back home from the war path. If another warrior or a young boy along for the first time makes the mistake of calling a bow a bow, or a spear a spear, then the Apache believe that's bad medicine and can cause things to go badly."

"To each his own," Newt said.

"Might not be that bad," Horn said, and held up his rifle. "I'm more partial to this Winchester than I am to most anything I ever owned, and I trust it more than the majority of people that I've ever met."

"You going to give it a name?" Newt wished Horn would quit talking. His knee was hurting worse and it put him in a grouchy mood.

"No need to be a smart aleck," Horn said. "But why not name this gun? Back when I was a boy I used to hear those stories about those old Indian-fighting long hunters like Boone and Crockett, and all those mountain men that came out West trapping beaver. Lots of them had a name for their rifle. Wouldn't have thought of not naming one, no more than you wouldn't name your child or have a woman without a name. A man that's proud of a thing or owns a thing should name it, or he doesn't think anything of it at all. You know, Tick-Licker, and Ol' Betsy, and Sweet Lips, and Sally, and Meat-in-the-Pot, and Thunder Stick, or some such like that. The Apache may have that right. There's power in naming your weapon."

Newt gave him a look that said he wasn't going to answer, and probably not talk anymore at all.

Horn plunged on, regardless. "You could name that fancy shooting iron on your hip if you wanted. People don't forget seeing a gun with grips like that, and you're a known man. You'd give them a name for when they talked about that gun of yours."

Newt frowned at him and shook his head and slowed his horse so that he fell back behind Horn.

Horn was nonplussed and continued to chatter. Newt tried his best not to listen. Billy had both arms wrapped about his waist, and he felt the child slipping to one side. He turned his head around far enough to see that Billy had fallen asleep. He reached behind him and righted the boy and noted that Charlie, too, had fallen asleep with his head resting against Billy's back.

Horn slowed and fell back beside him. He was still talking about guns and what he ought to name his rifle. Newt thought that Horn was a lot like little Charlie, in that there wasn't much that seemed to faze him. What kind of man could come out of a gunfight like it never happened and talk nonstop like that as if they were riding to a church social or a picnic?

"Is my talking bothering you?" Horn asked.

Newt rubbed his raw neck and shook his head. "No, you keep it up. You're putting the kids to sleep."

"Now, you listen. I . . ."

Horn never got to finish what he was about to

say, for at the same time they rode out of the mouth of the canyon into the oak grove, the brush cracked in front of them and rock rolled down the side of the canyon somewhere above them. Newt barely had time to pull up his horse and put a hand to his pistol before three Apache warriors stepped into the end of the canyon in front of them.

Chapter Twenty-one

Every one of the three warriors already had their rifles ready, and Newt had a feeling that there were more of them back in the trees or hidden somewhere above them on the canyon sides. One thing he was learning was that everybody in Sonora seemed to love ambushes and tight places to pull them off. He promised himself to avoid such places in the future.

"Easy, Jones," Horn said. "I'm pretty sure those are some of Gok's friends."

Gok said something to Horn and Newt, then rode on up to the three warriors blocking their way.

"What did he say?" Newt asked.

"Your Spanish isn't getting any better," Horn said. "I've never seen a man that talks less or with less knack for human language."

"What did he say?"

"He said to keep our hands away from our guns."

Newt rubbed the bottom of his pistol holster for a moment in thought and then rested it on his saddle horn. Billy squirmed, and Newt could feel the boy trying to hide behind him.

Charlie, on the other hand, leaned out around Newt so that he could see the Apaches better. One of the Apaches talking to Gok noticed Charlie and lifted his head as if he knew the boy and intended that subtle motion to serve as a greeting.

"You know him?" Newt asked.

"Yes, Chatto gave me to him. He's who taught me how to catch rats and cook them."

Newt was surprised that Charlie didn't seem angry or scared by the presence of one of his former captors, and possibly one who had participated in the murder of his parents. But he held his tongue, for he was too intent on what was going on with Gok and the other warriors.

After some talk, the warrior that Charlie pointed out motioned to someone up on the canyon sides, and before long four more warriors appeared. Gok called to Newt and Horn to move on, and they followed the warriors into the grove of oak trees. They soon came upon the Apache camp made beside a spring of water. There were no lodges and very little baggage. A few horses and scrubby Indian ponies were tied in the trees, but for the most part the Apaches seemed to have fled their last camp with only what they could carry on their backs.

A dozen or so women and at least that many children stood up from where they had been gathered around a fire cooking and eating horsemeat. The animal's partially butchered carcass lay nearby.

The children that he had rescued from the Hatchet leaped from their horses and ran among those around the fire. There was at first much keening and crying with joy, and then there was laughter. Even the warriors joined in. Gok's niece ran to one of the women, and the two threw their arms around each other. By their actions, and the presence of Gok nearby them, Newt surmised that the woman was the girl's mother. None of the Apache warriors said anything to Horn or Newt, and they seemed to have been almost forgotten.

Newt looked up to the smoke from the campfire floating up above the low trees. "If those Mexican soldiers had attacked me only a day ago and might still be looking for me, I wouldn't be building fires for them to see."

Gok started their way with a smile on his face. It took him longer than it should to get to them, for the Apache men kept stopping him to discuss things or to pat him on the back. Horn pointed to the smoke when Gok finally reached them, and Gok gave him a brief answer.

"He says that they have scouts out, and that Colonel Herrera's soldiers are camped many miles to the east," Horn said.

Gok motioned them to get down from their horses, and they did so. The Apache women and children were shy around the white men, but the men gestured to them to come to the fire and share in the horsemeat. They were cooking big chunks of the meat on the ends of long sticks held over the flames. When the meat was done, the men ate it directly from the end of the stick, tearing off bits of it with their teeth. The cooking meat juice dripping and splattering into the fire hissed and sizzled, and that sound mixed with the smacking and the belching, and the licking and sucking of hot, greasy fingers.

"Ain't you coming?" Horn had started forward, but noticed that Newt remained standing by his horse.

"I'm not eating horse."

"They're going to think you a weak man, or one that thinks he is better than them. And besides, this has turned into a celebration feast. If it was a real camp there would be dancing and drinking, and we would have to tell the story of how we got their children back."

"If us bringing those kids back isn't enough for them, then they can go jump on a cactus," Newt said. "I've already said it once. I'm not eating horsemeat."

Gok was watching them closely, and he said something to Horn.

Newt didn't have a clue what he had said, but he didn't wait for Horn to translate. "You tell him what I said."

Horn did as he was asked, but from his tone it was obvious to Newt that he gave Gok an answer that was softer and more political than the way Newt had actually said it. Gok broke into his native tongue again, and when he finished Horn was laughing.

"He says that there is a story among his people of a Yuma scout working for the army and helping to chase Apaches. He did not like to eat horses, either," Horn said. "The trail was rough, and the army had a horse go down with a broken leg. The Apache scouts with the army immediately butchered it and ate their bellies full. When the Yuma scout saw this he was upset and said, 'Poor horse, work for you all day. He fall down, then you kill him and eat. Damn! No good!'"

Even Newt laughed at that.

"Gok says that he only wanted to feed you if you were hungry, and that none of these people will think badly of *Shush Bijii* if he does not eat. You aren't Apache, and they are all used to the strange ways of white men," Horn said.

"What did he call me?"

"He called you what all of them are calling you, *Shush Bijii*. Bear Heart," Horn said. "Well, not all of them. I heard some of them calling you *Nantan Shush*. Big Chief Bear."

"That's what Gok called me the day we saw the bear, isn't it? And he said all that mumbo jumbo about bear sickness and magic."

"Yeah, Gok's told all of them about that, and what matters is that they believe him."

"I don't need another name."

"Well you've got one. Just go with it. That's a powerful name among them. It gives you some clout, and you don't have to eat horsemeat." Horn turned and started to head to the fire.

"What about you?" Newt asked. "You aren't going to eat that, are you?"

Horn looked back at him and grinned. "Like I been telling you, you need to work on your social skills. A man should never turn down a feast or a party."

Regardless of what Horn said, Newt noticed that he did not eat any horsemeat when he got to the fire. While he seemed a little edgy and less than his normal exuberant self, it was still a strange sight to see him visiting with the renegade Apaches, considering what he had suffered at their hands so recently. It was also strange to see them being so friendly to a white scout who had helped pursue them often and fought with them on many occasions. The more he watched, the more he began to think that Horn knew a few of them from the reservation.

Newt turned to help Billy and Charlie down from his horse, but found that Charlie was gone. He looked around for the boy and soon saw him standing with the same Apache man he had recognized earlier. The warrior had his hand on Charlie's head and was telling him something.

"Get down, Billy," Newt said. "I need to loosen the cinch on this horse and take him to water."

Billy shook his head. "I don't want to."

"Get down." Newt held out his arms to the boy but kept his attention on Charlie and the Apache while he waited.

"I don't want them to kill me," Billy said.

"They won't kill you. They won't hurt you at all. They're happy to have their children back, just like your daddy and grandma are going to be when I take you back to them in a few days."

Billy clammed up again, and Newt had to physically pull him from the saddle. Billy didn't fight him, but his eyes were watered up when Newt sat him down.

"They killed my momma," Billy said.

Newt looked at the fire and the group around it. "You mean you see one of them that did it?"

Billy rubbed at his eyes and studied the Apaches intensely. "No, but they look like them, and they eat horses like they did after they chased our wagon down."

"You don't have to eat horse, Billy. I'm not."

"They made me eat some. They hit Momma in the head with rocks, then made me eat horse right there where I could see her."

"That's all over now. I won't let any of them hurt you or make you do things that you don't want to."

Newt watered the Circle Dot horse at the spring, then led Billy under a shade tree where they sat down together while the horse grazed close at hand. Billy said nothing else, but every time an Apache adult walked nearby he leaned close to Newt and wouldn't take his eyes off of them.

Charlie walked over to the fire with the Apache he had been talking to. Newt tried to wave the boy over to him, but Charlie only smiled and went to stand beside Horn. He took up a stick with a chunk of raw meat and held it over the fire, and several of the Apaches pointed at him or called playful greetings to him. Horn was keeping watch on the boy, and that gave Newt some comfort.

Around the camp, the Apache children ran and played and squealed with delight, and some of the kidnapped children were among them. Newt was amazed at the resiliency of those kids, and could only hope that Billy had that same metal within him. The boy showed signs of getting better every day, but he was a long way from being what he likely was before he was taken.

Newt must have dozed off for a while, for the next thing he knew Horn was flopping down beside him. Charlie was with him. He put his hands on his little swollen belly and lay flat on his back. Billy had fallen asleep leaning against Newt's shoulder.

"I couldn't eat another bite," he said.

"You could thump this little horse eater's belly and it would sound like a ripe watermelon," Horn said.

"How come you didn't eat?" Charlie asked Newt.

"Charlie, I want you to stay with me from here on out," Newt said.

Horn noticed something in Newt's look. "Instead of napping over here you should have come over and talked with them."

"I've got nothing much to say to them. They got their kids back, and I'll ride on and that will be that."

"I get the feeling that you don't have any use for Apaches," Horn said.

"I don't have much use for *these* Apaches, no." Newt stretched his aching leg out straight in front of him.

"Gok was in on torturing us, and you still talk to him."

"Matter of necessity, but I won't be inviting him to sit down to supper when we get done with this trip, and he better not let me see him again after we part."

"Still . . ." Horn started to say.

"Say what you want to, but I'm sure there are those among this bunch that probably killed these boys' parents or would have if they had the chance. There's Gok and another one over there I see that burned the skin off of you, and they likely have done the same to others. They've killed women and children and raided ranches, and stolen anything they can lay hand to. I can bear being with them for now, but I won't be a hypocrite and act like I like them."

Horn cleared his throat, stalling and trying to get the words right for what he wanted to say. "Might be hard for you coming down here and seeing how it is, and you're right that some of the Apache have done horrible things, especially the Chiricahua. Crook's got that part right, and I don't see any way but to whip the troublemakers and kill them until there ain't none of them left that have any fight in them.

"But so have the Mexicans done bad things, too, and the same with our own people. You already know that. The Mexicans have kidnapped Apache children and killed women and burned villages, and our own army has done the same. We've strong-armed the Apaches' land away from them because we want it or need it; we've put them on reservations under a system so crooked and messed up that they starve and die of sicknesses that they've never known."

"If those were bad white men over there, or Mexican either one, I wouldn't have any use for them, either, no more than I do these Apache," Newt said.

Horn took a stem of dried grass and put it between his lips and let it bob around while he talked. "I guess what I'm trying to say is that there has been plenty of wrongs done on all sides. I've hunted bad Apaches and put a few of them under. Was glad to do it, but I've also known some good folks among them. I don't mean to sound like some Quaker Indian lover, but you can't ever forget that they don't think like we do. They've got their ways, and if you'll look close enough you'll probably find things that you like."

"They can have their ways, but that doesn't mean those ways are mine," Newt said. "They picked me for an enemy, and not the other way around. I don't know how to fight a man I like, and I don't know how to like a man that hurt me or my own."

Horn pitched his grass stem away and got to his feet. "Damn, Jones, do you know how much you

sound like an Apache right now? That's what I'm
talking about."

"Go on," Newt said. "No sense picking at this
anymore."

"Well, you're the one that keeps saying the only
important thing is to get these boys back home.
Two of those men over there were sent down here
by General Crook to tell these people that the
army has a troop of cavalry waiting for them at
the border. If you can bear not to start a fight
with these Apaches a little bit longer, it would be
safer for us and for the women and children if we
travel with them in force."

"Then that's what we'll do," Newt answered.

When Horn was gone, Charlie rolled over on
his side so he could look at Newt. "Mr. Jones, do
you have any family?"

"Some. Haven't seen them in a long, long time.
Not since I left home and came out West," Newt
said.

"What about your mother and father?"

"My pa's heart stopped on him while he was
plowing a field when I was fourteen, and my ma's
been gone for a few years now."

"You miss 'em?"

"Sure I do, time to time. I used to get letters
from my brother and sister."

"Do you ever think about going to see them?"

"Oh, I've thought about it, but I don't know
what I'd say to them after all these years. I'm different from them, and they've got their own lives
to live and families to take care of."

Charlie rolled onto his back again and stared up at the sky. "My sisters are bossy. They don't like me 'cause I'm the baby of the family."

"You've got sisters?"

"Yeah."

"I bet they like you just fine. The youngest one always gets picked on a little or spoiled."

"They never did like it out here after we left Kansas. Mother didn't like it, either."

"You like it though, don't you?"

Charlie only nodded and continued looking at the sky. After a while he asked, "Do you like it out here?"

"Reckon I do, the good parts, anyway."

"Me too," Charlie said. "Does it bother you, being by yourself?"

"Been so long at it that I guess I've gotten used to it."

"But does it bother you?"

"Mostly no."

Charlie sighed and then said, "Me neither."

"Charlie, I want you to stay away from that Apache man you were talking to. You stick close to me from here on out. You hear me?"

"He's not so bad. He treated me nice and taught me things."

"Charlie, those Apaches are who killed your parents. I know all this is hard for a boy your age to get a handle on, but don't you forget that."

"He didn't kill them, and he was the one that made the rest of them be nice to me," Charlie said. "He had his own little boy, but he died."

"He stole you."

"I remember them that killed Father and Mother," Charlie said. "I'll get them one of these days when I'm bigger if I get the chance. I don't know how I'll do it, but I will."

"You need to go back to be with your family. I hear your uncle and them are very upset and have been looking for you for a long time," Newt said. "You go back home and play with your friends and pester your sisters, and be a boy for a while. Maybe one day you'll be a judge like your daddy was."

"No, I don't want to be a judge. Father was always sitting in his office reading his books. I like being outside."

"You read plenty of those books and go to school if you don't want to end up like me."

"I want to learn to shoot a gun like you," Charlie said. "Father didn't use his much, and he didn't shoot good when Chatto came after us. I won't be like that."

"You'll think different when you've had time to grow. Guns and fighting aren't the measure of a man."

"Mr. Horn says—"

"Oh, so you're listening to Mr. Horn now?"

"He says . . . what did he call you? He says you're a thoroughly dangerous man. He calls you the Widowmaker sometimes when you're not around."

"He does, does he?"

"You got that name fighting."

"Any man can fight. What you want to do is be a man that does things or builds things."

"If I could fight like you I could get other little kids back that were stolen."

"Arguing with you is like arguing with Mr. Horn," Newt said. "What matters is that we're going to take you back home, and everything will be better and seem different in time."

Newt had been watching Gok while he talked to the boy. The old warrior had left his tribesmen and gone to sit under a tree alone. At first Newt thought he had eaten too much horsemeat and needed to take a nap, but he saw Gok watching the children play instead of sleeping. He seemed content and as relaxed as Newt had ever seen him.

Newt got up when he saw Horn nearby. He limped over to him and pointed at Gok. "You would never look at him right now and know what an old devil he is. Looks like nothing but somebody's grandpa."

"He's happy," Horn said. "The only warriors left in Mexico are loyal to him, but there is much bad blood between him and those back at San Carlos. Bringing those children back might help his name."

"What did he do to lose face?"

"Many things. He raids when many want peace, and he has lost many of their sons on the war path," Horn said. "Many don't trust his word anymore and think he puts himself above the people."

"That isn't all, is it?"

"No. Do you remember that fight I told you about when Colonel Herrera ambushed those Apaches and sold the women as slaves?"

Newt nodded that he did.

Horn continued. "Well so happens that Gok was there. And when the Mexicans set fire to the grass and brush to try and smoke the Apaches out, Gok suggested that the Apache infants should be strangled so that they did not cry when they tried to slip away under the cover of the smoke. And then he said that the women should be shot if they did not agree with him.

"Maybe he was frustrated and said that in anger. The heat of battle, you know. But the people heard him. His own cousin threatened to shoot him if he suggested anything like that again. The people remember those things."

"No wonder he wanted to get those children back," Newt said.

"I'd say that was the case, plus the fact that Gok has lost many of his own women and children over the years."

"Wily old devil, that's what he is."

"True, but you've seen how he dotes on that niece of his," Horn said.

Newt quit watching Gok and looked to the sun low on the western horizon. "When will we ride? Might be best if we travel by night."

"I agree, but these Apaches want to wait until morning."

"Why?"

"They won't say."

"Then we go on without them."

"Don't think that Colonel Herrera's regulars don't know that the Apache are likely to run for the border. That game's been played for a long time," Horn said. "The Colonel will have all the men he can patrolling between here and there and cutting for Apache sign."

"Just me and you and the boys," Newt said. "We could travel by night and lay up by day. Two nights from now we could be back in the States."

"The other thing we've got to worry about is that I don't know if this is the last of the Apaches down here," Horn said. "Might be more that haven't turned themselves in, and the way we have to go is right through their normal war trails back and forth across the border."

"So you're saying we go north with this bunch, even though a bigger party is more likely to be spotted by the Mexican regulars?"

"That's what I'm saying."

"They don't have enough horses. Those women and children on foot are going to move slow as molasses in wintertime."

"If the Mexican army gets after us, we cut loose on our own and run for the border."

"You're acting like Gok now."

"You said getting the boys back was what's important," Horn said. "All's fair in love and war and trying to get your ass out of Mexico, I guess."

Newt hobbled over to the Circle Dot horse and unsaddled him. He took his saddle and gear over to the tree and set it down. Charlie had gotten up while he was talking to Horn, and the boy had lain down close to Billy at the foot of the tree. Horn put a blanket over both of them before he lay down and did the same for himself.

His mind was racing with trying to foresee what could happen in the next two days, and he didn't think he would be able to sleep. But sleep he did, and he slept very soundly.

When he awoke an hour before daylight Charlie was gone, and so were some of the Apaches.

Chapter Twenty-two

Newt scoured the camp for any sign of Charlie, while Horn talked to Gok and the other people in the camp. Nobody claimed to have known that some of their people were going to slip away in the night, but they didn't seem bothered by it, either. Many of the Apache there were nervous about what would happen if they turned themselves over to the army and went back to San Carlos. Could they keep their guns? Would they be jailed? Would Nantan Lupan listen to their needs and let them live at a better place on the reservation? Would there be food enough to feed them, or would the agent picked by the Great White Father in Washington cheat them out of their beef allotments and rations? With such worries, none of those Apaches remaining in camp were shocked that some of their own had decided to go back up to the high country and continue to live the old way.

They knew that the two white men were upset about the loss of one of their boys, but none of them was willing to do anything about it. The camp was rapidly being packed and the remaining Apaches prepared to travel.

Newt was saddling his horse when Horn walked up with Gok following him.

"What are you doing?" Horn asked.

"What's it look like I'm doing? I'm going after Charlie," Newt said as he slung his saddle up on the horse's back.

Horn tilted his head at Gok beside him. "He says that they left early last night and have at least ten hours head start on you."

"They left on foot. If I hurry, I can run them down."

"He says that they will already be in the mountains, and that you should know that no horse can keep up with an Apache in such country," Horn said.

"Then I'll go to the mountains, and I'll run them down on foot if I have to. I'll crack the whole damned mountain wide open and pull them out if that's what it takes."

"Apache never were a horseback tribe. Oh, they'll use a horse same as anybody, but there's never been nothing born with two hind legs that can travel like one of them," Horn said. "Usually when we get in bad country our Apache scouts travel on foot, and I've seen them match a trotting horse all day long."

"We'll see."

"They'll leave little sign. When an Apache goes

to ground it's like trying to find a needle in a haystack, and you are no tracker."

"Then tell him to get on his horse and help me."

Gok and Horn spoke to each other while Newt cinched his horse's girth tight.

"He says that they are scared and can't be found right now," Horn said. "Even if he were to go with you he couldn't find them for a long, long time, and even then maybe not."

"We found him once; we can do it again."

Horn translated that and then what Gok replied. "Those were Mexicans that we tracked down and not Apache. Nantan Lupan's army had many, many Apache scouts and he couldn't find Charlie. He asks how do you think you could find the boy in so little time?"

"Did he know that they were going to take Charlie? You ask him that."

"He claims that he knew some were likely leaving, but not that the boy was going with them."

"I think he's a liar. You tell him that if you want to."

"He says that the boy had grown very close to the one he went with."

"What's that supposed to mean?" Newt quit what he was doing and looked directly at Gok. "That boy was stolen by your people, right here last night."

Gok had no clue what he had said, but he understood Newt's tone. He stared back at him but said nothing.

"Charlie went of his own free will," Horn said. "You know that."

"Like hell he did."

"The signs were all there for us to see. He didn't want to go back."

Newt jammed his rifle down in his rifle boot and looked at Billy beneath the tree. The boy was sitting up with his blanket still covering him and watching Newt.

Horn noticed him, too. "What are we going to do with him if we go after Charlie? Are you going to trust leaving him with these Apaches?"

"You stay here with him."

"You won't find Charlie. If we had a whole company of Apache scouts we *might* find him. *Might*, I say, but we don't. This bunch is ready to move north, and not one of them is going to help you. They don't think it's any of their business if some of the people don't want to go, and they think it only natural that an Apache father who lost his only son would want to adopt another boy like Charlie."

"Tell them that we'll tell the army that they took Charlie from us."

"If I say that, it's liable to get us killed," Horn said. "Gok is hiding it, but he's worried about that very thing. He wanted Charlie with us so he could say what a good heart his people had by bringing Charlie back. I think he would try to get the boy back if he thought he could."

"You tell him."

"I won't tell him that. Jones, there's nothing you

can do right now to get Charlie back. He wanted to go, for whatever his reasons were," Horn said. "And you can't save someone who doesn't want saving."

Newt frowned at Horn. "You know, Charlie said almost those very words to me once."

"He's an unusual kid."

Newt was tying his slicker behind his saddle, and he jerked the knot so tight on his saddle strings that he broke one of them. "He's just a messed-up little boy."

"Yes, but he's strong."

"He needed time to get his head right."

Horn cleared his throat. "I've seen captive children that plumb lost their mind and never would get it back. They couldn't take it. And I've seen others that turn more Indian than the Indians themselves. It's an odd thing."

"I've got to try to get him back."

"You're just mad and not thinking straight."

"Damned right I'm mad."

Horn put a hand on Newt's saddle, blocking him from finishing what he was doing. "Nobody thought Charlie McComas was alive. And he won't be to them. He's somebody else now, and I think that's the way he wants it."

"I should have kept a closer eye on him."

"We can put out the word that we'll pay a big ransom for him," Horn said. "That little bunch he's gone off with will have a hard time, and come a month or two from now they might be more than willing to trade Charlie back to us. We know who he went with, and there's no way they're coming back on the reservation without giving up the boy to the army."

Newt took a deep breath. "I've seen how hard it is to get anything back down here."

"When General Crook finds out maybe he will send some Apache scouts down here to find Charlie and try to talk those he's with into going back to the reservation."

"I failed him," Newt said. "The army failed him, and now I've failed him. He didn't have a chance."

Horn gestured at Billy. "There's a boy right there that's counting on you. I think he needs your help more than Charlie ever did."

Newt thought of Charlie McComas and then he looked at Billy. He knew Horn was right, but that didn't make it any easier to take.

Chapter Twenty-three

There were eight warriors and twenty-two women and children in the band that broke camp that morning. He put Billy up on a horse of his own, despite the boy's protests, and half expected to have to loan the Apaches the spare horses that Horn had rounded up after the first fight with the Hatchet. But he was soon surprised at how many horses the band had. Instead of the women and children being on foot as they often were, everyone had a horse to ride. He and Billy rode with Horn near the back of the line.

The belt of oak trees at the bottom of the mountain disappeared as they rode into the foothills south of the great bend in the Bavispe River. They hadn't traveled three miles when they came to a shallow, wide canyon. Although they could have avoided the canyon and a much better way would have been to go around it, the warriors guided them down a cut into its mouth.

Newt and Horn were still high enough above

the canyon to see down into it when Newt stopped his horse and stood in his stirrups for a better view.

"That dirty old devil," he said.

Horn stood in his stirrups and looked down into the canyon below them. The canyon bottom was crowded with horses and cattle. There must have been four hundred head of cattle and at least that many horses.

"Gok's bunch was holding out on us," Horn said. "They had these cattle gathered before yesterday."

"That dirty old devil," Newt repeated. "He's going to get us killed."

Horn acted as if he read Newt's mind and said exactly what Newt was thinking. "With a herd like that we're going to have to stick to the flat country and the easy ways. And there won't be any driving them at night."

"Yeah, and a herd like that is going to stir up a lot of dust," Newt said. "Easy to spot for anybody that's looking for us."

"You've got to admit, these folks are leaving Mexico in style."

"Whoever those animals belong to is going to be real mad in a real big hurry," Newt said. "That's what I'm thinking."

The Apaches pushed the herd fast, and as a result the first few hours on the trail were hectic, and at times comical. Their style of driving the stock was less centered around keeping the animals in an orderly herd, and more about never letting them slow their feet and basically chasing them ahead of the band. Stragglers and the lame were left behind, for there was no time to coddle or alter the pace for them. Cattle and several horses escaped at every challenging bit of terrain or when passing through heavy brush.

In that fashion, they drove the herd out of the foothills and across the Bavispe River onto the valley floor. Everyone was nervous to be traveling such open country, and more nervous about the great dust cloud they stirred up. Anyone who wanted to stop had to hurry to catch back up. Mothers nursed their children on horseback, and lunch was taken on the fly. When someone needed a fresh horse, one of the warriors would rope one and lead it out of the herd. The worn-out horse the Apache had been riding rejoined with the herd or was left behind. They changed horses often to keep up the pace, and the herd never stopped.

Most of the warriors rode at or near the front of the herd, and a couple of them ranged far ahead to serve as scouts. They camped in the broken country at the western foot of the Sierra San Luis, and by noon of the next day they were nearing the big arroyo of Cajón Bonito Creek east of where it joined the Rio San Bernardino.

Newt and Horn were riding on the upwind side of the herd when they saw two of the warriors racing their ponies back to them.

"That can't be good news," Horn said.

And good news it wasn't. The two warriors who had ridden ahead reported that Mexican cavalry and several Pima scouts were camped a little ways ahead, directly in their line of travel.

The warriors held a hurried conference, and some were for turning west, and some were for abandoning the herd and going into the mountains and crossing into New Mexico Territory farther east. However, it was Gok's argument that won them over. His fierce eyes flashed as he scolded them and his chin jutted forward at the finish of every closing word. They would go straight ahead, and they would go fast.

"What are they planning?" Newt asked.

Horn barely had time to answer him before the warriors were riding to the rear of the herd to join the women and children. "They're going to run this herd right through the Mexicans' camp."

"Is he crazy?" Newt scowled at Gok's back.

Horn got down from his horse and tightened his cinch, and then checked Billy's saddle. "You've got to ask that now?"

The Apaches already had the herd up to a trot. They crowded the weary drag animals and lashed at them with quirts and switches and the tails of ropes. The Apache women scolded the slow cattle like they would a disobedient child or a camp dog under their feet.

"It's a damned fool stunt they're about to pull," Newt said.

Horn got back on his horse and adjusted his reins. "Well, you better make up your mind in a hurry, 'cause this train's leaving the station."

"How many soldiers did they say were in that camp?"

"Plenty, and there's liable to be another camp to the west on the San Bernardino riverbed. I'm thinking that they're wanting to block every easy way to the border."

"They wouldn't bother two white men and a boy," Newt said. "We've got no part of this herd, or these damned fool Apaches."

"If that's Colonel Herrera up there, do you want to count on him letting us pass if he catches us?" Horn asked. "He'll have those Pima scouts up on every high point, and the odds of us passing through there without being seen are next to nothing."

"It's only a short run to San Bernardino Springs," Newt said. "If we ride hard they won't have time to do anything about it."

"And what if the army isn't at San Bernardino anymore? You think Herrera is going to let some imaginary line stop him if he wants to go across it?"

"He's got no call to be after us."

"Not unless he was really in on that slave trading and he's a little peeved that we interrupted his business," Horn said. "And what if his buddy, the Hatchet, is with him? Did you think about that?"

Newt scowled at him as he had scowled at Gok, and then he got down and tightened his own cinch.

"What are you doing?" Horn asked.

Newt went to Billy and pulled him off the horse he sat on. Without a word to him he stuck him behind the saddle on the Circle Dot horse. He

climbed up in front of the boy and jammed his hat
down tighter on his head. "What do you think I'm
doing? I'm getting ready to run like hell."

The Mexicans' camp was at the edge of a wet-
land marsh on the south bank of the creek in the
center of the wide shallow draw or arroyo that ran
down out of the mountains. Several single-file,
rutted cattle trails from the south merged together
into one and broke over the edge of the arroyo in
a wide gully that led down to the creek and the
Mexicans' camp, and it was along that course that
the Apaches aimed their herd.

The Apache women began to wave empty flour
sacks and rags tied on the ends of sticks at the
cattle, and the mass of the herd steadily built speed.
By the time it came over the lip of the arroyo it was
at a dead run. The Apache warriors yipped and
screamed at the herd to urge it on.

The Mexicans soldiers had virtually no time to
react. They and their scouts were caught taking a
midday *siesta*, with most of them napping or sitting
around their fires. The first one of the soldiers to
stand up at the sight of the herd coming over the
lip of the wash took a bullet in his throat and fell
to the ground, choking on his own blood and the
warning he had been about to shout. At that same
instant all eight of the Apache warriors plunged
their horses down the slope, firing their rifles
and carbines on the run.

The distance between the side of the draw and
the creek was so small that most of the lead animals

in the herd had too much momentum going and crashed right through the camp and splashed belly-deep into the bed of cattails and willows at the edge of the marsh. The animals knocked men down and trampled their gear. A white canvas tarp had been rigged into a tent awning, and the first wave of the herd became tangled in the tent ropes and yanked it down. More than a couple of the Mexican troopers were unfortunate enough to end up under the herd's hooves.

The rest of the herd veered east of the camp and ran up the wash. The soldiers' horses were saddled and tied to long picket ropes strung between iron stakes driven into the ground, and those animals jerked free and bolted in the confusion. They were soon running with the stampeding herd.

Newt and Horn pushed their horses into the middle of the herd, and all around them the Apache women and children were doing the same. They broke over into the arroyo amidst a cloud of dust and the throb of so many hooves churning the earth. Below them the camp was in a storm the likes of which Newt had never seen.

Newt got a brief glance of Colonel Herrera waving his saber around and shouting orders. His fancy uniform coat was torn and he was hobbling on one boot. One of his soldiers dropped his rifle and tried to flee into the marsh, but the colonel hacked him down from behind with the long curved blade. The colonel spun around on his heels at the same moment Newt flashed by him. Newt knew that the colonel saw him, for he grabbed at the pistol on his belt. But he was too late, and the herd had already carried Newt away.

Newt barely had time to look away from the camp before he saw one of the Mexicans' Pima scouts appear out of the dust ahead, aiming a rifle at him. Newt never heard the report of the gun, but he saw the powder smoke at the rifle's muzzle and saw the steer beside him take the bullet in the neck and tumble end over end.

Another steer crashed into his horse's shoulder and staggered it, and Newt felt Billy's arms tighten around his waist as the Circle Dot horse fought to regain his balance. Newt let the animal run freely, and they followed the mass of panicked cattle and horses as if all were melded into one fluid motion and motive to flee.

Somebody among the soldiers was blowing on a bugle, and Newt wondered what kind of soldier was fool enough to think he could organize anyone in that kind of chaos and confusion.

Newt and the boy had become separated from Horn, but Newt spotted him a little ahead of them. A fallen horse had caused a log jam in the flow of the stampede, and Horn had slowed some to navigate his way around it. A soldier on the ground at the edge of the herd swung a saber at Horn, and Horn blocked the blow with his rifle and jerked a foot free of his stirrup and kicked the soldier in the chest as he passed.

Horn was barely past the downed soldier when his horse went down in the front end and flipped end over end with Horn flying over its head and disappearing beneath the hooves of the stampeding herd. Miraculously, he popped up on his feet, minus his rifle and hat. A steer with massive horns knocked him down again, but somehow he staggered up again.

Newt was right upon him by the time Horn stood up, and there was no stopping to help him. The pressure of the herd and the force of its momentum were too much. Newt twisted in the saddle and saw Horn catch the mane of a horse than ran past him and swing up on its back like a circus trick rider.

The creek ahead angled in almost against the arroyo's bank, and the marsh gave way and revealed a shallow, rocky shoal of water. The herd veered of its own accord and splashed across the creek and started up the arroyo toward the mountains. Newt looked ahead to the crossing and hoped his horse wouldn't break a leg.

The Circle Dot horse hit the water at full speed and never stumbled once crossing to the other side. Behind them, guns were banging and he could hear Colonel Herrera shouting orders to his men.

Chapter Twenty-four

They crossed the border in the dead of night and made camp in the south end of the Animas Valley. There were no fires made, and the people huddled in their blankets and waited for daylight to come. Four miles or more away, the tiny orange glows of some other party's campfires were visible in the middle of the valley.

The Apaches that weren't asleep whispered to each other and watched the glow of those fires. Horn relayed to him that Gok said that the fires probably belonged to the American army. Gok claimed to be able to predict many things with his magic, yet neither he nor any of the warriors with him were confident enough that the fires belonged to American soldiers to ride into that firelight. Plus, all the Apaches believed that if it was the Americans, they might fire upon them if they surprised them in the dark with their arrival.

The day before had been too great of a victory to spoil their journey now.

A great victory—that's how the Apaches thought of running the herd through the Mexicans' camp. Newt had to admit it had been a bold thing, something he thought to never see again.

A third of the stolen horses and cattle had been lost in the stampede through the Mexican camp, yet not one man, woman, or child of the Apache were killed or left behind. In fact, other than a bullet burn on one warrior's shoulder and a woman with a broken leg where the horns of a steer had slapped her, the band had gotten through relatively unscathed.

There was no sign of pursuit by the Mexican soldiers, and that didn't shock Newt, for he had counted the number of saddled horses among the herd and knew the Mexicans were probably mostly afoot.

Newt couldn't sleep and sat with his back to a juniper bush watching those campfires up the valley. The sun would rise over the mountains soon. Billy leaned against him, sleeping soundly.

Horn was nearby. Apparently he couldn't sleep, either, for he kept moving around from one spot to another and occasionally mumbled to himself. Newt wondered if his foot was bothering him again, but he suspected Horn's bad mood had more to do with him losing his rifle and his horse in the run through the soldier camp.

Newt thought he saw streaks of light gray over

the mountaintops, and he rose without waking Billy. He saddled the Circle Dot horse, and by the time he was finished Horn was saddling the Mexican cavalryman's horse that had carried him away from the fight the day before.

"Do you think that's our army out there?" Newt asked in a whisper.

"Either them or more Mexican soldiers," Horn replied. "Nobody else would camp out in the open like that and build fires that big for the whole world to see."

"How far up is that pass you were telling me about?"

From the sound of it, Horn was scratching at his whiskers in thought. "You mean Skeleton Canyon? It's not far from here."

"We could go now. Slip past that camp while it's still dark."

Horn's silhouette tilted its head back and looked at the lightening sky. "We're about out of dark, and besides, you don't want to go through that canyon in the dark. There's a reason they call it Skeleton Canyon. It chokes down to nothing where it goes through the mountains there, and we wouldn't be the first fools to find our ending thinking we could just mosey on through it."

"What about that ranch you told me about? Isn't it somewhere up in this valley?"

"About a half a day's ride from here, but I don't cotton to just the two of us and that boy going it that way alone. These here with us aren't the only

Apaches still pilfering around, and this country right here is a veritable brick road for heathens and bad men crossing the border. What we do is wait and see if that's the U.S. Army out there."

Newt leaned against his saddle and waited. It seemed like an eternity before the sky brightened enough to be able to see any detail. It wasn't true daylight yet, but that gray light before true dawn.

Two of the Apache warriors came from the north on foot, and Gok rose up out of the rocks he had bedded down in and went to meet them. They had a long discussion before they began waking the rest of their people.

"We're about to get our answer," Horn said.

The Apaches mounted their horses. Although there were several saddled cavalry horses taken from the Mexican camp, none of the Apaches chose to make use of the saddles and still rode bareback or with only a blanket thrown over their horses' backs. Of all of them, Newt only saw three of them riding with saddles, and those had done that since they left the Sierra Madre foothills.

The young boys and the women began to gather the herd from where it lay bedded down by the river and to start it up the valley.

"There's our answer," Horn said.

Newt went over to Billy and gently shook him awake. The boy was still half asleep when Newt sat him up on his horse and climbed up behind him.

"That's the American army up there, Billy," Newt said as he pointed to the north where the smoke of campfires gone cold was drifting into the orange-streaked sky overhead.

Billy muttered something and then lay his head against one of Newt's arms. The boy's steady, slow breathing made Newt sleepy himself. He was bone tired and ready for it all to be over.

The entire band and the herd moved toward the army's encampment. Seeing the valley for the first time, Newt thought he had never seen a prettier piece of country. The floor of the valley where they were was broad and flat and shin deep in good grass. To the east were the high mountains that formed the Continental Divide, and to the west the Peloncillo Mountains divided Arizona Territory from New Mexico Territory.

The army's camp was beside a spring-fed pool at the end of an outcropping of lava rock that jutted out into the valley's western side. When they neared, the Apaches became skittish and held up a quarter of a mile out. An Apache scout came out to meet them and they all sat on the ground and held council.

An hour later they rode into the camp. Newt was surprised to see that there were only two tents. And he was more surprised that one officer, three soldiers, and a few Apache scouts comprised the entirety of the population. That officer was none other than the lieutenant that Newt had seen taking roll call back at San Carlos, and the same one that had refused him the use of any Apache scouts and sent the Indian policemen to make sure he left the reservation.

The lieutenant greeted the Apaches and went into immediate talks with Gok and the rest of the warriors. Newt noticed the lieutenant watching him while continuing his negotiations with the warriors.

Newt and Billy got off his horse and took a seat on an empty box beside the lieutenant's tent. From the trash and debris lying around, it was apparent that the lieutenant had been camped there a long while or it was a popular camping spot for anyone coming down the valley.

Horn sat beside them on the ground and took off both of his moccasins and unwrapped the filthy bandage on his wounded foot. After a while he leaned back with his arms behind him and his legs outstretched before him. He wagged his feet back and forth and studied them with a wry smile.

"I'll sure be glad when this bad hoof heals up," Horn said. "But I guess I maybe hold a record."

"How's that?" Newt asked.

"Well, lots of men have wandered around Sonora, but I bet I've limped over more of it than about anyone."

Newt knew that Horn wasn't looking forward to meeting with the lieutenant and was stalling. The Apaches were helping themselves to the lieutenant's supplies, and it was at that point that the young officer came over to where the two white men sat.

He was a stocky young man with a stiff posture. He glanced at Newt and the boy, and then his attention landed on Horn. Horn was still looking at his feet and intentionally didn't look up at the lieutenant or act like he was there.

"Mr. Horn," the lieutenant said.

"Why hello, Lieutenant Davis." Horn looked up with a sheepish smile and tried to appear surprised and innocent—both things that he failed at. "Fancy meeting you here. Why, I thought you'd be back at San Carlos counting Indians and breaking up *tiswin* parties."

"Oh, I bet you are surprised to see me here," the lieutenant said.

"Now listen, Lieutenant. It was like this . . ."

The lieutenant waved off whatever excuse Horn was about to give. "What I need you to do is to go over there and talk those Apaches into leaving their stolen livestock behind. Captain Crawford will have a fit if I let them bring them back to San Carlos, and the general won't be any happier about it."

"You mean I've still got a job?" Horn asked.

"Horn, you ran off from your responsibilities and the employ of the U.S. Army, and that's what we call dereliction of duty," the lieutenant said. "A man with sense wouldn't do that, but then again a man of sense wouldn't make a good mule packer. And you are a good packer, and fortunately for you, your Spanish is a lot better than mine."

Horn got to his feet with his moccasins in hand.

He started to leave but held up and pointed at the lieutenant. "Newt Jones, this here is Lieutenant Britton Davis. Lieutenant, this is Newt Jones and that young gentleman with him is Billy Redding."

Lieutenant Davis gave the boy careful study. "I'll send a rider ahead of us to wire the boy's father."

"Do you know where to send it?" Newt asked.

"Rest assured, Mr. Redding has been in contact with us. I've had messengers sent down here by him at least once a week."

"I was under the impression that he might be in the field looking for the boy," Newt said.

"He was, but he's not anymore. That bunch of drunks and blowhards he brought with him from San Antonio got themselves lost down in Chihuahua and then they ran out of water and horses and barely made it back to civilization in one piece," the lieutenant said. "I think they've had all the Apache hunting they want for a while."

"Where's William Redding?"

"He's in Benson, last I heard, but he has reminded me that any telegraphs addressed to him or the Southern Pacific Railroad will find him."

"Railroad barons," Newt muttered under his breath.

The lieutenant seemed not to have heard him or had no comment of his own that he was willing to add. "You've done something there; that happens rarely."

Newt knew that he was talking about Billy.

"Child captives are rarely recovered."

"It wasn't easy."

"I doubt it was. Geronimo has filled me in on the general events of your expedition, but I would like to hear it from you."

"Geronimo?"

The lieutenant gave him a funny look. "Yes, Geronimo. He told me that it was slave traders who stole the boy and not Apaches. He said that he rescued you from a band of hostiles and you accompanied him to recover the Redding boy."

"What the hell?"

The lieutenant's eyes shifted for an instant to Gok standing over by the tent. Horn started laughing.

"His name is Gok," Newt said.

Horn laughed even harder. "Jones, you have the worst ear and the worst tongue for human language on any man I ever saw. His Apache name is Goyahkla, but the Mexicans call him Geronimo."

"You never told me," Newt said, and the anger rising in his voice was plain to Horn.

"Well, I better be going over there and talk to Gok like the lieutenant says." Horn was looking sheepish again.

When Horn was gone the lieutenant said, "It seems that you have been made the butt of one of Horn's jokes. You aren't the first man to have that happen. He's a fine packer and a good man to have on the trail with you, but as you've seen his opinion of his own sense of humor is greatly overblown."

"Did Gok, I mean Geronimo, tell you that the

Apaches kidnapped this boy first?" Newt was still trying to get his brain wrapped around the fact that the man he had thought of as Gok was actually the famous Geronimo.

"No, but I knew he was stretching the truth, which is a trait he and Horn often share," the lieutenant said. "We already were sure that it was Apaches that took that boy there. Geronimo is just trying to curry favor with me before he goes back to the reservation."

Newt gave the lieutenant an account of his travels in Mexico, and before he was finished the young officer had taken a seat on the ground and was listening intently.

"Are you sure it was Charlie McComas?" the lieutenant asked when Newt was through telling his story.

"No doubt about it. Ask Horn."

"The general is going to be very surprised to hear that young Charlie is still alive. The newspapers and the people in Washington will have a field day with this."

"Newspapers?"

"General Crook has received a great deal of scrutiny for his failure to recover the McComas boy."

"Well, I didn't do much better than the general did."

"Mr. Jones, what you have accomplished is an extraordinary feat. Few men could have done what you did."

"I just kept my word."

Lieutenant Davis stood. "I must be getting back over there and see if Horn has had any luck talking that old devil into leaving this herd behind. All I need is the Mexicans running me down and finding their stolen livestock. And Lord help me if the newspapers get hold of it."

Newt reached down and adjusted the blanket on Billy until it covered him better. The lieutenant stopped and looked back when he was several strides away, as if he had thought of something.

"Could I ask one question?"

"What's that?"

"It's bad manners, but I would like to ask anyway."

"Go ahead and ask."

"How much are they paying you for getting this boy?"

"I didn't do it for pay."

The lieutenant nodded his head as if he had heard a different answer. "I understand if you do not want to say. I'm sure it must be a goodly sum to get you to do what you've done. I know I would not risk what you have risked for less."

Newt started to correct him, but the lieutenant was already walking away. Newt eased away from Billy and got to his feet. The boy was sound asleep again.

Newt stood there and watched Geronimo arguing with Horn and the lieutenant over the livestock, and without thinking he said the words he was thinking out loud, "Geronimo."

He must have said it louder than he thought, for Geronimo's head swiveled around in an instant and his eyes locked on Newt.

"Geronimo," Newt said again.

The old warrior nodded.

Chapter Twenty-five

Geronimo did not give up his stolen herd, nor did he give up his guns. Lieutenant Davis, with only three soldiers and Horn to aid him, escorted the Apache band through Skeleton Canyon into Arizona Territory and began the long journey to San Carlos. One of the soldiers and an Apache scout were sent ahead to the town of Willcox to send a telegraph to William Redding that his boy had been recovered.

Billy took a liking to the young lieutenant and talked more than he had since Newt had known him. They did not want the boy's family to see him in the condition he was, and the lieutenant had also ordered that the messengers bring back a boy's suit of clothes if such could be found.

Geronimo and Newt kept their distance from each other.

Six days later the party neared Willcox. The messengers had returned and said that William

Redding would be waiting there for them, and that other telegraphs had been sent to General Crook as Lieutenant Davis had ordered.

Newt helped Billy into his new suit of clothes, and with his face scrubbed and his hair combed the boy looked like so different that Newt could barely recognize him. Although the child was talking more, he still had the same scared expression on his face most times. And he often cried in his sleep. Newt wondered how long the nightmares would stay with the boy.

Lieutenant Davis intended to ride into Willcox with Newt, and while Newt was waiting for him to gather his things, Horn walked over to him.

"I've got to stay with the Apaches. Lieutenant's orders," Horn said.

Newt went to his saddlebags and pulled out the wallet that Redding had given him. Six hundred dollars remained. Newt counted out four hundred and handed the money to Horn.

Horn counted the money, shifting it from hand to hand. "You only owed me three hundred."

"That other is for Pretty Buck. You give it to his family or that girl he was sweet on."

"I'll do that."

Newt held out his hand and Horn took it.

"I don't know what to say," Horn said.

"Well, that's a first."

"I'd ride with you anytime."

"Same here."

"You ought to come up to the reservation when

you're through. I can probably get you on as a packer or maybe I could talk Sieber into hiring you on as an interpreter."

Newt laughed along with Horn.

Horn once more glanced at the money in his hand. "I'm going to buy me a new rifle gun with this, and then if it's a good gun I'm going to give it a name."

"Horn, the best thing you can do is quit the gun business. There's nothing in it but a noose or a killing at the end."

Horn laughed again. "Same old gloomy Widowmaker. Damned if I ain't going to miss that ugly mug of yours and all your brilliant conversation."

Newt went to his horse and checked his saddle. Gok came up on him so quietly that he didn't know he was there until he turned around and saw him. The old warrior said nothing for a long time, and Newt wondered what he wanted.

Geronimo finally reached out one hand, balled into a loose fist, and touched Newt on the chest. "*Shush Bijii.*"

And then Geronimo withdrew the hand and touched his own chest above his heart. "*Shush Bijii.*"

He gestured to Newt and then back to himself, yet did not repeat the phrase a third time.

Newt thought he understood and nodded his head. Both of them stood there for a while longer, looking at the horizon as if they could see something there.

In time, Geronimo pointed to the south. "*Enjuh.*"

"*Enjuh,*" Newt repeated. It is done.

William Redding's personal train car was parked on a siding next to the depot house when Newt rode into Willcox. The telegraph operator had made sure to tell everyone he could that the Redding boy had been recovered and was being brought to Willcox. There must have been a hundred people lining the streets when they rode across the railroad tracks. Some asked him questions or congratulated him, and others merely watched. A few people pointed at Billy and whispered to each other.

The marshal of Willcox, the mayor, a judge, and the town newspaper editor tried to stop them for conversation's sake, but Newt rode on. He could see Matilda Redding and her son standing beside the parlor car waiting for him.

Billy did not bail from his horse and run to them, but he did hold out his arms to his father when he came to lift him from the horse. His father hugged him tight, and Matilda wrapped her arms around both of them.

After the initial emotion of the reunion had calmed, William Redding Sr. ushered them all into his railcar. Lieutenant Davis politely excused himself, and Newt was left alone inside the car with the Redding family.

William Sr. sat on the couch with the boy on his

lap. Matilda surprised Newt and immediately hugged him the instant the door closed behind him. She wouldn't let go for a long time, and Newt felt awkward and happy and sad all at the same time.

When she let go of him and took a step back to look up at him, her eyes were full of tears. "Bless you, Newt. Bless you."

"I brought him back."

"I know you did."

"You'll have to go easy with him for a while," Newt said, looking at Billy. "He's had a hard time."

"I know. What about you?" She put both arms on his shoulders and looked him up and down. "I swear you've lost twenty pounds since I saw you last."

"No trouble."

She looked him square in the eyes and held her gaze. "Don't you go fibbing to me. It's a good, brave thing you've done."

"It wasn't nothing."

"Newt, I don't know how I can ever repay you. When we lost Billy and his mother I thought I was going to die."

"That's a bad feeling, I know."

William Sr. got up off the couch and came over and shook hands with Newt. "Thank you, Mr. Jones. Thank you."

"You're welcome."

"What Mother says is true. There's nothing that we can do that would ever express our gratitude."

"Just take care of Billy there. He's a good boy."

William Sr. smiled at his son, then went to his desk and drew out a ledger and dabbed a pen in the ink well. "I hope this will show our appreciation sufficiently."

It was then that Newt realized that William Sr. had opened a book of checks, or bank draft forms. He watched the man's right hand scrawl on the paper.

"Take this. And if it's not enough please let me know." William Sr. was holding out the bank draft to him. It was made out for one thousand dollars.

Newt didn't take the draft and stepped past William Sr. and looked down at Billy on the couch. "You be good now, you hear?"

"Yes sir, Mr. Jones." Billy got up and hugged Newt around the knees.

"And don't you be falling asleep on no horses. You could fall off and hurt yourself."

"I won't."

Billy still clung to him, but Newt broke free and handed him off to his father. William Sr. patted Billy on the head and offered the bank draft again.

"It's the least I can do," he said.

Newt took the wallet that they had given him back in San Antonio and laid it on the desk. "There's what's left of your expense money."

"There's no need of that."

"It's your money, not mine."

"But we owe you."

Newt looked at Matilda. "You don't owe me anything."

"I don't understand," William Sr. said.

"No, you don't know me, Mr. Redding. If you did you wouldn't offer me that money."

"I can't let you walk out of here after all you've done. I see that you are a man of pride and ideals, but every man has expenses and things he needs to attend to."

Newt held up a hand to stop him. "You want to do something? You let me use your line of credit over at the store across the tracks. It won't be much, just a few trinkets to trade, maybe a bit of staples for a week's trip, and a good pack mule to carry it all and a shoe job for my horse."

William Sr. held up the check again. "Just this."

"No, I've told what you can do."

William Sr. sighed. "Very well."

Newt tipped the brim of his hat at him and then to Matilda before he went out the door. As she had back in San Antonio, she followed him outside and watched him get on his horse.

"You're a good man, Newt Jones. I knew it the first time I laid eyes on you."

"I'm no good man."

"I don't care what you say. I see you, Newt. You're a good man, and there aren't enough of those to go around."

He turned his horse and rode across the tracks. Lieutenant Davis met him as he was getting off his horse in front of the nearest saloon.

The lieutenant had a telegraph in his hand. "I wouldn't go telling people about the McComas boy."

"And why is that?" Newt had an idea what the answer would be before he heard it.

"General Crook thinks that news of the boy being alive might stir up the public for no good reason and cause greater difficulty between the civilian public and the Apaches and the reservation."

Newt gave a bitter chuckle. "Let me guess. If I tell about Charlie he'll call me a liar in the newspapers and come up with some other story."

Lieutenant Davis looked as disgusted as Newt felt. "I'm only relaying his message, as per my orders."

"You need to get a new job, Lieutenant. How about you come have a drink with me?"

"Thanks but no thanks. I've got those Apaches waiting for me, and I'd better get them moving before the rumor spreads that Willcox is about to be massacred."

"So long, then. You tell old Nantan Lupan that he can kiss my ass," Newt said before he disappeared inside the saloon.

Two days later Newt rode out of Willcox leading a pack mule. Those that saw him said he had a hangover that would knock down an ox after doing nothing but drinking whiskey for two days straight, and that when the mayor tried to give him a citation from the city for his brave deeds in the recovery of the Redding boy he laughed at the mayor and shoved him out of the saloon. To all appearances, and to the city's disappointment, they found him to be a most unpleasant man— not at all in line with the rumors of his heroism and valor.

The last they saw of him he was riding to the south. Some said he was still too drunk to ride and let his horse pick the direction, but none of them really knew him.

Chapter Twenty-six

Newt rode into Galeyville on the east side of the Chiricahua Mountains two days later. It was a bitter cold, windy day—too cold for anybody to be outside to see him arrive. And there weren't many left in the town to see him even if the weather had been nicer. The town looked all played out, just like the silver load that had founded it.

There were no horses in front of the little false-fronted saloon, but the trickle of wood smoke floating out of the pipe chimney gave Newt hope for both a warm fire and something to warm his belly. He tied the mule to a fence post on the downwind side of the saloon and draped one of the horse's reins around the frame of the packsaddle and loosened the gelding's cinch.

Tucking his neck deep inside the collar of his coat against the bite of the wind howling down the street, and squinting his eyes against the dust, he went around the corner of the building and pushed the front door open. There was only one man inside, and he was sitting by the cast iron stove playing checkers with himself. He looked up and acted genuinely surprised to see anyone, and Newt assumed that he was the proprietor and bartender.

Newt stepped across the room, and the man by the stove got up and went behind the bar. Newt pointed at a bottle of Old Forester on the shelves of the backbar, and the owner took it down and poured him a healthy two fingers in a glass. Newt took the glass and went to stand by the stove.

"Haven't seen you around here," the owner said.

"Don't imagine from the look of things that you get too many new customers," Newt said.

"Town's about done. What brings you here?"

"Traveling."

Newt didn't want to talk. He only wanted to stand by the fire and have a few drinks before he moved on south. He didn't even know why he had come there, anyway. He hadn't known where it was, and simply struck the road to it and followed it.

"You haven't got trouble after you, have you?" the owner asked. "None of my business, but I'd as soon not have any brought on me."

"Nervous, ain't you?" Newt asked, and took a sip of his whiskey.

"Habit I guess. Curly Bill's boys back in the day always had somebody after them, and most that come here anymore are the kind that might be looking for a quiet place kind of out of the way."

"You think I look like trouble?"

"I think you look like a dangerous man."

"Thoroughly dangerous," Newt said to himself.

"What's that?"

"I said I don't have any trouble after me."

The owner left the bar and went to a window. The saloon only had two windows, and one of them faced up the street the way Newt had come.

"You say you don't have any trouble?" the owner asked. "Well then, what's that I see coming?"

Newt went to the window and saw the two horsemen coming down the street. He finished his whiskey while he watched them, then handed the empty glass to the owner.

"You know them?" the owner asked.

Newt took off his coat and laid it on a chair, then hitched his pistol to a better position on his hip and went out the door. He leaned against the front of the saloon and watched the two horsemen coming at a walk toward him. Even with the dust blowing, the red *serape* on one of them was easy to see.

When they were within fifty yards of him he saw that the man with the Hatchet was none other than Colonel Herrera in his blue soldier coat. Newt put his hand on his pistol and waited.

They pulled up not twenty feet in front of him, and it appeared that they didn't recognize him until they were that close. The colonel looked twitchy and nervous, but the Hatchet looked like he couldn't care less.

"Hello, Clagg," Newt said. "You looking for me?"

The Hatchet adjusted his glasses on his nose before he spoke. "Wasn't looking for you in particular, but I can't say that I'm unhappy to have run across you. I owe you one."

Colonel Herrera's horse was nervous in the wind, and it wouldn't be still. "You have ruined me."

"How's that, Colonel?"

"The governor fired him, and then those kids you took from me got to telling tall tales about how he came to visit me when they were with me," the Hatchet said. "You might say he's got a score to settle, too."

Newt expected the colonel to say something, but he did not. He only glared and worked his jaw muscles.

"You poked fun at me back in Bacerac," the Hatchet said. "I don't see you being funny now."

The wind banged an open door down the street somewhere. "You tell a joke and maybe I'll laugh."

Newt waited. He could see the colonel trying to get his hand closer to the open front of his coat and guessed he had a pistol under it.

"You are a . . ." The Hatchet lifted his right hand with the fingers pointing upward and made circles in the air with it. "What are the words?"

Newt was almost too late understanding that the hand in the air was meant to draw his attention, and he almost forgot about the Hatchet's left hand.

"*Bastardo!*" the colonel shouted, and reached inside his coat.

The Hatchet went for his left-hand gun at the

same time, and Newt's Smith was barely out of its holster when the Hatchet's first bullet hit the wall a hand's length away from his head. The colonel's horse was dancing in place, and he was having trouble getting his coat out of the way.

Newt thumbed back the hammer on the Smith and shot the Hatchet through the chest. The bullet twisted the outlaw in his saddle, and that movement caused Newt's next bullet to hit him high in the shoulder. The outlaw's horse reared, and he tumbled off its back into the street with a grunt.

Newt swung his pistol toward the colonel and saw that he was only then getting his pistol out. Newt cocked the Smith and leveled it at him.

"*Bastardo!*" the colonel shouted again, and brought his pistol up.

Newt shot him in the head.

He heard the sound of a pistol cocking and turned just in time to see the Hatchet on his knees with his pistol leveled at him. Blood was leaking out of the Hatchet's mouth, and his glasses were gone. His eyes were red and swollen, and the pistol wobbled in his hand.

"You can't kill me," the Hatchet rasped.

Newt put another bullet in his chest. The Hatchet slumped over and lay still.

Newt thumbed his empties out of the Smith and reloaded it while he watched Clagg die. "Like hell I can't. That was for Billy and Charlie."

When he walked back in the saloon, the two bodies lay only a few feet apart. The wind blew the

Hatchet's big *sombrero* down the street, rolling it like a cartwheel.

"Pour me another glass of whiskey."

The bartender was so nervous he was shaky, but he poured the drink.

Newt had the glass turned up but stopped short of taking a drink when he saw the Circle Dot horse looking in the front window. "Make that two drinks, bartender."

The bartender didn't understand, but he poured the second drink anyway. He stepped to the window and looked past the horse. "Damned but you got them both."

Newt tossed down his whiskey and set the glass on the bar. "Thoroughly dangerous man. Thoroughly, they say."

"What?" the man behind the bar asked.

"I said, do you think a horse will fit through that door?"

HISTORICAL NOTES

1. THE TIME PERIOD of this novel is purposefully set in the fall of 1883, as it lands chronologically after the first novel of the series and was the only date near to what I needed that fit the plot of the story I envisioned. I always try to insert a little fact and other bits of historical trivia into my novels, and the truth is that in the spring of 1883, General George Crook led an expedition into Mexico that was primarily made up of a large force of Apache scouts in the army's employ, a few American officers and troops, and a team of mule packers. The purpose of his campaign was in part to recover the kidnapped Charlie McComas. However, the major intent was to capture, kill, or receive the surrender of Geronimo and Chatto and other "renegades" and "broncos" who had fled the reservation at multiple times during 1882 and raided and plundered their way across parts of Arizona and New Mexico on their way south of the border.

Crook claimed that his expedition was a great success; however, he failed to get all of the Apache that had fled to Mexico immediately back into the

States and to the San Carlos Reservation. Although Crook did manage to run down and return 273 Apache women and children and 52 Apache men to the reservation, the fiercest of the warriors and some of their families remained in Mexico under the leadership of Juh, Chihuahua, Chatto, Naiche, and Geronimo. This ragged group of diehard holdouts was made up of some of the fiercest and most cunning fighters in the history of the Apache people.

Geronimo promised that they would return to San Carlos soon but claimed they needed time to try to find Charlie McComas to ease the Americans' hard feelings over his kidnapping and to gather up other Apache scattered and hiding in the mountains of the Mexican states of Sonora and Chihuahua. What Geronimo and the other warriors actually wanted was to buy time. They had tricked General Crook into lightening their burden of women and children and old men, leaving them free to raid the Mexican settlements and to have a last wild spree. And raid and plunder they did, throughout the summer and long into the fall and winter.

Most of the remaining Apache General Crook desired eventually honored their promise and showed up at the border ready to go back to the reservation by October 1883. Granted they showed up with herds of stolen livestock, counting on an army escort to help protect the spoils of victory taken from Mexico. Those Apache following Geronimo held out the longest and did not show up north of the border until February 26, 1884, when they arrived at the east end of Skeleton Canyon in the Animas Valley of New Mexico Territory driving hundreds of stolen Mexican cattle and horses. Mexican soldiers were out in force after them, and they quickly put themselves in the custody of a U.S. Army officer, although they did not surrender their arms. That officer was Britton Davis, a marginal character in my novel who appears briefly at the beginning as the officer taking roll call at San Carlos, and who is also present when the Widowmaker and the Apaches he is traveling with get back across the border.

Geronimo and others within the Apache party refused to give up the cattle, which they considered to be fair prizes taken from their traditional enemy. Davis acquiesced to those wishes and they all started back to San Carlos. But to throw more fuel on the fire, law enforcement officers or customs officials from Arizona Territory showed up on the way and wanted to impound or collect fees on the cattle. Davis, with only a few soldiers to help him, got the soldiers drunk so that another officer and Geronimo's people could sneak away with their livestock. It was that flight, however less hairraising than it seems, that was the inspiration for the expanded and fictional run to the border within this novel.

2. JUH—Historians can't seem to agree on how Juh, pronounced more like "Whoa," died. Juh was an admired leader of a group of the Nednhi

Chiricahua. But he was a heavy drinker later in his life. During the fall of 1883 he is said to have had a heart attack while crossing a river near Casas Grandes and drowned, or according to others, he was so drunk that he fell from his horse into the river and struck his head on a rock. The uncertainty of how he met his demise and that tiny bit of historical mystery was something I could not resist, and I placed the Widowmaker at that crossing and involved him in Juh's death.

3. The idea of the PHOTOGRAPH of Billy Redding saving the Widowmaker from death by Apache torture is based on an actual event.

Dr. Michael Steck was the first Indian Bureau agent for New Mexico Territory and the Apaches. Charles Poston, sometimes known as the "Father of Arizona," was a pioneer, explorer, mine developer, land speculator, town builder, and in his later years a writer and an influential proponent of forming the Arizona Territory. In July 1856, Dr. Steck took Poston to meet Mangas Colorados and other Apache leaders at the old presidio at Santa Rita de Cobre.

Poston had a few Texas frontier toughs with him who served as guards and teamsters for the two wagonloads of corn that were to serve as a gift to the 350 Apaches that eventually showed up for the meeting. The corn was soon made into *tiswin,* an alcoholic drink favored by the Apache. Poston and his Texans, not wanting to be rude, imbibed freely with the Apache warriors. A drunken target shooting contest between the Americans and the Apache warriors ensued. The Apaches were greatly impressed by the Americans' Sharps breech-loading carbines and Colt cap-and-ball revolvers, and Poston noticed them digging spent bullets out of the trees, so short of ammunition were they.

Other gifts besides corn were also in the wagons Poston brought to the meeting—cloth, beads, and other miscellaneous trade trinkets—but what the Apache liked were the matches. It would seem that we could learn much about the Apache of that era by the things from that meeting that they valued most, repeating firearms and matches.

But there was another thing in the wagonload of gifts that would have a long-lasting effect, especially for Poston. He gave away tintype photographs of himself as a gesture of goodwill and so that the Apaches might remember him. Little did he know, but one of those tintypes would later save his life. In the years following the meeting at Santa Rita de Cobre, Poston rode into an ambush unawares. The Apaches looking down on him were about to fire at him, but one among their number had one of the tintypes of Poston from the meeting back in 1856, even though he hadn't been there himself. He told the other warriors that Poston was known to be a good white man and for them not to shoot him. Poston never knew that the Apaches had the drop on him, for the warriors faded away without revealing themselves. It was years later before

Poston heard from another Apache how he was almost killed but saved by a photograph.

Not pertaining to the photograph, but also relative to one of the themes of this novel, during that 1856 meeting Dr. Steck noted that the Apaches were already declining in numbers due to the constant warfare with Mexicans.

4. TOM HORN—The formula for many western novels tends toward an almost invincible male lead character who has worked at many trades, is good at everything, can vanquish his enemies with utmost skill, and leads a life of adventure and danger. As that stereotype of the rugged American frontiersman and bigger-than-life tough man goes, perhaps no other historical participant in the days of the Old West fits the bill better than Tom Horn.

Horn fled his home in Missouri when but a boy because his father beat him. He worked his way west on his own, hired on as a teamster with the army when still only a teenager, trained under the legendary white scout and Indian fighter, Al Sieber, and became a mule packer and sometime scout during the Apache Wars. He fought in several skirmishes and battles with the Apache, and participated in major army expeditions into Mexico against Geronimo in both 1883 and 1885–1886. He eventually left the army to turn rancher, and in 1891 won the steer-roping contest at a rodeo in Globe against some of the best cowboys in Arizona. He hunted rustlers and outlaws, was at times a lawman in various capacities, claimed to have fought in the feud that turned into the Pleasant Valley War, served as Pinkerton, and ended his far-flung career and became a legend in Wyoming working for big ranchers who hired him to shoot stock rustlers with his Winchester rifle.

Throughout Horn's life, he was known as a talker and a storyteller, and sometimes he was not above stretching the truth for the sake of story or bragging a little. He was convicted for killing an innocent sheepherder's boy and hung at Cheyenne, Wyoming, in 1903.

5. CHARLIE MCCOMAS actually existed. The general details of the death of his family and his capture are basically as I have told it within the novel. The rest of his life, well, it may be stranger than any fiction I could create about him. His body was never recovered, and many different stories supposedly tell the real "truth" of what happened to him. Did he die at the hands of a rock-wielding Apache woman, or did he live into adulthood among the last wild Apache as many legends claim?

What is fact is that a few small bands of bronco Apaches remained hidden in the mountains of Mexico long after the Apache Wars were over and most of the world moved on to automobiles, radio, silent movies, and world wars. An Apache woman captured by Mexican *vaqueros* in 1915 claimed to have lived with a band that contained a white man with a red beard. In 1924 a tiny war party of these broncos killed a cowboy in the Animas Mountains in the southwestern corner of New Mexico and raided several ranches. The posse that went after them was unsuccessful, but days later two cowboys in Sonora supposedly did get a glimpse of the leader of the raiding party. That leader was a tall white man with long hair and a beard. Rumors and legends of such a white Apache were told from the 1890s well into the 1930s.

Another one of the McComas legends says that in 1940 a bronco Apache woman was captured and interrogated about the white Apache and claimed that he had been killed with a knife in a fight with another Apache man over a woman. The same legend tells that she guided her interrogators to a place near the Arizona line where Charlie's body had supposedly been thrown into a pit. The Americans found a skeleton in that pit and took it back to Douglas, Arizona, for examination. According to the examiners and the medical theory and techniques of the time, the bones were determined to belong to a white man.

6. GERONIMO—What can I say about this iconic and controversial warrior from the Apache Wars? Historians have already covered him well, and like all such famous men from the past, there is little to be said that hasn't already been beaten to death and that will not cause controversy among those who like to argue about such things. I admit to taking creative license with him for the sake of this novel, but as always with such a historical character, I tried to base him on what I learned of him from many years of reading—not only the events and

dates of his known life, but his actions. I make no judgments about him, for I did not live in his time, nor as the old Indian saying goes, did I walk in his moccasins.

Geronimo did suffer the loss of his mother, first wife, and three children at the hands of Mexicans at Janos, Chihuahua, in his younger years. His refusal to give up the warpath against Mexicans has often been attributed to this event. In his own words, Geronimo said that, "I have killed many Mexicans; I do not know how many, for frequently I did not count them. Some of them were not worth counting." He also bragged that he used rifles to fight American soldiers but only needed rocks to kill Mexicans. That hatred and the long warfare between the two cultures was a steady thread throughout the novel.

As in the novel, Geronimo is also seen as having lost face among his people, thus leading him to have to seek help from the Widowmaker and Horn to get the children back. Many Apache that were resigned to making the best of reservation life came to dislike Geronimo for his raiding and his recruiting of young warriors to go on those raids with him, many of which died under his leadership. Geronimo's kidnapping of Loco and forcing his band at gunpoint to flee to Mexico in April of 1882 resulted in Crook's campaign below the border one year later, and that manhandling of Loco turned even more of the Apache against Geronimo.

Perhaps the final straw came during a bloody

attack and ambush by Mexican soldiers under Colonel Garcia at Alisos Creek. Many warriors and women and children were killed or wounded in that fight, and the Chiricahua were put afoot while still under attack. Geronimo was so infamous among the Mexicans by then that the soldiers called to each other to get that devil Geronimo. And Geronimo proved his prowess on the battlefield that day, fighting like a madman and shooting a captain through the head at the perfect moment to stop a rush by the Mexican soldiers. But Geronimo showed another, less admirable side of himself that day. He was a perfect fighter, maybe, but by no means a perfect man.

The soldiers set fire to the countryside around the dug-in Chiricahua band in an attempt to flush them out, and it was during that fire that Geronimo suggested that the surviving infants be strangled so that their crying did not alert the soldiers while the warriors and the other people in the band strong enough to travel fled under the cover of the smoke. He also said that they should leave the women if they disagreed with strangling the children. Geronimo's own cousin, the famous warrior Fun, threatened to shoot him if he said such a thing again.

Geronimo seemed to have a dichotomous nature, to say the least. He was a man that loved his family so much that he declared war for life on all Mexicans; a man that had many wives and children that he was known to dote on in his elder years. Yet, he was also a man that would do anything to keep up the fight and to win, whether that meant kidnapping his fellow tribesmen, killing them, or strangling their children. He was a man who could be magnificently honorable and a liar at other times. It is that two-sided man who gave me the plotline of a Geronimo going after a kidnapped niece and to try to portray him in a way that the reader could not tell if he was doing it to regain status among his people or because he was heartbroken at her loss.

I wanted him to be as cunning and as wily as he really seemed to have been, and I wanted him to be the mystical and superstitious warrior shaman of great power that he was also known for among many of his people. Foremost, I wanted him to be as imperfect as I saw him, for perfect, flawless people do not exist nor do they interest me as a writer. Whether my fictional presentation of him is fair or not, or accurate or not, I will leave to the reader. I make no excuses for my work and can only say the one thing that I know for sure about the man. He was interesting, to say the least. Look at a photograph of him. Look into those eyes of his and tell me it isn't so.

Chapter One

The night was so pitch-black that not a single star shone overhead, and the wind howled like a banshee through the mesquite brush. Maybe that was what had Newt Jones feeling so edgy, or maybe it was the poke of gold tucked away in his saddlebags.

Either way, he was a careful man, and the sound of what he thought was a horse coming was enough to give him pause. He held the coffee to his lips and squinted through the steam lifting from the mug, cocking his head one way and then the other, trying to hear again whatever it was that was out there. The hissing, whipping flames of his campfire lit his pale blue eyes above the scarred knots of his cheekbones, and he set his coffee aside and took up his rifle, his thumb hooking over the Winchester's hammer, and the walnut forearm fitting into his other palm as comfortably as an old friend.

Behind him on their picket line, his horse and pack mule lifted their heads and cocked their ears forward in the direction of the sound of shod hooves clattering over the caliche rock ledge that banked the near side of the river crossing. Whoever it was, they were making no attempt to be sneaky.

When the horseman finally appeared in the edge of the firelight, he was a tall, broad Mexican; almost as tall as Newt, but wearing a wide-brimmed sombrero and with a set of pearly white teeth shining beneath his thick mustache.

"*Buenas noches.* May I warm myself at your fire?"

It was the middle of summer and far from a cold night. Newt's eyes searched the blackness beyond for signs of anyone else. When he was semiconfident that the Mexican was alone, he motioned with a lifting of his chin for him to dismount.

The Mexican noticed the rifle in Newt's hands and the careful watch he kept on him. He chuckled and nodded slightly as if he approved, and made a point to turn his horse and dismount where Newt could see him plainly, loosening his cinch and dropping his reins on the ground. "*¿Un hombre cauteloso, eh?*"

"Hmm?" Newt was so focused on the Mexican's every move that he only half heard him.

"You gonna take no chances."

"Always cost me when I did."

The Mexican's horse was well trained to ground tie, and even in the poor light, Newt could see that it was a good horse—big and strong, and a better mount than any he had ever owned. But that was nothing. The fancy saddle on its back was worth more than Newt had ever sunk into a piece of horseflesh. He grunted to himself and hunkered down again on the far side of the fire with his rifle laid across his thighs.

"*¿Con su permiso?*" The Mexican gestured at the coffeepot sitting on top of some hot ashes raked out of the flames.

"Help yourself."

The Mexican pulled his own enamel coffee mug from the long saddlebags behind his saddle and walked to the fire with his spur rowels rattling and raking the ground. They were the big Chihuahua kind, with the wide, heavy bands overlaid with silver and rowel spokes half a finger long. They left lines in the sand where they dragged, like tiny snake tracks.

"*Muchas gracias, amigo.*" The Mexican took up the coffeepot and poured himself some. "I have far to go tonight, and some coffee will help."

Newt merely nodded while he noticed the clean white shirt underneath the Mexican's embroidered and brocaded vest, and the row of silver conchos laced with ribbon that ran down each leg of his pants. A real dude, a man of means, or a man who cared a lot about how he looked and spent everything he could on his outfit.

"You wonder where I go?" the Mexican asked.

Newt wondered nothing of the sort, more concerned with where the Mexican had come from and whether or not he was alone.

The Mexican shrugged when Newt didn't reply, and sipped at the hot coffee. "I have a rancho to the east, but my sister, she lives in Socorro and is very sick."

Newt waited long to answer him, while the mesquite wood in the fire popped and crackled between them and the Mexican's dark eyes watched him. "Hope she gets well."

The Mexican nodded gravely, shrugged his shoulders, and made the sign of the Trinity in the air before him. "Maybe I don't get there in time. Maybe she die. Maybe I go there, and she already well. *Sólo Dios sabe.*"

Only God knows. It was a term Newt had heard many times since he had gone west. It was a perfect excuse for anything and everything in a hard country. Something bad happened and you blamed it on God. Some miraculous bit of luck came your way, and you counted it a blessing. More good than bad for most, but Newt couldn't complain. He'd finally had a bit of luck. What did they used to say back home? Even a blind hog finds an acorn every now and then? *Sólo Dios sabe*, sure enough.

It was a hundred miles up or down the river to anything that resembled civilization—nothing but burnt grass and scrub brush as far as you could see in any direction. If there was such a place as "nowhere," then he had found it. And yet, the Mexican's horse didn't look like it had come far, nor did the Mexican.

The Mexican uncurled a finger from the handle of his coffee mug and pointed at the jackrabbit carcass hanging over the coals on a leaning stick jabbed in the ground. "Your dinner?"

"It's not much, but I won't turn you away if you're hungry."

"You are very generous." The Mexican rubbed his belly and smiled again, as if to demonstrate how hungry he was. He jerked a leg off the rabbit and made a show of picking delicately at the meat and smacking in delight, as if it were the most exquisite thing he had ever eaten.

Newt grunted again, but with a little humor. A touch of a smile hinted at one corner of his mouth. Tough, stringy jackrabbit wasn't much, but it was better than nothing. And he was one to know, for until the rabbit darted from under the shade of a mesquite tree and ran in front of his rifle sights, he hadn't had anything to eat in a day and a half.

"I was considering eating my pack mule before that rabbit showed up." Newt didn't know why he said that, but he found himself relaxing his guard. That wasn't a good thing for a man camped alone on the Pecos. He cast a quick glance at his saddlebags out of the corner of his left eye and then looked back at the Mexican just as quickly.

"Your stock, they look tired." The Mexican pitched the rabbit bones aside after he finished picking them clean, and pointed to Newt's picket line.

Newt couldn't argue with that. Not that his saddle horse and the little pack mule had come so far or so hard, but neither of them were particularly good animals to begin with. But that's what a man got on short notice when he left in the middle of the night and in a hurry. Every miner in White

Oaks knew that you risked your poke and maybe your life riding in any direction out of town. There were some that made a living breaking their backs digging in the hard New Mexico ground, and some that made a living waiting beside the trail for some unsuspecting, prosperous sort to come along.

And that was why he had saddled up in the wee hours and rode like hell. Not north to the railroad at Las Vegas like most would expect, but south along the Pecos, hoping to strike the Texas Pacific line and catch a ride back East with his fortune intact and some crook wondering how he had gotten away.

"You look familiar," the Mexican said. "Do I know you?"

"Never saw you before." Newt ignored the hint and opportunity to introduce himself.

"You got one of those faces that makes me think I see you somewhere before. Maybe that's it," the Mexican said.

Newt didn't take offense, but there was a time when any mention of his battered face made him self-conscious enough to want to run his fingers over the knot of his oft-broken nose or trace the buckshot and gristle texture of the lump that was one cauliflower ear. Or it might make him want to hit that person in the worst way. A good, solid lick planted right on some unfriendly's nose always did short-term wonders for his temperament. But he told himself those days were long past and he had learned to dismiss the looks strangers gave him. He had fought for every one of those scars, and he'd be damned if he would be ashamed of them. Let them think what they wanted.

The Mexican continued to study Newt across the fire. The two of them stayed like that for a long while, staring while the mesquite wood crackled and the wind pelted them with sand. Newt found it odd to be at such a test of wills with a man he had only recently met, and a smiling, overly friendly man at that.

"Now I know," the Mexican finally said. "You fight that Irishman at Silver City a couple of years ago. What his name?"

"The Butcher."

"Yeah, that was him. You pretty tough. Thought you gonna win a time or two."

Newt let a hiss of air out between his teeth that was meant as a scoff. "He broke two of my ribs, my nose, and I couldn't close my left fist for a month."

"¿Cuántos vueltas? Thirty rounds?"

"Forty-five. That Mick bastard knocked me down nine times."

The Mexican remained squatting, but shadow-boxed and offered phantom punches over the flames. "That was a good fight. You never imagine some people you will run across. Like you, right here. Sólo Dios sabe. Widowmaker Jones in the flesh."

Newt frowned. It was a silly name, and not of his choosing. Seemed like all of his life he had been ending up with things he couldn't do anything about, trying to do things folks said he couldn't, and wanting what was always out of his reach. It wasn't some fight fan or newspaper editor that gave

him the name—only a dumb Welshman popping
it out of his mouth over a mug of beer in the midst
of a victory celebration years before. Such a name
shouldn't have lasted with only a half-dozen, not-
so-smart pick-handle men and hired muscle in the
saloon, and most of them too drunk or too battered to hear anything. But it did. Some things
you're stuck with, like it or not.

"What you make for that fight?"

"Not a dime. It was a hundred dollars, winner
take all."

"You like that kind of work?"

"What do you mean?"

"Beating people. Getting beat on."

"Money's hard to come by. Worked for the railroad some, dug graves one winter after that, and
worked with a blacksmith that following spring.
Ended up in a mining camp after that. Fought for
prize money here and there when I could and
worked as a mine guard and payroll escort when I
wasn't swinging a pick or handling a muck stick.
You know, whatever it took."

The Mexican nodded and pointed at where
Newt's hands were draped over the Winchester
cradled in his lap. "Big hands. *Manos de piedra* . . .
How do you say? A puncher's hands, no? All
scarred from the men you've hit."

Newt glanced at his battered knuckles. He'd
always had big hands. All those years ago, when he
left the mountains, his mother had stopped him
on the porch and taken hold of those hands. She

looked at them and then looked at him with that wise old look in her eyes.

"Newt," she said, "God gives every one of us something—some talent. Some he gives smarts and some he gives beauty or the knack to make money or build things. You, he gave hands made for fighting and a head as thick as a Missouri mule. Some would tell a hot-tempered man like you to ride easy out there where you're going, and I'll say the same. It's a far land and no telling what you'll run into. But I'll also tell you, when it comes to a pinch, you use what God gave you. Smite them that vex you to and fro, and lay about you with them hands. Samson didn't have much else but muscle and bone, and he did all right."

Newt laughed to himself and savored the old memory a bit before he answered the Mexican. "I've smote a few that vexed me sorely, and been knocked around myself more than once. You take your licks same as you give 'em."

"How did you come to that line of work? This pugilist business?" the Mexican asked.

"It just happened."

"You were fast when you fight the Butcher. Most big men aren't so fast as you."

"I've always had fast hands."

The Mexican nodded and clucked his tongue, as if it were something he already knew, and as if it confirmed something he already suspected—like a doctor adding up symptoms to make a diagnosis.

"You ask a lot of questions," Newt said.

"*Perdóneme.* I no properly introduced myself. *Me llamo Javier* . . . Javier Cortina."

Newt immediately recognized the name and started to raise his rifle, but it was too late. The pistol appeared in the Mexican's hand as if by magic, cocked and pointed leisurely across the fire at him with the nickel plating on the steel shining in the firelight like some kind of talisman.

Cortina laughed. "A good fist is something, gringo, but it don't reach so far as a bullet."

Newt's hand crawled up the stock of his rifle toward the trigger guard.

The Mexican extended the pistol and pointed it at Newt's forehead. "Don't try it. You fast, but not fast as me."

Newt cursed under his breath. Damned Cortina sitting there smiling like he was doing him a favor holding a pistol on him. The thievingest bandit on the border, they said he never met a horse he couldn't steal, a woman he couldn't bed, a priest that he couldn't make cross himself, or a man that could run him down or best him with a gun. Of all the people to ride into his camp, and him stupid enough to let his guard down.

"I should have known you right off."

"Don't take it so hard," Cortina said. "Maybe you come through this alive. I get your gold, you know, and you get to keep your life. Fair trade."

"I don't have any gold."

Cortina clucked his tongue and shook his head. "I follow you all the way from White Oaks. Maybe if you wanted to keep it a secret you shouldn't have a drunk for a partner. That Yaqui Jim, he buy everyone in the house rounds and pay for it with gold. All the people, they know Yaqui Jim made a strike."

"You kill Jim?"

"That Jim, he don't listen to reason good."

Newt had always worried that Jim couldn't keep things quiet, despite all the promises he made when they found the pay streak. Nobody would have ever believed the two of them would find anything when they quit their mine guard jobs and headed up the side of the mountain to do a little prospecting. What did a barroom thumper and a half-breed, drunk Indian know about ore? Everybody expected to strike it rich, but few ever did.

But Newt and Yaqui Jim had—a little pocket on the side of the mountain not yet claimed by the company and with a little ledge laced with gold. It was only a small find, and it had been their plan to high-grade it and get gone before the bushwhackers or company men snooping around found out about it. They were so close to getting away with it, but Jim always loved a bottle and wanted to celebrate and show off a little.

There were more riders coming through the brush—a lot of them. Cortina heard them but, smiling smugly, didn't even look their way.

"What say you lay down that rifle and get your poke for me? Save me the trouble of digging through your things," Cortina said.

"Go to hell."

"You first, señor."

Cortina's pistol roared, and that was the last thing Newt remembered until he wasn't dead anymore.

Chapter Two

Bullets hurt like hell going in, but they can hurt worse later. A lot worse, until you can't think and until you don't know where the hurt begins and ends and you would rather be dead than suffer so. But then again, the only good thing about that kind of pain is that it lets you know you aren't dead. If you're a stubborn sort, hurting like that will make you mad enough to fight through it, if only because getting to your feet is the only way you can find the son of a bitch that did it to you and do worse to him.

Newt Jones woke with his face in the dirt, and it was a long time before he could recall how he came to be in such shape. There was a bullet hole through his chest, still intermittently and slowly seeping blood. There was a lot of blood—some wet and sticky and heavy, and other blood, older, dried and matted and mixing with the sand and forming a pasteboard crust of the front of his shirt. Yet, he was still alive. Cortina's bullet had passed through him like a hot knife, but somehow it hadn't killed him.

Cortina and his men had taken everything he owned: his livestock, his gun, his gold. Made a fool of him. The damned gold. The most money he ever had. Blood and sweat and backbreaking work. The thought of losing it hurt almost as bad as the hole in him.

At least Cortina had left his boots on his feet. There was that, even if he was too weak to walk. As it was, it took him half an hour to crawl the fifty yards to the river's edge. Most times, he would have complained about the bitter Pecos water, but it tasted like heaven. He drank and drank and then dunked his head under until his mind was clearer.

It took him most of the afternoon to rebuild his fire from the feeble coals left from his previous one, and to bathe his wounds. The second day he smashed a rattlesnake's head with a rock. There were plenty of snakes.

The third and fourth day he ate more snake and took stock of his situation. He had nothing but a sheath knife and the clothes on his back, and it was a long way to anywhere from where he was. The closest settlements were a few little Mexican sheepherder villages back up the river to the north. And then there were Fort Stockton and Comanche Springs somewhere south of him, and the old mail road, running west to El Paso or southeast to Del Rio. Cortina's gang's tracks were headed due south.

He was no scout, but from the sign they left behind, he guessed there were at least five or six of them riding with Cortina. Most likely, every one of them was as salty as Cortina. A man in Newt's condition wouldn't stand much of a chance against them. The smart thing would be to walk north and count himself lucky that he might live. A smart man would do that, no doubt.

On the fifth day he started south, following the river and walking in the tracks of the man he swore to kill. He was in no shape to walk fast, but he walked as best he could. Every step he took was a challenge in itself, and his chest ached like he had been beaten with a sledgehammer. He wasn't a praying man, but more than once he scowled at the sun and asked that if he had one thing left granted to him, then let him come face-to-face with Javier Cortina one more time. Revenge and getting his gold back was the way it should be, but if it came to that, he would gladly settle for nothing but revenge. Cortina should have known that if you're going to kill a man, you better make sure he is dead.

Chapter Three

It wasn't much of a tent, as circus tents go—a round thing with the brightly colored panels long since faded to dull pastels, and tears here and there sewn over with mildew-stained patches. One of the stakes had pulled loose from the sandy ground, and the Arabic-styled top that should have formed a needle spire at the center support pole instead sagged deeply. Still, it was perhaps the only circus to ever visit the little Mexican village, and the people who filed inside stared at it admiringly.

Kizzy Grey peeked out of a crack between the wall of the tent and the wagon tarp draped over a stretched rope that served as a screen and a dressing room. Some two dozen Mexican families were crowded together on the small section of bleachers on the far side of the tent from her, their eyes dark beneath the flickering lantern light, and their expressions almost somber, as if they weren't sure what to expect. Some of the children tugged at their parents' sleeves and pointed at the murals of

African elephants, crocodiles, immense snakes, sword-swallowers, fire-breathers, and other exotic circus themes painted on plank signs scattered around. Most of the peasant farmers and villagers had likely never seen anything approaching an elephant, nor were they apt to. Billed as a circus or not, the Greys had never owned an elephant, no matter what was on the signs. Although they had once owned a monkey and used it in the show until it bit a customer one night in Kansas City and the drunken Italian track layer pulled a club out of his coat pocket and killed the poor, ill-tempered thing.

The signs were what they were. "Ambience" was what her father used to call his painted flights of fancy—creating hope and setting mood—rather than false advertising. In Kizzy's mind they were an outright lie, but a harmless one if a lie could be such.

There had been a time when the Incredible Grey Family Circus had played before the big crowds in the big towns. But everything fell apart. Since then, it was more of the same, traveling the roads and settling for anyplace that would have them and doing their acts for whatever the local citizenry had to shell out, which of late hadn't been much.

Kizzy turned and stared at the rusted little money box on the table behind her. The night's take for the gate wasn't more than a handful of pesos and not near enough to feed their animals or to keep up with repairs. She shrugged her thin shoulders without realizing she did it. It wasn't all bad. One old woman had bought her family's way into the show with a chicken. At least they would eat well for a meal.

Kizzy double-checked herself in the mirror, dabbing at a stray strand of black hair before tugging on her hat. She smoothed the front of her dress, frowning at a stain on it and wondering if she had made the best selection from the open chest full of costumes beside her. Her father had claimed that he paid a genuine Indian maiden to tan and sew the buckskin together. The snow-white, fringed dress was a pretty thing, with embroidery and fancy stitching across the chest and beadwork at the sleeve cuffs and on the hem of the skirt. She loved the dress, even though her father hadn't really gotten it from any Indian maiden. She had known that, even when she was only ten. He had really paid a Jewish seamstress in Chicago fifty dollars to make it. The buckskin wasn't really buckskin, and the cheap suede was worn smooth in places from the days when her mother wore it.

No matter, it was still an impressive costume. She took both of her pistols by the butts and lifted them a little in their holsters, adjusting the gun belt cinched around her narrow waist until it felt comfortable. She looked into the mirror one last time and pressed her lips together to smooth the red lipstick on them, blowing a kiss at herself before she walked out before the crowd.

"Ladies and gentlemen, lords and ladies," her voice rose to the sagging tent top. "Perhaps since mankind first captured fire or mastered the art of shaping flint, there has been no greater moment than when he first sat astride a horse. Until then, his spirit was incomplete; until then, the horse's spirit was incomplete. In that moment, when the horse first moved beneath him, the partnership was forged. Man and beast racing over the plains, swift and sure, stronger for one another. Nothing so mighty, they became like the wind."

She paused dramatically, noting that none of the crowd seemed to speak enough English to understand everything she said, but her tone obviously had their attention. Half of pandering to any crowd was always about the showmanship, anyway, rather than the words.

"And in time, many men came to ride the noblest of the beasts, but every once in a generation there was born a special rider and a horseman like no other. And ever more rarely a horse was born to match him. And once every century, or two or three, that special horseman and that special horse came together and magic was the result. Man and horse working together, until the giant, beating heart throbbing beneath the rider's legs flowed into him and they breathed and lived as one."

Fonzo timed his entrance perfectly. All six of the horses loped through the open tent door in a perfect line, side by side, with their long manes dancing with each stride and Fonzo standing with a foot each on the backs of the middle two, riding standing up, Roman style, with a long set of reins attached to the halters on those two horses.

Two times, he took them around the ring, and then on the third revolution he steered to a low jump made of a small log resting on end braces some two feet off the ground. All six of the horses sailed over the jump with their front legs folded under them and their nostrils flared. Fonzo stayed standing, even through the jump, and the crowd clapped when he landed without a hint of losing his balance and his knees absorbing the shock.

Kizzy smiled. No matter how many times she saw them, the six snow-white horses were truly beautiful. If her father had done one thing for the family show—for her and Fonzo—it was that. Ten years he had spent searching for matched animals, so alike in size and looks that anyone not a horseman might not recognize a difference in them at a glance. Every spare coin her father had ever been able to put together, he spent on those horses: Bucephalus, Herod, Mithridates, Sheba, Solomon, and Hercules. Blood and sweat and tears, and all the years putting the show together, making it something, all represented in horseflesh.

Her attention switched to her brother. Fonzo was as nimble as a cat, slight and wiry and athletic, with grace and balance oozing from him as effortlessly as quicksilver sliding over glass. For all the trouble he often caused her, she would still be the first to admit that he could ride like no other, as if he were born on a horse, or as if he were once a part of the horse and some appendage that had been removed and found its proper working once returned to the body from whence it was taken.

Fonzo guided the horses around the ring one more time, the horses keeping perfect pace and spacing, and their noses even, like they were bound together with invisible harnesses. The second pass over the jump, Fonzo floated up, his feet losing contact with the horses' backs. The crowd gasped, thinking he was about to be thrown to the ground, but to their amazement, he landed on two different horses and rode around the ring smiling and waving one hand at the crowd as if it were nothing.

The somber faces of the crowd turned to smiles and they pointed to him and laughed in wonderment. Fonzo leapt to the ground without even stopping the horses. They continued to circle him until he picked up a braided, long-handled buggy whip and whistled to them and cued them with some motion of the whip that only he and the horses understood. As one, they shifted into a single-file line, and with a second signal they stopped and faced inward to him at the center of the ring, like wagon spokes surrounding him. He raised both arms high overhead, and all six horses reared on their hind legs and pawed playfully at the air.

While the other five waited, one of the horses then came slowly forward and bowed to Fonzo with one of its front legs stretched out before it and the other bent beneath it. Fonzo swung onto

its back and led the other horses around the ring
again at a fast lope.

Riding bareback, Fonzo took a double handful
of mane and swung off as if he were going to dismount on the run. The instant his feet hit the
ground he bounced back up and landed again on
the animal's back. The second time he did it he
twisted and contorted his body so that he landed
facing backward.

Once the crowd had quieted, Kizzy stretched
one arm toward her brother in a dramatic pose.
"Another round of applause for Fonzo the Great
and his magnificent horses."

Fonzo leapt from his horse and joined Kizzy in
the center of the ring, the horses still revolving
around at his bidding. He motioned for the crowd
to quiet.

Fonzo's voice rose high and clear in the confines
of the tent, only slightly deeper than his sister's.
"And man soon found that the horse was good for
war, and the mighty men of old broke themselves
against each other in one wild charge after another, sword in hand and a swift warhorse beneath
them, until empires were made, and a time came
when a warrior was no warrior at all unless there
was a four-legged brother beneath him and carrying him into battle.

"Weapons of steel, sword and mace, required a
strong arm, and the mighty usurped the weak, and
giants ruled the world until here, on the frontier of
the New World, an invention was made—a weapon

so great, so cunning and minuscule, yet deadly, that history would be changed. The American cowboy likes to say that Samuel Colt made all men equal, but it is not only men that can handle a gun." Fonzo turned and bowed to Kizzy. "I give you Buckshot Annie, at the same time the prettiest woman west of anywhere, and the finest marksman to ever lift a firearm."

Kizzy bowed deeply in an imitation of the courtly dip of someone paying homage, as if the crowds were kings and queens instead of dirt-poor peasants and subsistence farmers. When she raised her head again to face them, she smiled and blew another kiss.

Fonzo went back to the circling horses and swung up on one on the fly. As soon as he was astride, she began to pitch him a series of red, shiny glass balls, one at a time. He caught them on the run, one-handed, stuffing them into a leather bag at his waist.

Kizzy stood with her back to the crowd and slowly drew the pearl-handled Colt revolvers at the same time. She let them dangle at arm's length beside her thighs, standing unmoving except for her eyes tracking her brother as he went around her. The next time Fonzo passed before her he tossed one of the glass balls high above him and she shattered it with one shot from her right-hand pistol. On his second pass he tossed two balls simultaneously and she busted those, too, with a shot from each gun.

The crowd had grown deathly quiet, but she was used to that. She suppressed the smile building on her lips and holstered her left-hand gun and waited for Fonzo's next pass. That time, he launched four balls into the air, and she shot from the hip without even taking aim with the pistol sights. She worked the trigger on the double-action Colt Lightning so fast that the four shots almost sounded as one. All four balls shattered, and brightly colored bits of glass showered down like falling stars.

Fonzo dismounted again and the horses raced out the open door and left the tent. He ran to her side and they gave the crowd another bow. As if it had taken the farmers and goat herders that long to get over seeing such a slip of a young girl shoot so, they finally erupted into a round of applause.

"Pretty good stuff when you can impress anyone on the border with your shooting prowess," Fonzo said under his breath as they bowed again.

Kizzy smiled demurely at the crowd, and her eyes strained upward toward the ceiling of the canvas tent. She was a far better than average shot, but none of the spectators ever seemed to notice the tiny holes all over the roof of the tent or the unusually quiet pop her .38s made. Busting such glass balls out of the air with regular bullets and black powder charges would have been a feat of marksmanship, indeed, but the lead birdshot and reduced loads she reloaded her cartridges with, much like small shotgun loads, made it a far easier thing. And the less powerful shot loads were much safer for work inside the tent or around crowds, rather than sending stray bullets speeding to who-knows-where to hit who-knows-what. However, the scattering of the pellets over the last year since they had added her act had pinpricked the tent with holes to the point it leaked like a sieve on a rainy day, and the tent was getting in pitiful condition as it was.

They shook hands with the villagers as they filtered out of the tent, and Kizzy did a few more trick shots with real bullets under the open sky, where she could pick a safe direction in which to shoot. Normally, Fonzo would have mingled through the crowd to find one or more men with enough faith in their own marksmanship to think that they could best a girl in a shooting match, but there wasn't enough money in the village for anyone to make any kind of a wager.

Fonzo let the children pet his horses, and even gave a few of them a ride, smiling even though not many months ago he would have charged four bits per person to have their photo taken sitting on one of the horses. But the camera was ruined when one of the wagons overturned crossing the Rio Grande a month before, and there might not be four bits left in the entire village.

The sun was going down when their guests finally filtered back to their village of mud-daubed picket huts, eroded adobe walls, and bleating goats. Fonzo traded a stained and frayed red velvet jacket that his father had once worn as ringmaster, along with four pesos, for the services of two of the village men to help dismantle and pack the tent. It was long after midnight before the tent was loaded into one of their wagons, and it cost them two more pesos to buy some hay for the horses.

The more elaborate of their two wagons was a gaudy thing, with high wheels, a bright red paint job, and gold pinstriping on every edge. It was what Kizzy's people called a *vardo*. It had plank sides and a shingled roof, and inside it was their living quarters—a narrow bed on each side, cabinets for storage, and a small kitchen area and stove for cooking when the weather was too bad to build a fire outside.

The night was too hot to light the stove, and Kizzy butchered the hen and baked it in a Dutch oven at a fire she built beside the wagon. She had already finished her portion of the chicken and carried water to the horses from the river to their picket line by the time Fonzo and his helpers were through packing up the show. He joined her at the fire, and she noticed the weary way he walked.

He nodded at the money box she had set on the camp table beside their fire. "How much?"

"After the cost of the hay and what you paid the men to help take down the tent?"

"How much?"

She pointed at the half-picked carcass of the hen grown cold on the plate she left out for him. "You get half a chicken."

He shrugged. "Oh well, but please tell me we have a little wine left."

She lifted a pottery jug and held it close to her ear while she shook it. "There's a swallow left. Maybe we can find someone down the road that might have a little fruit to sell so that you can make us some more."

He picked at the cold chicken, brooding and lost in his own thoughts. She noticed the way his eyebrows tilted in together above his nose, like their father's had when he was deep in thought. After a while he stood and paced around the fire.

When he spoke again he switched to the Roma tongue without thinking. Although they had both been born on American soil and were as comfortable with English as any language, it was an old habit when they were alone with each other. When their parents were alive they all had spoken the language of their people among family settings. And it had other advantages when strangers were around, as it was often of benefit to them to converse where the *gadje* couldn't understand what was being said. In addition to the Gypsy language, both of them spoke a smattering of French, a thing rarely used, but their mother had insisted on it, as it was the land of her birth. To add to the confusion of their multilingual skills, there was the bit of Spanish picked up during their time below the border. Without either of them realizing it, they often mixed words of many languages in the same breath, or hopped from one to another at whim.

"Homemade wine not fit for human consumption, and a bit of cold chicken. What's happened to us?" He lifted both arms wide and then let them drop with a slap against his hips.

"You know what happened."

"I think we ought to go back to the States. There's no money down here."

"And who in the States wants us, and what money were we making north of the border?" she asked, cocking one eyebrow.

"What about the invite to Monterrey?"

She picked up the money box and rattled the few coins in it as she had shaken the almost empty bottle of wine. "I don't think there's enough here to get us there."

He walked to the edge of the firelight where his white horses stood watching him from their picket line. He picked up a brush and began to rub it over the back of one of them—a gelding slightly larger and heavier than the rest of them.

"Hercules looks like he's lost a little weight," she said.

"They've all lost weight, and I fed them the last of the corn this morning."

"We'll get by like we always do."

He whirled and threw the brush across the camp. "It isn't fair."

"Nothing is fair."

"How many people will be at that bullring in Monterrey?"

"I'm told that it can seat a thousand people, and the crowds are always large," she said. "I can get you the letter from the promoter if you want to read it again."

"How much up front did he offer us?"

"Only a cut of the gate after each show. Ten percent. We perform two acts a day in between bullfights. No guarantees of any kind."

"Getting there is a week's trip, at least."

"President Díaz is supposed to be at the fights, and the U.S. ambassador to Mexico and other dignitaries, also. I imagine it will be a big crowd," she said. "Maybe the kind of crowd that could put us back on the map."

He paced more, and she suppressed a smile the sight of him brought on. He had both arms folded behind his back and was bent at the waist, his face turned down to the ground and his brow furrowed in thought. A pacing general on the night before a battle wouldn't have looked more serious.

In an instant, his demeanor changed and he stopped in his tracks and turned to her with an impish, boyish smile lighting him like a candle. "We'll give them a real show. I'll break out the new acts I've been practicing and some special stuff for the bigger arena. And we can think up some new things for you. Maybe you'll rethink some of my suggestions."

She couldn't help but sigh. For almost a year since their parents had passed on, Fonzo had been trying to get her to add what he called some "William Tell" parts to her portion of the show—shoot an apple off his head or a coin out of his hand, much like some of the other traveling sharpshooter acts did. He had persisted so in his arguments that she had finally agreed to practice such. Their second day of practice with her shooting a silver dollar out of his outstretched hand, she took the tip off his right index finger. The sight of him bleeding and the scarred nub of that finger, minus its last joint, was more than she could take. She knew she was an exceptional shot, but it felt foolishly dangerous to risk his health. He was the last of any kind of kin or family she had on the earth, unless she counted some distant cousins, equally as nomadic as she and Fonzo, and long since out of contact.

The shadows of two dogs crept into the edge of the firelight. Both of them were big and hairy with broad heads, outsized feet, and jaws like bears. The smaller of the two was brown and the larger one was white. They lay down at her feet on either side of her, and one of them, the white dog, carried a dead rabbit clamped in its jaws.

"Look at that," Fonzo said. "Even the dogs eat better than we do."

She reached down and stroked both the dogs' heads. "Did you ever think of giving up this life?"

"And do what?"

"I don't know. Maybe live like normal people and stay in one place."

He laughed. "We're Roma."

"There are Gypsies that don't live on the road. You've met them like I have."

"What would we do to make a living?"

"I wouldn't call what we make now a living."

"I like performing, and you do, too."

"That's not what I mean. Don't you ever think what it would be like to have a real house? Maybe something solid for once. A place to winter, at the very least."

"Sounds boring."

"Maybe."

"And what about the first time someone accuses us of some petty theft, or places blame on us whether we're guilty or not? Don't you know? We Romani are supposed to be a shifty lot. Witches, thieves, and fortune-tellers. I think I'll go find some children to kidnap."

"Don't be so dramatic." She took up her little squeeze-box accordion and began to play a wistful tune that her mother had taught her.

"Quit that. It's bad enough without you playing that stuff."

"I like that tune. It makes me think of Mama."

He sat down on a campstool and listened to her play awhile. "Look at us. We're everything Gypsies are supposed to be. You playing that thing, and both of us without a penny to our names and wondering where we can go to snatch a little coin from someone's purse."

"We'll get by."

He jumped to his feet, the passion in his voice raising it half an octave. "We're going to Monterrey. I won't take no for an answer."

She watched him storm off into the night, smiling to herself. Fonzo liked to announce everything, as if he made all the decisions. But in truth, she had intended to point the wagons that way in the morning anyway. Maybe Monterrey would turn out like they hoped, but that was the thing about being Roma and circus people. The next place down the road was always the same thing as hope.